Charles Star

Sally Myers

Carrie McLaren and Jason Torchinsky

Ad Nauseam

Carrie McLaren started *Stay Free!* as a zine in Chapel Hill, North Carolina, in 1993. She speaks regularly on the topic of advertising and media. Jason Torchinsky has been a key contributor to *Stay Free!* since its inception.

Ad Nauseam

Edited by

Carrie McLaren and

Jason Torchinsky

FABER AND FABER, INC.
An affiliate of Farrar, Straus and Giroux
New York

Ad Nauseam

A Survivor's Guide to American Consumer Culture

Faber and Faber, Inc.
An affiliate of Farrar, Straus and Giroux
18 West 18th Street, New York 10011

Grateful acknowledgment is made for permission to reprint the following:
illustration on page xv by Heidi Cody; photographs on pages 20–21 by Sally
Myers; photograph on page 93 by Michael Colton; photograph on page 176
by William Moree; photograph on page 289 by Amy Feitelberg; photograph
on page 323 by José Melia. All other illustrations are by Jason Torchinsky.

Library of Congress Cataloging-in-Publication Data
McLaren, Carrie, 1949–
    Ad nauseam : a survivor's guide to American consumer culture /
Carrie McLaren and Jason Torchinsky.
        p.   cm.
    Includes articles from their blog, Stay Free!
(blog.stayfreemagazine.org), with some articles written for the book.
    Includes bibliographical references.
    ISBN: 978-0-86547-987-6 (pbk. : alk. paper)
    1. Consumption (Economics)—Social aspects—United States.
2. Advertising—Social aspects—United States.   3. Marketing—Social
aspects—United States.   4. Social influence.   5. Social values—United
States.   I. Torchinsky, Jason, 1971–   II. Title.   III. Title: Guide to
consumer culture.   IV. Title: Consumer culture.

HC110.C6M353   2008
306.30973—dc22

                                                              2008041564

Designed by Ralph Fowler / rlfdesign

www.fsgbooks.com

10   9   8   7   6   5   4   3   2   1

For Our Parents

Contents

3. Consumer Culture and Society

4. Behind the Scenes

5. Down the Memory Hole

6. Adventures in Medialand

Foreword

by Rob Walker

Active vs. passive: that's the crucial dichotomy everybody talks about in discussions of media culture in general, and the commercialized subset of that culture in particular. I believe I first encountered *Stay Free!* in 1997 (that's the date on the oldest issue I still have, at any rate). An independent publication finding its audience against astonishing odds, it was certainly the opposite of passive. I loved it and remained a devoted reader of the print version and its online successor. It was smart and funny and entertaining and original: well researched and serious when it needed to be, and sharply satirical and almost reckless when it didn't. Extremely informed interviews from scholars coexisted with smart-ass pranks. And the writing, by Carrie McLaren, Jason Torchinsky, and their colleagues, always took an approach to commercial and media culture that was active in the very best sense of the word.

Many of the finest examples are collected here, along with new material that lives up to that standard. Everything in *Ad Nauseam* is about questioning what most people take for granted, laughing at the stuff you're meant to accept soberly, and taking seriously the things you're not intended to notice at all. This is done in a variety of ways. The opening overview of ad history is indispensable—and is followed promptly by an attempt to train a dog to like iPods that makes some surprisingly effective points about marketing and the human animal. McLaren's piece about subliminal advertising is the most insightful take on the subject I've ever read, and Torchinsky manages to make a visit to a sponsored party at the Playboy mansion provocative in an entirely different manner from what you might expect. Throughout, it's a book of thinking about the news and entertainment we're offered and, in particular, about the commercial expression that underwrites so much of it. It's a book, that is, of thinking about what we're really not supposed to think about—and inspiring the reader to do the same.

It's a sad fact that while the shaping of consumer culture is an incredibly important topic that touches all of our lives on many levels, the vast majority of commentary about it is written by a group of people whose opinions are decidedly skewed. These are the marketing professionals and gurus whose assessments of commercial persuasion in American life invariably boil down to Seven Tips for Selling More Whatever to today's savvy consumer. Whatever value that sort of thing may have for the trade, it's not very useful to the other participants in consumer culture: everybody else. We could use more voices on the subject whose end goal isn't landing new clients or scoring a corporate consulting gig.

So as refreshing as it was to encounter such voices when I first did, and with the way the commercial and media landscape has changed in recent years, it's flat-out energizing to read them now.

To explain why, I have to say something about the cheaper, less useful senses of "active" that have come into vogue in the twenty-first century. Frequently, these uses involve squishing that word into the much-ballyhooed idea of the *interactive.*

Thanks to interactiveness, you can, for instance, respond directly to an online opinion you disagree with: type "Your an idiot" into the comments field, and you have just participated; you have interacted; you have been not-passive. In the realm of consumer culture it means, say, complaining via Twitter that you have lately received a very poor latte from a famous coffee chain. If that coffee chain has employed someone to monitor brand-specific tweets, then perhaps you'll be contacted and score a compensatory coupon. (And maybe you'll tweet about that, thereby completing the transformation of your interactivity into word-of-mouth marketing.) Or maybe you don't have a complaint, you have an idea for a whole new style of caffeinated beverage you wish this coffee chain would sell. No problem. Stop by the new website the chain has set up where you can log on and share your profitable idea. Big ups: you've *interacted* with a brand.

Fine. (I guess.) But passing this sort of thing off as empowerment, democratization, or progress presents a few problems. It shamelessly misrepresents the world prior to comment fields and social networking sites and so on as a place where we all stared slack-jawed at *Gilligan's Island*, nobody disagreed with whatever the evening news anchors had to say, and everybody bought the products that were advertised on television for the simple reason that this is what the advertisements told us to do. This suggests not only that nobody knew how to think, but also that this sorry state of affairs has been resolved only because we are now "allowed" to comment, "given" interactive new techno tools, and "provided" opportunities to express ourselves. In other words, even our newfound unpassiveness has been handed to us from without.

If you find the theory that an active response to commercial culture is a recent gift from corporate America a little suspect, if you prefer a version of unpassiveness that's a little more genuine, well, you've come to the right place. Of course I'm not suggesting that you'll simply agree with every opinion or conclusion in the pages ahead. What fun would that be? I'm suggesting you'll find yourself doing what I did when I first came upon *Stay Free!* years ago: learning new things, forming new opinions, having a well-placed laugh or two, and thinking. That's the whole idea—or that's what I think, anyway.

Rob Walker is *The New York Times Magazine*'s "Consumed" columnist and the author of *Buying In: The Secret Dialogue Between What We Buy and Who We Are.*

Preface

A few years ago, I spent a semester trying to teach Nike-wearin', iPod-swingin' American high schoolers what it meant to live in a consumer culture.

The class began with a simple exercise. I showed slides of twenty plants and trees common in our Brooklyn neighborhood and asked the kids to name as many as they could. They stared at me blankly.

Then I showed a slide of the alphabet, in which each letter had been lifted from the logo of a common household consumer product. This time, the kids proudly shouted out the brands associated with each letter. They got nearly all of them right (and I suppose can be forgiven for missing the "U" in Uncle Ben's).

These kids—and the zeal with which they devoured "American Alphabet"* as opposed to, say, the actual landscape around them—seemed alien to me. But the truth is that high school students like these aren't all that different from most Americans. Whether living in cities or suburbs, we're surrounded by

*The title is from the original artwork by Heidi Cody that this exercise is based on.

logos as well as flora. Yet, we're much more familiar with the former, because that is what our culture emphasizes. The ads, logos, and other symbols that we encounter thousands of times each day constitute an education of sorts, but it's a hidden form of teaching. Ask most Americans over the age of twelve whether advertising influences their decisions and they'll tell you: "Advertising doesn't affect me. I just ignore it."

People make similar assumptions about television and other media. We all too often assume that only the unstable, ignorant masses are seriously influenced by what they read, watch, or listen to. The media industries encourage these assumptions by trumpeting Americans'—particularly young Americans'—ever-increasing "media savvy."

Ad Nauseam is guided by a singular proposition: to show the varied ways that this culture *matters*. The task is made more difficult by the fact that the particular culture we're concerned with—consumer culture—is generally not recognized as "culture" at all. We're not merely talking about pop culture here, or American culture (although there is a great deal of overlap). We're talking about a culture *centered on buying and selling*, a culture defined primarily by pecuniary interests.

In confronting consumer culture in all its guises, *Ad Nauseam* tends to focus on advertising—and by "advertising" we mean to use the term not merely in the form of the magazine pages you thumb through to get to the table of contents, or the fifteen-second interludes between TV programs, but in the broadest possible sense. As an industry, advertising has evolved over its hundred-plus years to pervade and transform all aspects of American life. You can actually see this process take shape by examining print ads over the course of the last century. These mini-portraits of American life reveal a decided trend: first, the "reason-why" direct appeal disappeared, followed by the text, then the product. By the 1980s, a typical ad—still distinguishable from media "content"—would contain nothing more than a logo superimposed over a photo of a sexy woman, happy couple, or puppy.

Today, as we progress deeper into the twenty-first century, the trend continues apace, only by now the ad itself has disappeared as all popular media—film, magazines, television, pop music, and websites—have come to function as ads. As in the plot of the sci-fi B movie *They Live*, Consume! is implied in every media message. Every hit on the radio brings to mind a corresponding car commercial. Online book reviews scan with an imaginary "Click here to purchase at Amazon.com" button. An invisible FOR SALE sign hangs over everything the Desperate Housewives keep in their impressively expensive closets.

The evolution of advertisements has a corollary in the evolution (or, if you prefer, de-evolution) of our brains. We're surrounded by so many commercial messages that in order to be productive human beings, we've tried to cope. We've become experts in making snap judgments, in tuning things out. We'll consider "new and improved" a selling point the first time but learn to ignore it. Twelve-story billboards that initially catch our eye inevitably become invisible. We stop opening e-mails with headers that resemble spam. The more ads proliferate, the more we rely—the more we *have* to rely—on defense mechanisms.

We've also learned, for example, ways of distinguishing what advertisements actually *mean* from what they *say*, nuances that you won't find in any schoolbooks. My friend Paul once joked about the "new" Soft 'n Creamy brand of Breyers ice cream. "So, was all the ice cream they made before hard and crusty?" he said, laughing. His observation struck me as funny at the time. But later I remembered that I had actually wondered a similar thing *when I was six years old*. Seriously perplexed by the major laundry detergent brands boldly declaring themselves "new and improved," I pestered my mom to tell me what was wrong with them before. Upon learning that these descriptives were essentially meaningless, I did what every forward-thinking person does: I ignored them.

Inculcating this kind of skepticism is the foundation of a burgeoning media literacy movement, where well-intentioned critics point to disbelief as the necessary prescriptive for ad-land. "Don't trust advertising," they say. "You can't believe what you read or watch. The media lie."

A well-developed sense of skepticism is, of course, crucial in navigating consumer culture. But skepticism turns out to be a surprisingly limited tool: it gets exhausting quickly. If the typical American sees three thousand ads every day, it's unlikely she'll notice more than ten, let alone have time or energy to analyze them. Besides, as anyone who's ever been sucked into a senseless novel or scary movie knows, there's pleasure in getting snookered from time to time.

For many years, I self-published a magazine called *Stay Free!* that sometimes ran parodies of popular advertisements. One such parody, designed to resemble a Gap ad, portrayed a young man who had just hung himself, alongside the familiar slogan "khakis swing." My contributors and I intentionally left the Gap logo off, but it didn't matter. Everyone we talked to who saw the ad immediately thought of the Gap. Some peo-

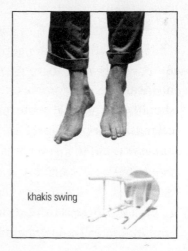

khakis swing

ple even mistook the parody for the real thing. A coworker of mine at an urban design magazine congratulated me for snagging a Gap ad! This woman wasn't stupid. She just didn't consciously process the image. Like the students rattling off the brands in "American Alphabet," she reflexively identified the look and feel of the image but never really thought about it.

What we aim to do with *Ad Nauseam* is encourage readers to "think about it"—to make people conscious of the things that they are usually unconscious of, if only for a moment. How does advertising really work? How does it shape not merely our product purchasing but the ways we define community, friendship, and family? What does it mean to live in a consumer culture?

The consumer world, after all, isn't the only world possible. But Americans young and old are like the students in my high school class: fish who can't see the water . . . and, okay, every so often we'll read an eye-opening article and notice the tide, but critical analysis of commercialism is one message that bears repeating again and again. In fact, it *must* be heard over and over if it's going to challenge His Master's Voice, that endlessly chattering loop: advertising.

What Is Stay Free!?

A familiarity with the magazine that spawned this book is by no means necessary for appreciating it, but a bit of background should help provide context. *Stay Free!* began life as a free, local music zine in Chapel Hill, North Carolina, around 1993. The name was chosen as a spoof on the faux feminist name of a popular brand of maxipads. If companies can steal ideas from women's activists, we reasoned, *why not try to steal them back?*

In 2005, we launched a blog, *Stay Free! Daily*, that covers issues similar to those covered in the magazine: marketing misdeeds, corporate shenanigans, advertising schemes, and the occasional item related to Brooklyn, where *Stay Free!* headquarters are now located. We eventually decided to go "paper free," putting out what would be the final issue of the magazine in 2006 and focusing on the blog, which continues on at blog.stayfreemagazine.org.

About This Book

Roughly 70 percent of the articles in here originally appeared in the pages of *Stay Free!* in one form or another. Many have been updated, several have been entirely rewritten, and a few are published in their original form. For those of you who care about things like sources, we've listed the *Stay Free!* issue number and approximate date of previously published stories at the end of each piece, as well as the author's name when the article wasn't penned by one or both of us. Entries that have no such citation are original to this book.

In order to understand consumer culture, you need to first understand modern advertising. So, in terms of organization, the first section looks at how advertising works—and not merely how advertising does what it is intended to do (sell products) but what it does in the process of doing it. Most people have a very limited—and wrong—understanding of advertising. They assume that commercials succeed by prompting viewers to run off to buy the advertised good. The enlightened ad agent, however, merely hopes to win the attention of prospective buyers by momentarily knocking them out of their media comas. Contrary to popular belief, the vast majority of consumer advertising isn't designed to persuade anyone of anything, but merely to link a favorable (if arbitrary) image to one's brand and to keep it "top of mind" among potential consumers.

In the second part, we look at how rampant consumerism affects individuals and their psyches. No one is immune from advertising's influence. To be not influenced is to be nonsentient. Every time you're distracted by the blinking banner ad—every time you glimpse a naked torso—you're being influenced, regardless of whether you end up buying the advertised good. In fact, altered purchasing habits are only one possible effect of advertising, and a minor one at that. Here we look at how consumer society shapes our behavior, our personal goals, and our attitudes toward our fellows.

In the third section, we take a step back from the individual and consider how consumer culture affects society at large. Nothing is wrong with buying and selling. How else would we secure our morning bagel? The problem starts when the profit motive invades places where it has no business being: schools, courtrooms, and hospitals. The situation is complicated by the fact that advertising has increasingly received First Amendment protection, so that sellers are free to advertise however they like, but you aren't free to get away from it. The result? A society that favors noise and idiocy over logic and quiet contemplation.

Having addressed the basics, we start exploring some of the details in the fourth section. Here we go behind the scenes of the media machine, looking at places and processes that the normal human never sees or ponders: a Nike shop designed exclusively for celebrities, market researchers paid to spy on shoppers, and the creation of corporate-sponsored holidays.

In the same way that going "behind the scenes" sheds light on the consumer world, history presents a mind-altering side to the story. But the commercial media system we know and love is aggressively ahistoric, largely because true warts-and-all history interferes with selling. We explain this in the fifth section, drawing on history as a means of understanding a present where Einstein sells khakis and "freedom" can be purchased with a zero-percent-interest credit card.

The final chapter is often one in which authors outline solutions to all of the problems they've detailed. We're not going that route because there is no grand panacea we can honestly prescribe. Instead, for the sixth section, we've collected a few minor acts of protest: people who have found creative ways to subvert, exploit, or merely survive the marketing machine. None of these examples are going to change the world but they at the very least suggest possibilities for entertainment not centered on consuming.

Introduction

In his cult classic movie *Idiocracy*, Mike Judge portrayed a future society so anesthetized by advertising that people have given up all intellectual pursuits to devote their time to TV, money, and hand jobs. Though riddled with slapstick and potty humor, Judge's fable provides us with an important cautionary tale. What happens to a society when it lets corporate marketing dominate its culture? When everything from hospitals to schools to city parks is mined for its profit potential?

What happens is that the governing body resembling democracy quickly devolves into idiocracy. Whereas in a democracy, constituents are defined by their connection to others ("citizens"), in an idiocracy they are defined by their propensity to buy things ("consumers"). Whereas a democracy is governed by rational thought and debate, an idiocracy is fueled by emotion and impulse.

This idiocracy isn't merely part of a speculative future; it's already here, invading our schoolbooks, computer screens, and municipalities. Perhaps the scariest thing about *Idiocracy* the movie is how much it looks like our reality: with newscasts filled with highway chases and celebrity profiles, public pay phones that work only as billboards, and elected officials who mouth nonsense while nakedly fronting for industry.

Ad Nauseam is our attempt to teach readers how to look more critically at consumer culture. But we don't want this goal to be mistaken for an end in itself; learning the methods and madness of media mechanizations is only the first step. In order to truly understand unchecked consumerism, we need some sense of an alternative—something to compare it with. And in order to get that sense, we need to start placing some boundaries on the marketing machine. In other words, we need to take action. To that end, we've included information about nonprofit, activist organizations at the end of this book, so that readers so inspired can get involved in battling the powers that be. Only by challenging rampant commercialism and limiting its reach can we hope to ever understand consumer culture and our place within it.

—Carrie McLaren

Ad Nauseam

How Advertising Works

1.

The Evolution of Advertising

ADS ARE PREDATORY. This is not necessarily a bad thing, as some of my favorite cats are predatory. But ads are not only predatory, they're mercenary: hired guns paid to hunt down our desires and bag them for dollars. Like any good predator, advertising evolves along with its prey. Ads in their primeval form merely needed to alert a potential buyer of what was being vended—a shoe or a dismembered pig, for instance. Just enough to get the idea across. As competition grew, so did the need to create demand; hence modern advertising was born. If we start the modern era of advertising around the late 1800s, an evolutionary path can be plotted and expressed as a series of broad caricatures.

The Polite Pedant (Late 1800s to 1900s)

Print ads from this early era have the tone of a helpful, avuncular acquaintance, someone who is humble about taking up your precious time but feels compelled to describe in great, tedious detail the relative benefits of a particular product. You can almost imagine him, dressed soberly but very dapper, hat in hand, earnestly and a touch apologetically enumerating every possible item of worth about face soap or bolts of cloth. You'd likely smile and nod, not offended, with every fiber of your soul fighting off the warm blanket of sleep.

A bold choice for a camera company, the complete lack of images. The sober, informative tone of this 1891 ad is indicative of the era, and of special note is the motto: "You press the button, we do the rest," followed by "or you can do it all yourself." This is a company too polite to even insist upon its own slogan.

PHOTOGRAPHIC OUTFITS

THE KODAK

Combines in one compact instrument all the attributes of a view or hand camera.

For snap shots in the street, tripod work in the field, or flash-light pictures at night, it is not equaled by any other instrument.

It is the only camera that exposes continuous films with certainty, and without abrasion of the sensitive surface.

Being simple and certain, it is adapted to the use of both young and old, novices or experts, and is fast superseding other cameras the world over.

The KODAK is made in various styles and sizes, to suit all tastes, and, while being preëminently a film camera, it is also fitted with a glass plate attachment for those who desire.

Any number of exposures can be made with it, and removed for finishing without disturbing the rest of the load.

Every KODAK is carefully tested in actual use before it leaves the factory. No imperfect lens or faulty mechanism can pass our inspectors, and it is owing to the great care taken in our testing department that good results with the KODAK are almost invariably secured.

" You press the button,
We do the rest,"

or you can do it all yourself.

THE EASTMAN COMPANY,
ROCHESTER, N. Y.

115 OXFORD STREET, LONDON.
4 PLACE VENDOME, PARIS.

When you write, please mention THE CENTURY.

Dec. '91.

The Expert (1920s to 1940s)

It didn't take advertisers long to realize that a well-reasoned argument was still just that: an argument. And arguments can be lost, which begs the question: Why do something unless you know you can win? Why bother presenting facts to make a case when you can neatly circumvent all that messy reason and appeal directly to emotion? With the popularization of Pavlov, Freud, and the nascent field of psychoanalysis, advertisers realized that you can give people reasons to do things that don't really make sense, as long as they play to a person's deep-seated drives and insecurities. It's kind of like being able to hack into brains: say the right thing, from a position of authority (perhaps wearing a white lab coat), and you can create an army of self-conscious zombies, ready to buy anything they can to get rid of their horrible breath or coarse hands.

In this 1941 Listerine ad, that speckled circle resembling a diagram of samba steps is in fact a scientist's-eye view through a microscope, showing the many wee beasties that do abominable things to your scalp. And since it's through a microscope, you know it's from a scientist, and you'd better damn well listen. He's so very much smarter than you, and you're only hurting yourself by not, um, rubbing mouthwash on your head.

Pretty as a Picture (1940s to 1950s)

People aren't that crazy about reading long blocks of text about products. Better to show them! Advertising, while never afraid of images, starts to realize their true power. Make them big and colorful. And don't focus on the product; focus on the consumer, who is by now enjoying the wild, unrestrained happiness that can come only with choosing a quality drain unclogger or a pair of insoles.

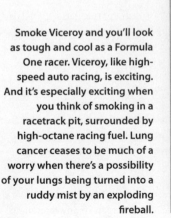

Smoke Viceroy and you'll look as tough and cool as a Formula One racer. Viceroy, like high-speed auto racing, is exciting. And it's especially exciting when you think of smoking in a racetrack pit, surrounded by high-octane racing fuel. Lung cancer ceases to be much of a worry when there's a possibility of your lungs being turned into a ruddy mist by an exploding fireball.

The Double Agent (1960s to 2000s)

Blatant advertising styles were becoming a joke, but where there's a joke, there's laughter; and where there's laughter, there's either a recording of laughter or, better yet, people—people who can be made to buy things! So why be laughed *at* when you can laugh *with*.

And so was born a new persona for ads: an intelligent friend, a pal who's a bit smarter, hipper, and more attractive than you but likes you anyway. He tells you, in a witty way, why you might want to buy a Volkswagen as both of you laugh at those ridiculous Chevy ads with their smitten bimbos and tailfins. The fools, you and your pal laugh, right before he suggests what kind of vodka a young, urbane sophisticate such as yourself may enjoy. The Double Agent is cunning. He's genuinely funny and engaging, but deep down he only wants you for one thing.

Think small.

This ad of Volkswagen's legendary 1960s campaign is iconic. It popularized a style of hip self-deprecation that flatters the consumer for his resistance to advertising—all the while selling to him. Call it the anti-gimmick gimmick.

The Mystic (1990s to 2000s)

Recent changes have made ads the most effective consumer-consuming creations ever known. Building on over a century of experimentation, ads now work from deep within your mind. Ads no longer need to engage in such mundane activities as showing the product, telling what it does, or making any claims of value. Sellers catch more prey by blurring the boundaries between advertising and not-advertising. Product placement, viral marketing, and friend-to-friend shilling is all part of the new form—a being that has reduced itself down to a single cell that permeates the air you breathe, the sounds around you, the classrooms you endure, and the movies you watch. It's a fully ingrained part of the fabric of life.

There's no ad here, just homework. We've got our McGraw-Hill math textbook and we're learning how to divide wholes into parts, and those parts are M&M's—small, convenient, tasty, fun to eat, melting only in mouths, not hands, available in peanut as well as plain varieties.

The Psychology of Advertising

WE'RE ALL APES

I N O R D E R to understand how advertising works, we need to first realize how it *doesn't* work. Many people assume that commercials succeed or fail based on whether viewers rush out to buy the particular product. They assume that if they don't like an ad, can't remember the brand, or consider the whole affair inane, they're not affected by it. All of these assumptions are based on an outdated model of advertising as a form of persuasion. But advertisers discovered long ago that persuasion is terribly limited in its ability to push product. Persuasion engages rational thought. When your potential consumers start thinking, they're as likely to consider the bills they need to pay, the crap they can't fit in the closet, the calories they need to count, or the appointment they're going to miss. In other words, thinking consumers buy less. Persuasion is also a relatively slow process. In a sped-up world with zillions of ads competing for attention, there's no time for it.

The vast majority of consumer advertising today, then, isn't designed to convince anyone of anything. Rather, advertising relies primarily on the power of suggestion (or association) to create a psychological link between some favorable image and one's product. Nike = inspiring athletics; Lexus = luxury;

Marlboro = manly. Unlike persuasion, suggestion doesn't require our active attention. If some guy in a suit said to you, "Wear these Nike shoes and you'll be like an athlete," you'd never take him seriously. Such a claim is verifiably true or false, and the question of whether something is true or false prompts that troublesome habit of *thinking* ("Is it true?" "What does that mean?").

Suggestion, however, inspires belief by not asking for it, by averting the questioning process. Nike's ad agency produces jaw-droppingly beautiful images and emotionally rich, provocative commercials punctuated by contained moments of rebellion. Repeated often enough, the linking of Nike with inspiration and triumphant athleticism gets drilled into your brain, becoming more accessible than your father's birthday.

The basis for association is Pavlovian. We consumers are like dogs who dance excitedly when someone pulls the leash out. Advertisers take greatest advantage of us by capitalizing on our animal behaviors—and by "animal" I mean rooted in our biology, behaviors that are innate. Much of what we consider to be advertising clichés are strategies based in these biological drives: the human appetites for food and sex (not necessarily in that order). I'm talking phallic beer bottles, mouthwatering "money" shots of hamburgers, and big-breasted models pitching everything from skateboards to kitchen gadgets. Appeals using sex or food are among the most obvious tactics, yet people seldom recognize their unconscious effect. In a classic study, a group of men was shown a car ad featuring a sexy young woman and another group of men saw the same ad without the sultress. The men who saw the ad with the girl "rated the car as faster, more appealing, more expensive-looking, and better designed than did men who viewed the same ad without the model." Naturally, these men later denied that the presence of the young model had any influence on them.[1]

Food and sex are just the tip of the iceberg. Advertisers aim to reach our inner animal through instincts more subtle than our appetites. For example, humans are much more likely to notice an object if it moves. A cockroach could remain on a wall in my office for hours if it stayed in place, but I will scream bloody murder when it crawls, even if it appears only out of the corner of my eye. Darwin tells us that this tendency is a holdover from our hunter-gatherer past, when we needed to spot prey and potential enemies alike. Alas, in the modern office or home, this inclination is decidedly less helpful, protecting us from cockroaches and falling light fixtures but not much else. Instead, it renders us vulnerable to marketers, who exploit it with flashing banner ads, gigantic video billboards, and TV "news" crawls.

Advertisers similarly exploit humans' animal instincts by taking advantage of our inner copycat. Humans—even some of the most rugged of individualists—look to others for clues on how to act. Our copying begins at infancy, when we acquire language, the ability to walk, and social skills from family members. Things aren't much different as adults: we yawn when someone around us yawns, look up at a building when

Marketers love to appeal to our animal instincts, be they for plump, juicy burgers or pea-brained, scantily dressed blondes. The image at right is taken from Paris Hilton's once-controversial Carl's Jr. commercial.

A Brief History of Advertising Suggestion

Stage 1

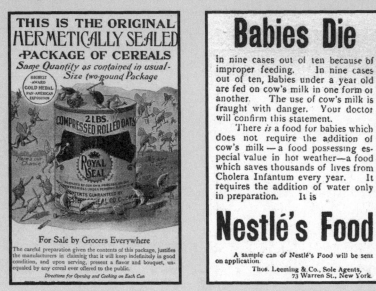

In the days before Pavlov, ad men didn't quite "get" how suggestion worked, as is demonstrated by this unappetizing visage (above left) of insects surrounding Royal Seal brand oats, from the 1890s. Apparently, the Great Western Cereal Company thought that nothing said breakfast like a roach infestation. Similarly, a misguided attempt to scare parents off of cow's milk (above right) had the unfortunate side effect of scaring them away from Nestlé's Food as well. As Charles Austin Bates pointed out in *Good Advertising* (1896), the copywriter would have been much better off with a headline such as "Save Babies." Consider, for example, how this ad must have appeared to a barely attentive newspaper reader who merely glimpsed the large headings.

Stage 2

By 1919, advertisers were taking note of developments in psychology and experimenting with suggestion. This ad illustrates an important advance: instead of associating the product with dead babies or vermin, it links toothpaste with something *positive*—happiness. Yet, its literary approach, requiring the audience to read a half page of uninspired copy, means that only active readers will make the connection. In other words, while giving a nod to Pavlov, the ad agents missed an essential point: suggestion works best when the audience isn't conscious of it.

Stage 3

This car ad (1926) one-ups the toothpaste with a crucial addition: a photo showing the car as the vehicle of choice for rich white people. Still, the photo remains dominated by cumbersome copy, including one phrase ("social asset") that reads as if ripped straight out of a psychologist's notebook.

Stage 4

Introducing naked association. Copy is now more or less superfluous: if you removed it all and left only the logo, the ad would convey essentially the same point. Unlike earlier copy, the text in this 1964 ad has a humorous, vaguely self-conscious tone, as if to apologize for assuming the reader is so base as to fall for a sexual appeal.

Stage 5

If people were not familiar with advertising, they might look at this 2007 ad and think the person here is Yves Saint Laurent—or,

perhaps, a creature from the future. But modern consumers instantly identify this as a fashion ad. As advertisers have improved methods of suggestion, audiences have evolved to interpret them.

YVESSAINTLAURENT

we notice others doing so, and laugh more when others are laughing (whether live or canned for lousy TV sitcoms). More often than not, we're unconscious of our copying. Ever find yourself applauding a show and pausing to think, "Wait. That sucked"?

Marketers exploit such copycatting in a number of ways. Most noticeably, ads are loaded with images of people wearing things the sellers want you to wear, or doing things they want you to do. Other tactics are both more ambitious and subtle. Nike hires good-looking fans to wear its clothes and cheer at the Australian Open.[2] Liquor companies hire foxy young trendsetters to prominently order their brands in popular bars. And new forms of word-of-mouth marketing ("buzz," "viral"), where companies enlist everyday people to model and promote products to their friends, are springing up like cancers.[3]

Marketers often link copycatting with yet another animal drive: we're naturally drawn to good-looking people. Although the evolutionary basis of this instinct is arguably reproductive and therefore sexual, it carries over into a preference for attractive animals of all sorts: the handsome men and women working at Banana Republic, the adorable babies in the GAP Kids catalog, and the fluffy kittens in the animal shelter pamphlet. While this inclination in itself is no shocker, what is surprising is how powerful it is. We not only prefer attractive people, we unknowingly attribute to them all manner of positive traits. Study after study has shown that humans are more likely to vote for good-looking people, more likely to give them jobs, more likely to consider them intelligent and kind, more likely to deem them not guilty in a court of law, and on and on and on. There's even evidence that parents and teachers are nicer to kids who are cute.[4]

These animal instincts—toward attractiveness, copycatting, flashy objects—are among the most universal and the most easily exploited by marketers, but they are far from the only examples. You could fill an entire library with the books and articles that have been written on consumer psychology.

Like birds and bees, humans are instinctively drawn to certain colors. Unlike birds and bees, humans are self-conscious, and that consciousness prevents us from acknowledging such unconscious influences. To wit: Market researcher Louis Cheskin once conducted an experiment in which he mailed out to test subjects identical samples of an underarm deodorant packaged in three different color schemes. He told the subjects that the deodorants were different formulations and asked them which they preferred. The response? People considered color scheme B best, with its pleasing fragrance and long-lasting effectiveness. Color scheme C was deemed less effective, with a stronger aroma. And color scheme A was practically toxic. As Thomas Hine notes in *The Total Package: The Evolution and Secret Meanings of Boxes, Bottles, Cans and Tubes*, "several users developed skin rashes after using it and three had severe enough problems to consult dermatologists."[5] Yet, the typical deodorant buyer would deny that something as mundane as package design could shape his or her experience in such a way.

We can study our animal nature, try to memorize marketers' tricks backwards and forwards, and we'll never come close to immunizing ourselves from their influence. For one thing, there are simply too many unconscious influences to possibly identify, let alone count. Hidden influences are as varied, fleeting, and infinite as sensory experiences. We may be the most intellectually evolved creatures on the planet, but we instinctively respond to colors, shapes, and scents.

All of which is to say that marketers have biology on their side. Darwinian evolution—our genetic heritage—can't evolve fast enough keep up with culture. It took untold generations for evolution to rid us of our fangs and tails, and only a couple of months for pop-up ads to spread. In order to adapt, then, we can't rely on natural selection; we have to learn on our own.

And learn we do, sometimes consciously, sometimes not. We install software to block banner ads. We use TiVo to record TV programs in order to skip the commercials. We develop "banner blindness" to online web ads, instinctively directing our gaze away from them. We notice a twenty-story-tall billboard the first time we see it and then it becomes invisible to us.

The adaptations we muster are inevitably quick fixes. Once we adapt to a particular ad tactic, once we develop a strategy for avoiding it, advertising responds in kind; then we have to learn a new trick, and the cycle repeats. For example, consumers eagerly embraced TiVo and other DVRs in part because they allow them to fast-forward through commercials. The advertising industry responded in two ways. One, it started focusing more on product placements, because ads embedded in programming can't be skipped. And two, marketers started to make the spots they do run entertaining enough to draw an audience in their own right.

As a devoted TiVoer myself, I can say with authority that these strategies work. I'll break from fast-forwarding when I see, say, a new Mac-versus-PC commercial with John Hodgman and Justin Long. I'm certainly not alone. In fact, many people go the extra step and post favorite commercials on blogs and websites such as YouTube and MySpace. The Internet itself feeds the trend by allowing advertisers to get even more creative as they target smaller and smaller groups of people. Some of what you can find online is the weirdest, funniest, edgiest material you could imagine coming out of corporate America. A Budweiser spot created for the Internet takes place in an office where employees have to put a quarter into a "swear jar" every time they cuss; the money will go to buy "something for the office . . . a case of Bud Light or something." Suited-up professionals, filmed in a hilariously dry manner à la *The Office*, are shown mouthing four-letter words, so that, in the end, they can all share a Bud together. A Coca-Cola spot featuring White Stripes hipster Jack White has a catchy '70s-style jingle and surreal freeze-frame hippie-dippie scenery. Somehow it all works beautifully.

Such commercials—alternatively hilarious and poignant, silly and politically charged—suggest a future advertising where suggestion is taken to another level: where it's not so much about defining one's brand identity as sexy or delicious, but with positive experiences more generally. If a busty woman sitting in a red car is Beginner's Suggestion, this is Advanced. It assumes a consumer who is already inundated with red cars and beautiful women and is therefore resistant to such pitches . . . which isn't to say he's not still an ape.

Advertising

THE ULTIMATE DOG WHISPERER

ADVERTISING IS kind of like dog training. To train a puppy, you give it a small treat when it does something you want. And repeat and repeat. You later work in a cue that Pup can associate with staying and getting a treat. The cue could be any number of things: a command ("Stay"), a bell, a light tug on the collar. Eventually, with enough repetition, the dog will respond to the cue even without a treat because it associates the action with something good happening. Over time, dogs can be taught ever more complicated behaviors in this way. The same principle underlies modern advertising. Just as dogs can be taught to associate an arbitrary cue with sitting, humans learn, through advertising, to associate Coke with good times and Macs with creativity.

While techniques used in dog training can be useful in marketing to humans, we decided to test whether the converse is true.

Introduction

This study tests whether dogs can be made to desire an arbitrary object such as an Apple iPod (30GB, video-capable model) using proven marketing techniques. Dogs share key qualities with humans that make them highly susceptible to marketing: an intense desire to be liked; common anxiety; a drive to consume, even to excess; and the ability to learn through conditioning. Potential barriers include an inability to read or carry things, and the fact that they always seem to be broke.

The Experiments

Subject: Dirty Girl, a ten-year-old terrier mix known to enjoy leisure items (chew toys).

Test 1. Product introduction

Researcher called subject to the kitchen, a place previously associated with the distribution of desirable consumer goods (dog treats). Researcher displayed iPod to subject, who inspected it via olfactory means. Interest was lost soon afterwards.

Test 1

Results: Desire levels substandard. More aggressive promotion required.

Test 2. Use of influential authority figure

While petting and praising subject, primary caregiver (Sally) enjoyed use of the product.

Results: Ambiguous. Attention to the product was sporadic, and the subject seemed more preoccupied with receiving attention and affection from caregiver.

Test 3. Use of peer as marketer

Beezus, a Pomeranian alpha dog, was given the product and instructed to use and enjoy it around the subject.

Results: Initially, the subject displayed a great deal of attention. However, physical deterrents prevented the peer (Beezus) from properly wearing the product for longer than five minutes.

Test 3

Test 4. Use of innovative packaging

Product was slathered in a mix of ground beef and butter.

Results: Product, with marketing modifications, was placed five feet from subject, where it was apprehended

orally and manipulated for a great deal of time before being placed in a subject-dug hole under a shrub. Closer inspection revealed that all packaging had been removed and a puncture to the product's screen had damaged it considerably. A successful demonstration of proven marketing techniques.

Test 4

Image Is Everything

WHY THE ADMAN PREFERS PICTURES

Y EARS AGO, *Stay Free!* ran a fake ad that parodied a then-popular whiskey campaign. The original ad touted the brand as the choice of "sophisticated" drinkers, so we tweaked the copy to say what no sophisticated advertiser would ever say: "Remember how liquor used to make you vomit?"

Like the Gap parody mentioned earlier (pages xviii–xix), the Dewar's rip-off was mistaken by some readers for real. One subscriber even accused us of selling out. Any decent parody risks misinterpretation, but what made this one ripe for confusion is the imagery: the Dewar's parody looked virtually identical to the original ads. In order to get the joke, the audience would have to read a few words. And therein lies the snag.

Over the hundred-plus years of modern advertising, there has been a decisive shift away from using words in ads to using images. Pictures and words communicate differently, and pictures are better at selling.

Unlike written language, images can be recognized in an instant. They require no education, so any healthy person, whether infant or elderly, can appreciate them. Language, on the other hand, unfolds only over time. Letters combine to form words, and words combine to form sentences and paragraphs. Where images communicate meaning in an instant, this process is more like a game of connect the dots. With language, an "image" or idea is only complete after some degree of decoding.

The lure of images is largely emotional. A photo of a whimpering, wounded puppy can alone make one weepy. To have the same impact using language would require telling a story. And for that story to be emotionally moving, it would need to "set the scene"—to bring a visual to mind. Visuals seem more "real," more credible, to us. Vision is a primary source, a primal sense. Language is easier to discount because it invariably reflects someone else's subjectivity.

Which isn't to deny language its strengths. Logic and rational thought depend on language. Words allow us to specify cause and effect; to state something's relationship to the past or future; and to distinguish potentialities from possibilities and probabilities: *If I can afford it, I'll visit Paris this summer; but if I lose everything, I'll give up and go to Jersey.*

There's really no way to communicate even an expression as seemingly simple as this using only images. Unlike connecting words and sentences, the relationship between images is vague and open-ended. A television screen may cut from a woman crying to a man on the phone at work. Viewers make assumptions about the connection (romantic relationship? sexual harassment?), and producers have established certain conventions that play to those assumptions, but there is no "propositional syntax" equivalent to print. The ambiguousness of imagery is another quality that makes it ideal for propaganda: advertisers can establish a relationship between things without having to state the relationship outright, without having to make a claim. What's true for video is true for images in print. By merely placing a logo or product alongside a favorable image, advertisers allow viewers to make the connection on their own, to read their own meaning into it.

These characteristics combine to make imagery so powerful that when visuals compete with language for attention, visuals usually win. The classic illustration of this is a news story by CBS's Leslie Stahl that ran in 1984. Stahl's report criticized President Reagan for funding cuts harming the elderly and disabled. Footage showed Reagan visiting nursing homes and interacting with the handicapped, undercut by Stahl's disturbing findings. But after the story ran, Reagan's campaign rep shocked Stahl by calling to thank her. No one listens to the words, he

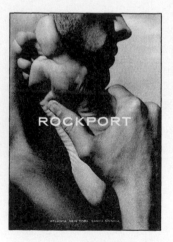

Rockport is casual yet intense sexuality. Rockport has nothing to do with anything mundane. Rockport is about you, your beautiful body, the beautiful people who long for intimate contact with you, confidence, power, and a cool, detached yet untamable lust. Rockport is the feel of perfect skin sliding against perfect skin; of the hard pressure of muscle against soft, yielding flesh; of the grazing of lips against body, of pressure and release, of passion, ROCKPORT® and of intense attraction. You want what Rockport can give you. You want to be a part of Rockport so badly it aches deep inside you. It pulls you, tempts you, forces you, with the powerful and welcome pressure of a lover's hand on the back of your neck. Rockport will take you and give you pleasure you have never known. Other beautiful people will see what Rockport has done for you, and want you in the most basic, primal ways. Rockport makes shoes, and you should buy these shoes.

A picture is worth 1,000 words . . . or at least 165. That's how many it took us
to translate the actual Rockport ad (above left) into a text-only copy
(above right). In the process, the libidinal tone of the original becomes
more or less a joke. While this seemingly ironic edge can make for unusual and
affecting advertising, it's an entirely different beast from the original.

said. And he was right. A subsequent CBS study "found that less than 25 percent of Stahl's audience understood her message while most thought that her piece was a positive news story on Ronald Reagan."[1]

In other words, better research and stronger fact-finding wouldn't have helped Stahl make her case. What her report needed was different visuals. If she had swapped out the stock footage of Reagan meeting and greeting for footage of bedsores, rotting bandages, and suffering children, she would have conveyed a different message. What Stahl needed, in other words, was an ad strategy.

Truth in Advertising Case Study

BABY VIDEOS (OR, HUMANS' CAPACITY FOR BELIEVING THE UNBELIEVABLE)

HOW DO YOU DRIVE a child psychologist crazy? Mention the multimillion-dollar market for baby videos.

According to advertising, Baby Einstein videos help develop "your toddler's speech and language skills." BabyFirstTV "encourages children to develop language" and Brainy Baby's Peek-A-Boo video "helps nurture such important skills as object permanence, communication skills, cause and effect."

Apparently nothing teaches communication skills like solitary, sedentary watching.

So here's your lesson in truth in advertising: there is none. The only formal study on the relationship between baby videos and language skills to date found that for infants eight to sixteen months, watching videos was linked to lower vocabulary skills.

This is a classic case of false advertising, in which an advertisement makes a misstatement of fact. But for every commercial that flat-out lies, eight* cleverly conceal the truth in a subtle, legal manner.

*Rough approximation. I made this statistic up.

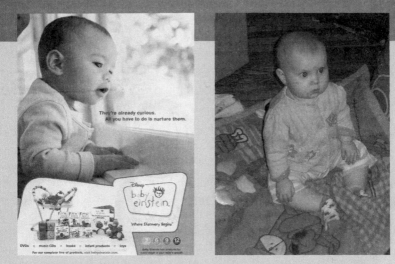

How does Baby Einstein advertise its DVDs? By showing kids enjoying life outdoors, playing with parents, and interacting with the real world—everything *but* sitting glassy-eyed in front of the tube. Notice how the ad (at left)—published after a children's health group filed a false advertising claim against Baby Einstein—suggests that the products are educational without stating that claim outright. Right: Ariel Harrington Wright, seven months, watches a Baby Einstein vid.

The most common way is to simply replace words with images, which have a handy way of making the matter of truth or falsity irrelevant. By juxtaposing a product logo with some desirable image, advertisers can prompt their audience to "fill in" the meaning on their own. Oddly enough, this projected image is often the virtual opposite of the thing as it is. A typical sport-utility vehicle ad, for instance, will show a pristine lake or mountainous terrain, creating a romantic vision of man in touch with nature. In the real world, SUVs are far more often to be found at suburban shopping malls than remote forests—which, incidentally, are becoming even more remote thanks to environmental destruction by SUVs.

Similarly, cigarette ads often show rugged, athletic types hiking, sailing, and mountain climbing—instead of the typical easily winded, yellow-toothed smoker.

So what's the one thing you'll never see on the website for a baby video company? A picture of a baby watching a video. Instead, you'll see kids petting farm animals, frolicking in the sun, playing with their parents, and reading books.

Baby video advertising projects an image of healthy, happy children experiencing life to the fullest. If that image is repeated often enough, it becomes linked in the public mind with baby television. But with the sudden rise of the baby vid industry, I get the feeling that repetition isn't the only thing driving sales. Another important factor is at stake: the public's burning desire to believe the claims about baby video.

The Power of Belief: A Parable

The following ad—a spoof on get-rich-quick schemes—was once posted in the window of a bank as an example of how *not* to invest one's money.

 We are starting a cat ranch in California with 100,000 cats. Each cat will average 12 kittens a day. The cat skins will sell for 30 cents each. One hundred men can skin 5,000 cats a day. We figure a daily profit of over $10,000 . . . Shares are selling at 5 cents each, but

the price will go up soon. Invest while opportunity
knocks at your door.[1]

> The California Ranching Company

This ad was placed next to another sign, which read:

> Some gullible people will try to buy this stock. It is a
> foolish fake, of course, but no more foolish than many
> "wild-cat" schemes being promoted today. Don't hand
> your money over to any unknown glib-tongued salesman.[2]

In other words, "Invest it with us instead!"

The cat ranch ad was just as ludicrous in the 1940s as it is today. Yet, the lure of a novel moneymaking venture turned out
to be so compelling that the bank's effort backfired. Several
people who saw the sign approached the bank tellers and asked
them if they could invest in cat ranching! So many people mis-
read the sign, in fact, that the bank had to take it down.

I experienced a similar phenomenon myself while working
for a record company in the mid-1990s. At the time, mainstream media was abuzz about the Internet and its revolutionary powers. As the label's webmaster, I thought it'd be fun to do
a spoof of Internet hype and came up with a parody of a chat
room featuring one of our most popular bands, Pavement. Pavement wasn't popular in the way that, say, Justin Timberlake was
popular. But the indie rockers had a huge and fervent following
among people who take rock music seriously.

Which, as it turns out, is ironic. The Pavement Chat was ab-
surdly billed as a twenty-four-hour! Seven days a week! Non-
stop! Chat with the band! With no interruptions! On the chat
web page, Pavement members were shown sitting at computers, a scene that I had crappily pieced together in Photoshop.

The chat itself invited users to submit questions via a form and the "responses" from the band appeared on-screen. (Those of you of a certain age may remember a program called Eliza; it was very similar.) I wrote the responses by cobbling together quotes from various Pavement interviews, and made the rest up. A few key words (tour, album titles, etc.) would trigger related but Dada-esque chunks of dialogue.

Pavement was often labeled "postmodern," and so I thought this stunt would get a big laugh and introduce fans to our new website. What I hadn't anticipated was people mistaking it for real. They did. I fielded e-mails for a week explaining to confused fans that the chat was run by a robot. *The New York Times* ended up publishing an online feature about the Pavement "hoax."

What especially surprised (and delighted) me was that the techno-utopians at *Wired* magazine were among the duped. In other words, even the most tech-savvy of readers ignored the obvious signs of satire and saw what they wanted to see. There is nothing the Internet can't provide, or so they thought.

All of which is to point out that the amount of nonsense that people are willing to believe is directly proportional to their desire to believe it. This is a widely accepted truth among admen, but the rest of us have a hard time acknowledging it in ourselves.

Which brings us back to baby videos. To understand their popularity, one must consider the context in which they are used. Parents of infants are starved for free time. In many cases, they can't afford child care and are working overtime to stay financially afloat. For single parents it's even tougher. The ability to occupy the kid for a few minutes in order to make dinner feels less like a convenience than a dire need.

This borderline desperation makes Baby Einstein's sales job

a cinch. Parents are willing and eager to believe that videos help babies learn. This allows them to avoid the guilt that comes with using television as a babysitter. It allows them to believe that they are doing something for their children instead of for themselves.

If baby-video makers changed their advertising and started touting their programs as cheap babysitters instead of something that benefited children, they would sell a lot less product. So they have responded to public concerns by marketing themselves as the opposite of a babysitter—as a "fun" tool for helping parents and babies interact. Viewing guides recommend that parents and babies watch together. (This way, if parents decide not to watch, it's their own damn fault!)

Of course, as anyone who has ever tried it knows, television is a lousy tool for communicating. Infants tend to stare at the screen as if mesmerized. A parent who truly wants to interact is better off with toys, picture books, or perhaps a cardboard box. But that truth, spoken only by child psychologists and nagging do-gooders, will not be televised.

The Sea Monkey Effect

Remember when you were a kid and saw an ad for sea monkeys in some magazine? Those sea monkeys looked amazing: raising little families, building huts, living, loving–all in a plastic tank. Then remember when you got them and found that they were just ugly crustaceans that died in two weeks? That was a hard lesson: the difference between perception and reality. Sadly, we are forced to learn this lesson again and again, even in the world of food.

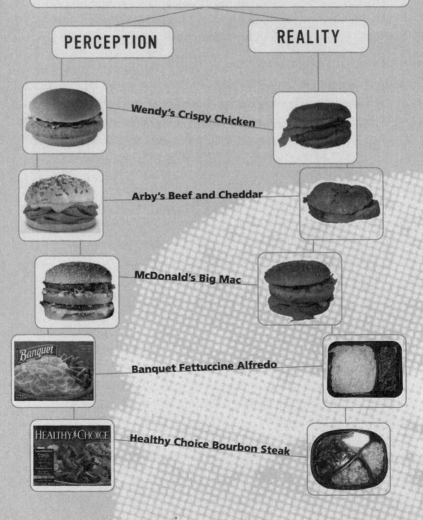

PERCEPTION

REALITY

Wendy's Crispy Chicken

Arby's Beef and Cheddar

McDonald's Big Mac

Banquet Fettuccine Alfredo

Healthy Choice Bourbon Steak

Brand Magic

To a martian visiting the United States, Ensure and Nutrament would seem like virtually identical products. It's easy to see why: both are an inelegant mix of sugar, oil, and vitamins (and roughly the same amount of sugar per serving as ten Oreo cookies).[1] Both come in various flavors and provide dinner-in-a-can. But though the ingredients are similar, Nutrament and Ensure have different identities. Whereas Nutrament is targeted to low-income, inner-city consumers, Ensure is for the elderly and dyspeptic.

This is the magic of branding. The adman Rosser Reeves once took two quarters out of his pocket and said that his job was making people believe that one was better than the other. A lot of consumer products are, like quarters, virtually indistinguishable from others in their category. Ensure and Nutrament are one example. Disposable razors are another. The same for most shampoos, soaps, and other personal grooming products: except for minor differences in fragrance and lather, they are identical.

The Rosser Reeveses of the world distinguish goods by inventing personalities

Before becoming the meal du jour among inner-city crackheads, and before the ideal female body type was borderline anorexic, Nutrament was marketed as a way for skinny teens to gain weight.

for them based on the target consumer. The ad industry calls this branding maneuver "positioning" a product in the marketplace. Since positioning has little to do with the material qualities of the product, companies can change a product's positioning without changing the actual product—and earn a windfall in the process.

Consumers weren't buying Norelco's electric shaver when it was introduced in the 1950s because shaving with rotary heads took longer. To goose sales, Norelco's advertising director came up with a brilliant plan—he changed the razor's name to Speedshaver—and sales took off.[2]

Perhaps the most famous re-positioning is that of Marlboro cigarettes. When the brand was introduced in the 1920s, it was the first cigarette with a filter tip. The ad agency targeted "decent, re-spectable" women by calling Marl-boros "mild as May." After a good run, sales began flagging in the 1950s, so Marlboro was reposi-tioned to appeal to a generation of World War II veterans who now found themselves in emasculating office jobs. An ad campaign intro-duced a new, virile Marlboro, one

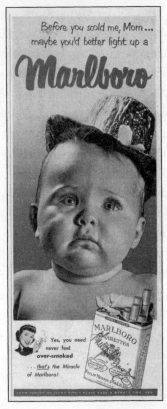

Before the Marlboro man was born, marketing for the cigarette brand— such as this ad from 1950— targeted women.

featuring tattooed military men, firefighters, and other tough guys. Then the Marlboro Man rode in on his horse, and the brand has remained the top-selling cigarette ever since.

But back to liquid meals. No one remembers it today, but Nutrament was originally touted as an aid for skinny teens to bulk up. Although the drink was initially pitched to girls, it found a more receptive audience among athletic-minded boys. In the 1970s, football trainers routinely handed out Nutrament to players before games. By the mid-1980s, however, sports nutritionists had pigeonholed the drink as a mere sugar rush, and the bottom fell out of the market.

But every cloud has a silver lining. For executives at Bristol-Myers, makers of Nutrament, that silver lining was the fact that sales turned out to be unusually strong among certain minorities: Hispanics and West Indians, for example. Nutrament was then repositioned as a meal in a can for the urban poor. Since 1993, the company has spent millions of dollars repackaging and marketing the drink on inner-city billboards, magazines, and radio programs that cater to this group.

The Wall Street Journal quoted a couple of satisfied customers: "'When you're on drugs, solid food isn't easy to get down,' says a 39-year-old welfare recipient . . . 'It's easier to drink something, and I definitely make sure it's something that's good for me.'" A homeless street musician volunteered, "I mix it with Baileys Irish Cream and ooh la la." *The Source*, a hip-hop magazine, named Nutrament one of "36 Things That Blew Up or Succeeded Because of Crack."[3]

Naturally, Bristol-Myers denied that the company targeted drug addicts or the homeless, although one spokesperson allowed, "It certainly wouldn't surprise me if drug addicts buy the product."

Key Questions

1. A pioneer in the psychology of packaging design, Louis Cheskin once tested color schemes by sending three underarm deodorants to experiment subjects. The deodorants were, in fact, identical: only the color of the packaging varied. How did people respond?

   a. Subjects preferred the first deodorant tested, regardless of color scheme.

   b. Subjects preferred the second deodorant, finding that the first one irritated the skin and the third one was strongly aromatic but ineffective.

   c. Subjects did not notice a difference between deodorants.

   d. Subjects preferred whichever deodorant was packaged in their favorite color.

2. This 1970s ad for Like cola, from the makers of 7UP, was intended to:

   a. Co-opt the burgeoning women's movement.

   b. Mock the burgeoning women's movement.

   c. We have no idea, but probably both.

   d. Confuse the Soviets.

The first soft drink just for girls

3. What emotional state did a Harvard Laboratory for Decision Science study find was most conducive to spending money?

   a. Happiness.

   b. Sadness.

   c. Fear.

   d. Envy.

4. Which of the following figures was NOT cited on the Direct Marketing Association website as the total amount of sales from telemarketing in 2001?

   a. $93,800,000,000.

   b. $296,000,000,000.

   c. $390,000,000,000.

   d. $410,000,000,000.

5. According to a 2008 study by BIGresearch, how do TV viewers spend time during commercial breaks? Match correct percentages:

   a. Talk with others in the   i.   5.5%
      room or by phone

   b. Mentally tune out   ii. 30.2%

   c. Channel-surf   iii. 33.5%

   d. Regularly fully attend   iv. 41.2%
      to commercials

6. When local weekly magazines in medium-size American cities have their annual "best of" issues, and select large chain restaurants such as McDonald's over locally owned,

independent establishments for categories such as "best burger" or "best fries," it makes one want to:

a. Cry.

b. Laugh, then cry.

c. Retch.

d. Kill.

7. Which of the following is NOT included as part of the "Megastar Package" sold by Celeb-4-A-Day, a service selling "personal paparazzi" to Los Angeles civilians?

a. Bodyguard.

b. Up to two hours of "Paparazzi Treatment," including fake reporters who ask questions, photographers vying for coverage, and people shouting your name.

c. Two weeks at Promises Rehabilitation.

d. A personal publicist to escort you to events.

8. Which of the following are NOT actual commercials?

a. After a golden retriever pees on an SUV tire, the car, a Dodge Nitro, brutally electrocutes the pup.

b. In a spot for SKY Football, a man dives to catch a dog that has leapt from a burning building, to much applause, then punts the dog as if it were a soccer ball.

c. An office worker attempting to file live cats hits the Staples "Easy" button, which sends the cats through a paper shredder.

d. The sunroof of a Ford SportKa cuts the head off a cat, whose body then falls to the ground.

Answers

1. B. Thomas Hine, *The Total Package*, p. 212.

2. C.

3. B. From the "Misery Is Not Miserly: Sad and Self-Focused Individuals Spend More" study by Cynthia E. Cryder, Jennifer S. Lerner, James J. Gross, and Ronald E. Dahl, *Psychological Science* 19, pp. 525–30.

4. D. Chris Hoofnagle, "The Direct Marketing Association's New Math," *Denialism Blog*, scienceblogs.com/denialism/2008/02/the_direct_marketing_associati.php (February 8, 2008).

5. a. iii; b. ii; c. iv; d. i. "BIGresearch Releases 11th Simultaneous Media Survey" www.bigresearch.com/news/big012208.htm (January 22, 2008).

6. Trick question. One wants to do all these things.

7. C. www.celeb4aday.com/EventLA.html.

8. C.

How Consumer
Culture Shapes
People

A S I WRITE, media outlets from *60 Minutes* to *The Wall Street Journal* are flooded with news reports of the same story: twentysomething "millennials" raised on a diet of warm fuzzies and ego-building are a disaster in the workplace, needing constant praise and attention from their superiors.

A *Wall Street Journal* columnist blames twentysomething narcissism on Mr. Rogers (unfair), boomer-style permissive parenting (getting warmer), and relentless self-esteem building (warmer still). What the press reports seem to have missed, though, is the fact that the generation in question is the first raised in an environment of unabashed marketing.

In 1980, corporate lobbying managed to get Congress to abolish the Federal Trade Commission's authority to regulate advertising to children. With no watchdog in sight, an entire industry developed to market directly to kids. Full-length commercials began masquerading as TV cartoons. Channel One was launched as an in-school, ad-industry-funded TV "news" network. And junk-food marketing skyrocketed. The most common message of marketing to tweens and teens: *Your parents are idiots, your teachers are dull, you're so much cooler than everyone else. But we understand you and know what you want— product!*

Should it be any wonder, then, that a crop of employees raised on this stuff expects to be flattered and coddled by their (obviously retarded) superiors?

Of course, there is more to this story than what corporate recruiters have to say. Bashing the youth, after all, is an age-old tradition. But there's no need to blame this rampant narcissism on young people. Imagine a planet—any planet—where the inhabitants were bombarded with thousands of marketing messages daily: at work, at home, while traveling. Ads everywhere. All the time. To keep it simple, we'll pretend that this propaganda is just like the stuff we see all the time. After one hundred years of this assault, what kinds of traits might you expect the aliens to exhibit? For starters, it's a good guess that the creatures would be inclined to obsess over minor physical flaws; they'd be self-centered and self-absorbed; their language would be peppered with pithy catchphrases and slogans; they'd have short attention spans, limited vocabularies, difficulties with logical thought, and an unhealthy fixation on material success. Sound familiar?

In this section, we plan to show that these aliens are us. Here we look at the subtle ways that advertising causes a slow-creeping brain death, shaping our thoughts and emotions through mindless repetition.

Your Ad Here

AS ADVERTISERS RACE TO COVER EVERY AVAILABLE
SURFACE, ARE THEY MAKING US INSANE?

I N 2005, a man auctioned off his head on eBay. He was followed by a woman who auctioned off her belly, a student who auctioned off his back, and a young couple who auctioned off their baby. Thus began the boom in "body advertising"—that is, the selling of ad space on one's person.

By now, these stories are old news. What new ad medium can possibly be next. Ads on gas pumps? Urinals? The bottom of each hole on the golf course? Been there, done that. Perhaps the only real challenge would be to find spaces *without* advertising.

Naturally, advertisers aren't limited by physical surfaces (or lack thereof). Voice mail, in-store radio, even fragrances are used

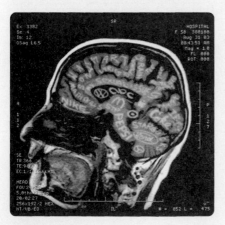

as ads, luring bystanders into retail stores and eateries. Nor are advertisers constrained by laws. "Street blimps"—large flat billboards on wheels—drive around cities despite ordinances banning them. Companies paint ads on sidewalks and streetposts, and indulge in the equally illegal "wild posting" of flyers. Billboard owners poison trees that interfere with the sight lines of their signs. The fines paid by transgressors—usually a fraction of what legit advertising costs—are prefigured in the budget.

The catch-all trade term for this kind of advertising is "ambient," or, as the British refer to it, the "pavement and urinals" category. Although it has been around for decades, the category has exploded in recent years. Although the causes are many, the forces behind ambient are inherent in the advertising process. Advertising works somewhat like bacteria: After its hosts (consumers) are exposed, they become immune, so new strains of ads must develop and grow. These new strains are quickly copied, adding clutter, requiring new strains to emerge. Over time, advertising clutter leads to diminishing returns for individual campaigns. The more advertising expands, the more it *must* expand. The cycle accelerates, and what was formerly considered unethical, offensive, or gauche is out of necessity gradually mainstreamed.

Take bathrooms. When Zoom Media, a company that places

**"Advertising in the Near Future,"
as portrayed in *Puck*, 1895**

advertising in restaurant and club bathrooms, launched in 1991, no company wanted to promote its brand near the crapper. The promise of reaching a captive, targeted audience eventually made converts, though, and Zoom reaped millions.

Similarly, ads have spread to territories formerly kept in check by some vestige of ethics: school buses and textbooks, historical monuments, doctors' offices, even whole cities. Sacramento, California's "Capital Spirit" plan pitches city services and assets such as zoos, parks, and even the police department as marketing opportunities for corporate sponsors. In Manhattan, trees along Twenty-third Street are adorned with small signs bearing Old Navy logos. It's no surprise, then, that ambient advertising is also known as "ad creep," a phrase that single-handedly suggests both advertising's growth and its creators. And though the term, like ambient, is new, its roots run deep.

In 1759, Samuel Johnson wrote in *The Idler* that "advertisements are now so numerous that they are very negligently perused." This was over a century before anything that could be considered an advertising industry existed, but almost as soon as it did (by the 1910s and '20s) admen warned of "saturation," or what is now called "clutter." The key difference between then and now is that, formerly, the media used by advertising—newspapers, radio, television—were commonly understood to be public goods. Admen felt obligated (if only out of legal concerns) to keep public interests in mind. The new breed of ad "creatives" are not nearly so encumbered, giddily promoting their ability to reach a "captive audience" with "forced media." Incidentally, said selling point also happens to be one of the main problems, as critics see it: people can't get away from this stuff. When serving as director of Commercial Alert, a nonprofit watchdog group, Gary Ruskin sent a letter to ad agencies inquiring: "Do you recognize any place to be off-limits to advertising? In your view, where should your industry draw the line?" He received no response. Advertisers have the freedom to advertise, apparently, but you aren't free to avoid it.

Not that you would want to. To hear the marketers tell it, advertising is a gift, relieving you of the agony of a reflective moment during that fifteen seconds of waiting for your cash at the ATM. The Outdoor Advertising Association of America calls billboards the "art gallery of the roadways and the theater of the streets." (The same organization once published a study showing that billboards improve safety by preventing "mild disorientation" and "excessive fantasy formation" in drivers.)

Advertisers insist the response to ambient ads is "tremendous" (Zoom Media) and "overwhelmingly positive" (beachn billboard.com), that ambient ads are "hot and chic . . . cool and hip" (Starcom Worldwide), and that criticisms are minimal: a few grumpy ATM customers here and there. At the same time they recognize that ad fatigue is real. People are said to see upwards of three thousand ads a day, and tuning out most of them is necessary to stay functional. *The Wall Street Journal* reported that following a Coca-Cola-sponsored racing event that was littered with Coke signs, giant inflatable Coke bottles, and a Coke logo covering the middle of the racetrack, only one-third of the attendees could name Coke as the sponsor.

Advertising is, to some extent, a victim of its own success. And to maintain the same level of success, it evades public criticism by rendering that criticism moot—by blanketing the environment so that there is no escape. In so doing, ambient's biggest impact may, ironically, be the most invisible. In the same way that advertising can determine what people will or won't see on the news, ambient advertisers aim to control what they will or won't see outside, at work, or wherever.

Far from shying away from this dystopic vision, corporations embrace it. Compaq chose ATMs and elevators for its "Non-Stop" ad campaign because, according to one spokesman, "we wanted to send a message that we're everywhere, that we're unstoppable."

A guerrilla campaign for CFRB, a Toronto talk radio station, was even more direct. CFRB's ad agency Roche Macaulay & Partners Advertising told *Strategy*, "We wanted [the campaign] to become part of the cityscape—a universal thing like homelessness and crime that everyone has an opinion about." In other words, controversy sponsored by CFRB. So Roche Macaulay blanketed Toronto with signs bearing such questions as: "How far away do you think the nearest crack house is?" and "Could you live on this street corner for a week?" After at least one billboard drew angry calls from residents, Roche Macaulay cheered. Apparently, when people complain, it shows they're awake and consciously viewing the brand.

A trade ad that appeared in *Advertising Age* and *Brandweek* in early 2001 for Captivate, a company that sells commercials in elevators

Even better than merely saturating the environment is getting people to interact with it. Floorgraphics, a company that places "adhesive billboards" on grocery store floors, designed a "Got Milk?" ad to look like a puddle of spilt milk, complete with an actual milk carton lying on its side. Unwitting supermarket shoppers would hunt down store employees and point out the "hazard" to them.

Such tactics may seem innocuous (even funny) as isolated incidents; the problems are apparent only when ads are multiplied by thousands and force-fed to the public.

"There's a negative correlation between all that advertising hoopla and interesting ideas we can create ourselves," says the longtime *Village Voice* ad critic Leslie Savan. Incessant advertising, she adds, "drains us and depresses our ability to think that life can be fun and interesting outside of what corporate culture brings. It's as if the color has drained out of our brains onto the signs on the floor."

As Savan suggests, our minds and spirits are the ultimate media for sale. Left unchecked, ad glut will only worsen, and any downtime people have in between absorbing media messages will be defined as waste. Thus, rather than measuring ad growth by fruit stickers and gas pumps, we should start looking at declines in IQ points and pulse rates. Once every conceivable surface has been taken, advertising's growth can come only at the expense of our own.   [*Stay Free!* #18, Spring 2001]

A Slow-Creeping Brain Death

IS CONSUMER CULTURE ROTTING OUR MINDS?

IT IS COMMONLY SAID that advertising, television, and the broader media culture have a "dumbing-down" effect on American culture. Indeed, even a momentary glance at prime-time television or the covers of popular magazines makes it hard to avoid the suspicion that there is a vast conspiracy to make Americans stupid. However, seldom does anyone ever pause to delineate how stupid we are becoming and why. We thought we'd do our part by discussing a few ways that America's ad-saturated culture is rotting our brains.

Part I: Ubiquitous Marketing Increases Mindlessness

A funny thing happened on my way back from a plant shop the other day. I had purchased three large planters, stacked them inside each other, wrapped them in a clear blue bag, and lugged them with me on the subway. The planters were heavy, so I sat them on the ground next to me.

The first time it happened I shot the transgressor a dirty look. A businesswoman mistook my planters for a trash can and threw her used tissue in them. But then it kept happening:

commuters tossed napkins, lunch bags, and, yes, more dirty tissue into my pots.

For those of you unfamiliar with the mores of the New York subway, there are no trash cans on the trains. Yet, the shape of my package and the fact that it was wrapped in a clear bag somehow signaled "trash" to people and they absentmindedly followed their instincts.

Mindlessness—this habit of acting without thinking—afflicts us all and, sadly, seems to get worse with age. A ten-year-old is less likely to mistake orange juice for milk and pour it in her cereal than a forty-year-old is (I can personally vouch for this). Humans are constantly ordering and categorizing experiences to make sense of and cope with the world. Once you touch a red-hot stove top, you know not to do that again. When the sky is covered in clouds and the air feels heavy, you come to expect rain. Learning in this fashion is a sort of stereotyping. *Racial* stereotyping has given stereotypes a bad reputation, but in fact we wouldn't function very well without them. You cross the street when you see someone walking a pit bull ahead of you. You are allergic to perfume, so you avoid sitting next to heavily made-up women on the train. You decline to rent an apartment in a building after you spot a rat in it. Pit bulls, heavily made-up women, and rodent-filled apartments all conjure stereotypes in these instances. Many pit bulls are harmless, loving dogs, the woman may also be allergic to perfume, and that rat you spotted could be an escaped pet, but the stereotypes are nonetheless helpful in navigating the world and making things go smoothly.

The more experiences we have, the more we tend to rely on these heuristics—mental cues that serve as shortcuts to thinking. In other words, the older we get, the more mindless we're likely to become. While this is a natural result of aging, it is also heavily influenced by culture and environment. People tend to be much more mindless at work than at play, for example, particularly when required to perform repetitive tasks. They tend to be more mindless when focused on meeting a future goal. And they tend to be more mindless when multitasking, or "doing many things badly at once."

Finally, people are more likely to be mindless when constantly barraged with meaningless messages designed to exploit their attention. In other words, they are more likely to be mindless in a media-and-marketing-saturated culture.

As soon as humans are able to grasp the concept of advertising, they learn to discount certain messages and, eventually, to ignore them. In children, this starts around second or third grade. By the time kids reach adulthood, they've mastered the art of tuning out. While avoiding ads can be an active, conscious process—purchasing ad-blocking software or a DVR to fast-forward through commercials—it is more commonly done out of habit, by rote. Mindlessly. Readers avert their eyes from newspaper ads. They skip the first few pages of a magazine to get to the table of contents, and then they skip the pages they instantly recognize as ads.

Sometimes these efforts backfire. A heuristic that may usually be helpful in avoiding ads can also lead you astray. You may miss a phone call from a traveling friend by assuming that the 800 number meant it was a telemarketer. E-mail messages with blank subject lines, unfamiliar sender names, or colored text trigger a "spam" reflex in some users, prompting them to hit "Delete" without actually reading. (And by "some users," I mean me. I have unwittingly trashed an untold number of personal missives from acquaintances in the process.)

The consequences of ad avoidance are perhaps more serious with more invasive—and more ambiguous—forms of adver-

Natural Schemes

You know who has an awesome marketing campaign? Nature. All the big tricks: sex appeal, hunger, the desire not to be torn apart and eaten—Nature was the first to use them all.

Camouflage

Chameleons

"Advertorials"

Occasionally you'll find yourself reading an article in a magazine when something starts to eat at you: Why is the type and page color slightly off? What's this moron's fascination with doing business in the UAE? Is there anything in Dubai this guy doesn't like? When that happens, friends, take note: you've seen a wild advertisement camouflage itself to fit in with editorial content.

Mimicry

Hawk Moth Caterpillar (mimics a snake)

Junk mail offers

Whereas mimicry in nature is usually a defense mechanism, the ad biz uses it to ensnare prey—by disguising advertising as something useful. Ever heard of a Federal Expeed or a Unified Package Service? When companies send you actual checks, do they really print the fact on the envelope?

Sweet Things

Fruit

Entertainment and freebies

Just as nature uses delicious fruit to prompt creatures to transport her seeds, so advertisers occasionally provide something enticing in hopes of us spreading their metaphorical seeds. These enticements can take almost any form, from a colorful sweatshirt to a funny commercial.

Parasitism

Tapeworms, fleas, lampreys

Product placements, celebrity endorsements

A tapeworm has it all figured out: it just hangs out, enjoying the warm splendor of your alimentary canal while you do all the work of moving, eating, and metabolizing. Like a chump. A deal this good doesn't go unnoticed, which is why advertisers have found hosts of their own for their form of parasitism. The tapeworm of advertising subtly works its way deeply into the entertainment you take in, and you then take in the hidden messages of consumption. Brilliant, huh?

tising. Our work spaces—computer screens—are covered with
floating, animated ads. Movies are loaded with unzappable
product placements. Living, breathing human advertisements
now populate bars, sports events, and streets, secretly promoting their clients' products. Offices, apartment buildings, even
historic sites are wrapped in skyscraping billboards. To avoid
such tactics, we have to not only constantly redirect and divert
our gaze but learn to ignore and discount large swaths of our
surroundings. (I once ignored a man on the street because I assumed that he was handing out retail flyers; a few seconds after
walking past him, I realized he was asking for directions.)

The number of times the average person makes a split-second
decision to avoid an ad is nearly impossible to quantify—not
that journalists haven't tried. Media reports will routinely cite
the number of ads people confront, but these stats are effectively arbitrary. When a skyscraper, a ticket stub, newspaper ed-
itorials, computer hardware and software, your ballpoint pen,
and your daily e-mail are all ads, the question is less what to
count than what *not* to.

So in keeping with today's rigorous journalism standards,
let's say the average American confronts three thousand ad messages per day. Even the most reflective or ad-loving soul auto-
matically tunes out the great bulk of them without thinking.
While it's as impossible to quantify that time as it is to count ad
impressions, I think it's safe to say that we're talking about a lot
of wasted mental energy.

The good news in all this: mindlessness does not equal stupidity. Like ignorance, hangovers, and headaches, mindlessness
is a temporary condition. Lurking in the brains of even the most
comatose consumers is the potential to wake up and experience the moment, to confront the demons overrunning our
computer screens and magazines and to embrace life at its

fullest. Then again, for those of us living under unprecedented amounts of ad creep, it's a lot easier to just tune out.

Part II: The Incredible Shrinking Attention Span

In 2005, an article about a new study on the effects of e-mail use spread across the Internet. According to the news reports, research conducted for HP found that e-mail is "a greater threat to IQ and concentration" than smoking pot. I was one of many bloggers taken in. The study did happen and it did link e-mail to lower concentration and a temporary decline in problem solving, but the press grossly exaggerated the findings. The author of the study, in fact, later described it as "the bane of my life."

Even after learning how shoddy journalism misinterpreted this research, I had no trouble believing the underlying point, because it confirmed long-held suspicions about what my own Internet habits were doing to my brain. Before I started blogging and web surfing, I would sit and read books for hours. Now that seems next to impossible. I check my e-mail on average about every two minutes. The only time I can concentrate enough to read anything substantial is when I go on vacation and unplug.

Of course, it would be a mistake to make any general pronouncements based on my own mental atrophy. But, as it turns out, I'm not alone. "Our attention span gets affected by the way we do things," Ted Selker, head of the Context Aware Computing Group at the Massachusetts Institute of Technology, told the BBC. "If we spend our time flitting from one thing to another on the web, we can get into a habit of not concentrating," he said.[1]

While it's commonly understood that Americans' collective attention span is on the decline, there has been very little substantial research on the subject. A couple of studies have linked infant television viewing with attention disorders, but neither is comprehensive. By far the strongest evidence comes from the people who've worked for decades in public speaking, market research, television production, sociology, and education who all say the same thing: attention spans are shorter than they were, say, twenty years ago.[2]

While there is no single or simple cause of this decline, there are a couple of unavoidable components. The first: the rise of electronic media and computer technology.

Americans have a fundamentally different way of interacting with and learning about the world than we did a century ago. Back then, a person had to seek out helpful information: to read widely and to talk to others. When radio came along, listeners would set aside time to stop and listen to a favorite program. Today, with the vast explosion of information sources, one's task is less to seek out than to *filter out*. A Google search for "Einstein" returns over forty-six million pages of results, including info on computer software, a restaurant, a health-care network, and baby toys. Finding reliable health-care advice means learning to identify the few trustworthy websites from the thousands of snake oil sellers, hippies, and hypochondriacs. The average white-collar worker in 1910 probably got a couple of pieces of mail a day. The average BlackBerry-toting worker today gets roughly one hundred e-mails a day.[3]

Both "seeking" and "filtering" can be mastered as critical skills, but the first requires active engagement and sustained attention; the latter can also be done passively. You can't read a book without paying attention. If your eyes merely trace the page without mentally absorbing the message, you haven't actually read. But you can skim a list of web links, perform a

Google search, listen to an iPod, or watch TV with half a brain. In fact, prevailing evidence suggests that most people do.

The rise of electronic media is intricately tied to the second factor in declining attention span: the media's underlying commercial imperative. While it's possible to conceive of a media system not driven by the profit motive (government applications were key in the development of radio, television, and the Internet), in America the two go hand in hand.

The bottom line for such commercial media is not providing helpful information or challenging the audience intellectually or emotionally: it's making money. And in order to make money, you need to get the audience's attention. If you don't get attention, you aren't in the game.

The easiest, cheapest way of getting attention is to produce stimulating material: sex, violence, dramatic music, car chases, and explosions. Alas, things are often stimulating when they're new but fail to maintain interest. Small wonder, then, that American programming has gotten faster, busier, and racier over time; there's more profanity, sex, and graphic violence in

Newspaper websites often come complete with ads blocking their stories, as if begging web surfers not to read.

the mainstream than there was thirty years ago, and there was more then than there was thirty years before that. After all, if you shout "Hey!" and someone doesn't respond, you shout it louder, faster, and in more varied ways until they do.

This process behind commercial entertainment is a feed-back loop. Viewers stop paying attention to certain kinds of material, so producers amp up the stimuli. This works, at least initially, but makes the older, slower programming even less engaging . . . which is to say, people have a harder time sitting and paying attention to it. The new stimulus quickly becomes old news.

MTV launched in 1981 as the premier source of music videos, but by 2000 it was unable to sustain itself with its bread and butter. Young audiences wouldn't sit through whole videos anymore. Instead of airing full videos, the network started showing only short bits of them at a time. The typical length of an (unwatchable) full video? About 3.5 minutes.

Music videos are far from the only thing disappearing. A business consultant and former journalist recalls:

> When I started with ABC News the network had a
> 50-second limit on the length of radio news reports. By
> the time I left ABC News nine years later, the maximum
> length of a radio news report was down to 24 seconds,
> and today (some years later), the average length of a
> soundbite on commercial radio news is less than
> 6 seconds and the length of the newscast as a whole
> (where newscasts still exist at all) has often been reduced
> by 90 percent or even more.[4]

Newspaper stories, the average length of a film or TV "shot," radio commercials: all shrinking.

Perhaps none of this would be a problem if everyday life consisted of watching TV, playing video games, and web surfing. As long as one remains connected and stimulated, the effect on our psyches is invisible. Which may be one of the reasons that, increasingly, people in public are never very far away from a screen. Airports, bars, Laundromats, banks, and even doctors' offices use TV and Net connections to keep customers happy while they wait.

But everyday life, despite our best efforts, is not like life on-screen. Our novelty-seeking brains have trouble finding the same kind of stimulation off-screen as on-. "The problem is that people think of novelty as a stimulus," Ellen Langer, a social psychologist who studies mindlessness, told me in a phone interview. In other words, we've become accustomed to being

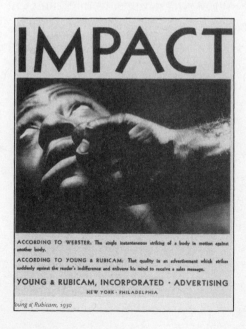

"Enlivening the mind"!? In this rare moment of candor from 1930, ad agency Young & Rubicam equates soliciting consumers' attention with punching them in the face.

entertained by things outside of ourselves—fast-cut editing and flashy visuals, for instance—rather than drawing on our own imagination and creativity.

"The trick is to teach people that *they* are what make things interesting," said Langer. "One could read the same book many times, or could see the same television program over and over, and bring to it something different each time."

The problem, then, isn't that movies, TV, and video games make people stupid. These media have the potential for teaching us new things, for opening our minds and challenging our thinking. The trouble, rather, is that time in front of the screen all too often displaces the activities that would allow us to fully appreciate it: reading books, creative writing, or traveling, for instance. Reading allows us to develop an inner language to help sort out our thoughts. It helps us to identify possibilities and probabilities, to link causes with actions, to think and to reflect. Similarly, creative writing and editing flex our imaginations and help us develop an inner dialogue. Even just sitting and doing nothing can help someone get more out of the media by encouraging him to draw on his own resources to conquer the inevitable boredom. In the end, it all boils down to letting interesting things come out of your head instead of simply allowing them to barrel toward it.

Part III: Talk Is, Like, Y'know, Cheap

Media stories, academic studies, and cranky old people decrying the inarticulate nature of today's youth are easy to find. Annoyingly, they often seem to be right—though, to be fair, I'd hesitate to single out kids. I haven't heard the word "literally" used properly in years by anyone, regardless of age.

One statistic, cited frequently in these depressing sorts of articles, states that the average teenager in 1950 had nearly double the daily working vocabulary of a 1990s teen. Now, there's no actual basis for this claim,[5] but for the sake of argument, let's say I believe it. The question, of course, is why the drop.

Teenagers now are certainly not inherently stupider than 1950s teens, what with their sock hops and jalopies; but modern teenagers have many more options open to them when it comes to finding ways to not learn more words. More important, most of those options convey a wide spectrum of ideas and stories and concepts with no words at all—and it works pretty damn well.

Teenagers in the 1950s had television and movies, of course, but nothing like we have now. They had no video games, no twenty-four-hour television, only three or four channels, no iPods, and so on. These things don't make people stupid; they merely provide alternative forms of communication: audio, visual, experiential, along with a readily accessible toolbox of easy, crafted elements that can be substituted for actual thought and expression.

Let's take a popular example: someone wants to convey disgust or shock, so he says, "I was, like . . ." and then, instead of using specific terms to describe their state, he will gasp, or say one syllable ("uh" or "wha") while making a face that mimics some quality of the state he's describing. It's essentially adding a multimedia element: instead of just saying what he felt, he's showing a clip. An emoticon.

I've seen this used since junior high school, which for me took place in the 1980s, a time when modern levels of media saturation were really getting started. This sort of nonverbal expression isn't done to save time, as usually a single word would replace the relatively time-consuming pantomime, but rather to give conversation added impact. Other media-inspired conversational add-ins, such as the sitcom-derived long, drawn-

out "Oooookaaaayyy . . ." used in lieu of actually considering
an idea or statement that at first blush seems unusual, and
other mass-media-spawned audio cues (i.e., shouting "TMI"
for "Too much information" when one is told personal or awk-
ward facts) are similar in form and use. Essentially, these are
spoken audio "samples" that have preestablished associations
that can be plugged into conversations to give an illusion of wit
without actually having to think of anything clever.

The modern media world treats long passages of speech
with disdain; a common criticism of certain movies is that they
are too "talky," a charge I suspect was never leveled at Shake-
speare. Kids now grow up in a culture that has amazing resources to make media visually and aurally very compelling;
verbal eloquence is simply not a mainstream goal. Commercial
media, instead, provide a readily available toolbox of easy-to-
remember catchphrases and quotes.

How many of us have known groups of dorks who will
quote lines from movies at one another with wild-eyed glee?
No jokes or commentary is even needed: just a rapid-fire back-
and-forth of well-known movie lines is enough to get all the
laughs. There's no work here; it's just an easy plug-and-play
path to witty banter. Quotes from commercials and other advertising are often traded with the same delighted abandon as
those from movies or television shows, with no differentiation.

In some ways it's like the desktop publishing revolution of
the mid-1980s. For the first time, tools to create professional-
looking documents came into the reach of the average person.
With an array of tools readily available, zines and documents
were created by many, many more people than ever before—
and 80 percent of them were crap. Same goes for the World
Wide Web: once tools to make web pages and later videos became easily accessible, an explosion of production resulted,

with some gems surrounded by copious amounts of crap. In the case of everyday conversation, the constant flow of advertising and entertainment provides a common pool of resources anyone can dip into freely and gain an easy way to give one's conversation a simple, thought-free means to laughs and attention.

Perhaps the modern vocabulary has shrunk, but the amount of what's being said certainly hasn't, and the voids left by all those wonderful but elusive words has been filled by premade, punchy zingers, easy and free for the taking. What's left after that is light not just on words but on worth.

When I realized this, I was, like [opens eyes and mouth wide while exhaling audibly].

Language Skills
Then and Now

SURE, every decade carping eggheads complain
that people are getting dumber and dumber . . .
but we've got proof! Here are representative examples of presidential speeches, bestselling novels, and standardized English
tests from various points in history alongside their modern
equivalents. You'll notice that in the more recent excerpts, the
grammar is less complex, the vocabulary is simpler, and the act
of consuming plays a more central role.

Exhibit I: Presidential Debates

Abraham Lincoln (debating Stephen A. Douglas), July 17, 1858

> With respect to the evidence bearing upon that question
> of fact, I readily agree that Judge Douglas and the
> Republicans had the right on their side, and that the
> Administration was wrong. But I state again that, as a
> matter of principle, there is no dispute upon the right of
> a people in a Territory merging into a State to form a
> Constitution for themselves without outside interference
> from any quarter. This being so, what is Judge Douglas
> going to spend his life for? Is he going to spend his life in
> maintaining a principle that nobody on earth opposes?

Does he expect to stand up in majestic dignity, and go through his apotheosis and become a god, in the maintaining of a principle which neither man nor mouse in all God's creation is opposing? Now something in regard to the Lecompton Constitution more specially; for I pass from this other question of popular sovereignty as the most arrant humbug that has ever been attempted on an intelligent community . . .

George W. Bush (debating Senator John Kerry), October 13, 2004

Bob, we relied upon a company out of England to provide about half of the flu vaccines for the United States citizen, and it turned out that the vaccine they were producing was contaminated. And so we took the right action and didn't allow contaminated medicine into our country. We're working with Canada to hopefully—that they'll produce a—help us realize the vaccine necessary to make sure our citizens have got flu vaccinations during this upcoming season.

My call to our fellow Americans is if you're healthy, if you're younger, don't get a flu shot this year. Help us prioritize those who need to get the flu shot, the elderly and the young.

The CDC, responsible for health in the United States, is setting those priorities and is allocating the flu vaccine accordingly.

I haven't gotten a flu shot, and I don't intend to because I want to make sure those who are most vulnerable get treated.

We have a problem with litigation in the United States of America. Vaccine manufacturers are worried about getting sued, and therefore they have backed off from providing this kind of vaccine. One of the reasons I'm such a strong believer in legal reform is so that people aren't afraid of producing a product that is necessary for the health of our citizens and then end up getting sued in a court of law.

But the best thing we can do now, Bob, given the circumstances with the company in England, is for those of us who are younger and healthy, don't get a flu shot.

Exhibit II: Standardized Tests*

Stanford Reading Achievement Test, Grade Four, 1964

Test 2: Paragraph Meaning
Although we cannot always see the difference with the naked eye, stars are of different colors, and astronomers with <u>49</u> to aid them can see this. Since heat produces light, one thing that the different <u>50</u> of the stars tell us is the <u>51</u> of each star.

49	1 telescopes 2 colors	3 eyes 4 charts		1 2 3 4 49 ○ ○ ○ ○	
50	5 colors 6 lights	7 astronomers 8 telescopes		5 6 7 8 50 ○ ○ ○ ○	
51	1 distance 2 size	3 temperature 4 weight		1 2 3 4 51 ○ ○ ○ ○	

The flowers of trees differ widely in their size and prominence, so that, while we all know the flower of the cherry tree, we may never have noticed that the oak has a flower. Yet, if we could trace back the history of every acorn, we should soon find that the oak does have a <u>52</u>. The size and appearance of what we call a flower usually depend on the part we call the petals, but these are not necessary parts of a flower at all; and there are many flowers which have no <u>53</u>. All <u>54</u> have flowers of some sort. They may be large or small, but they exist.

52	5 flower 6 trunk	7 seed 8 root		5 6 7 8 52 ○ ○ ○ ○	
53	1 color 2 petals	3 stems 4 size		1 2 3 4 53 ○ ○ ○ ○	
54	5 plants 6 petals	7 parts 8 trees		5 6 7 8 54 ○ ○ ○ ○	

FIGURE 1. Comparison of Reading Achievement Tests, Grade Four: 1964 and 1982. (A, Stanford Achievement Test: 6th edition. Copyright © 1964 by Harcourt Brace Jovanovich, Inc. Reproduced by permission. All rights reserved. B, Stanford Achievement Test: Copyright © 1982 by Harcourt Brace Jovanovich, Inc.)

*These test examples were taken from Jane Healy, *Endangered Minds: Why Children Don't Think and What We Can Do About It* (New York: Simon & Schuster, 1999), pp. 30, 34, 35, and originally published in Stanford Achievement Test: 6th edition, 1964, by Harcourt Brace Jovanovich, Inc.

Stanford "Advanced" Reading Achievement Test, Grade Nine, 1988

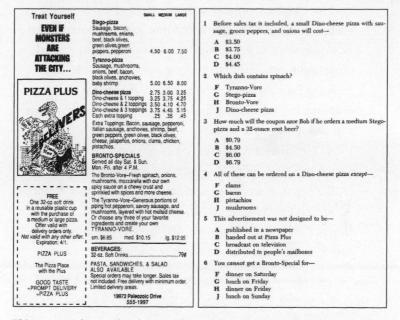

This test example was taken from Stanford Achievement Test, 1988, by Harcourt Brace Jovanovich, Inc.

Exhibit III: #1 Fiction Bestsellers

Excerpt from *The Virginian: A Horseman of the Plains*, a "Colonial Romance" by Owen Wister, 1902

Some notable sight was drawing the passengers, both men and women, to the window; and therefore I rose and crossed the car to see what it was. I saw near the track an enclosure, and round it some laughing men, and inside it some whirling dust, and amid the dust some horses, plunging, huddling, and dodging. They were cow ponies in a corral, and one of them would not be caught, no matter who threw the rope. We had plenty of time to watch this sport, for our train had stopped that the engine might take water at the tank before it pulled us up beside the station platform of Medicine Bow. We were also six hours late, and starving for entertainment. The pony in the corral was wise, and rapid of limb. Have you seen a skilful boxer watch his antagonist with a quiet, incessant eye? Such an eye as this did the pony keep upon whatever man took the rope. The man might pretend to look at the weather, which was fine; or he might affect earnest conversation with a bystander: it was bootless. The pony saw through it. No feint hoodwinked him. This animal was thoroughly a man of the world. His undistracted eye stayed fixed upon the dissembling foe . . .

Excerpt from *Blood Brothers* by Nora Roberts, 2007

Inside the pretty kitchen of the pretty house on Pleasant Avenue, Caleb Hawkins struggled not to squirm as his mother packed her version of camp-out provisions.

In his mother's world, ten-year-old boys required fresh fruit, homemade oatmeal cookies (they weren't so bad), half a dozen hard-boiled eggs, a bag of Ritz crackers made into sandwiches with Jiffy peanut butter for filling, some celery and carrot sticks (yuck!) and hearty ham and cheese sandwiches.

Then there was the thermos of lemonade, the stack of paper napkins, and the two boxes of Pop Tarts she wedged into the basket for breakfast.

"Mom, we're not going to starve to death," he

complained as she stood deliberating in front of an open cupboard. "We're going to be right in Fox's backyard."

Which was a lie, and kinda hurt his tongue. But she'd never let him go if he told her the truth. And, sheesh, he was ten. Or would be the very next day.

She put her hands on her hips, a pert, attractive blonde with summer blue eyes and a stylish curly perm. She was the mother of three, and Cal was her baby and only boy. "Now, let me check that backpack."

"Mom!"

"Honey, I just want to be sure you didn't forget anything." Ruthless in her own sunny way, Frannie unzipped Cal's navy blue pack. "Change of underwear, clean shirt, socks, good, good, shorts, toothbrush. Cal, where are the Band-Aids I told you to put in, and the Bactine, the bug repellant."

"Sheesh, we're not going to Africa."

I'm with the Brand

THE CONSUMER AS FAN

O<small>F THE PEOPLE</small> who remember watching MTV's *FANatic*, a late-1990s reality show that hooked up obsessed fans with their idols, perhaps one half of them live in my house. The show's weakness—its remarkably repetitive storylines—was also what made it interesting to this marginal demographic (me). In every episode, some fan, upon meeting Celebrity, gained composure long enough to launch into a spiraling testimony about how Celebrity had changed Fan's life. Sometimes there was a former drug problem, dead parents, depression, or poverty. In the midst of the catharsis, the stars came off as normal, reasonable, even dull.

Though very MTV, formula alone couldn't account for the stunning similarities of the testimonies, which usually included bromides gleaned from the star's lyrics or quotes: Follow Your Heart; Strivers Achieve What Dreamers Believe; Be True to Yourself, Stay in School, Love Your Mother.

Watching these testimonies to Celebrity night after night had a funny way of undermining the very myth that made them work: the belief that the particular object of affection *mattered*. The inspiration could just as well be a college professor, Jesus, or a brand of tennis shoes. In fact, the pithy lessons gleaned from celebrities resembled ad slogans. The *FANatic* narrative, in the end, was like that of commercials, with stars working magic in the same way that products do. As an old Sprite campaign said, "Image is everything." Nike, Macintosh, Coke, Pepsi, Disney: whatever works for you.

She never would have made it on *FANatic*, but Heather Denman drinks fourteen cans a day, paints her fingernails with Pepsi logos, chooses her dates based on whether they drink Pepsi or Coke, and surrounds herself with Pepsi paraphernalia. The good people at Pepsi have even flown her to Hollywood for a promotional party.

Diehard Macintosh users are known as evangelists for their zealous promotion of Macintosh products and circulation of lists such as Famous Mac Users and Why Mac Kicks Windoze Butt. Among Nike devotees, getting a tattoo is practically de rigueur. One fan sent me a letter she'd written (but never sent) to Nike chronicling her battle with drug abuse and eventual recovery through softball. She writes: "I am one of your most loyal customers. My closet is full of shoes and clothes. I guess one could say I have traded addictions. At least this one is healthy."

The fact that consumer brands should inspire fans as devoted as those of musicians and celebrities makes sense in a way. Hollywood and Madison Avenue have long competed for each other's territory. Movies are long commercials; commercials are quickie movies.

Oprah, Madonna, and Tiger Woods are not only themselves products (or brands) but ads. Buy the album. Watch the show. Wear the cologne. A recent *New York Times* article suggests that Rosie O'Donnell—herself a vocal fan of theater—is the best ad Broadway could have, in the same way Oprah is the best ad books can have. This isn't strictly endorsement, which assumes that the one doing the endorsing is outside the picture. This is more like borrowing Snap! Crackle! and Pop! to sell milk instead of cereal. As *Advertising Age* puts it: stars today don't sell brands, they *are* brands.

And brands, in turn, are human. Personification—the most obvious method by which brands acquire social traits—is nothing new: the Geico gecko is only a recent addition to the pantheon starring Mickey Mouse and Tony the Tiger. Market researchers frequently strategize by asking consumers, "If Noxema were a person, what kind of person would she be?" "If you were at a party, whom would you rather talk to: Cadillac or Volkswagen?" Why? Because no one buys yellow carbonated sugar water or four-wheeled hunks of metal. They buy Mountain Dew or Saturn.

Of course, most Pepsi drinkers don't collect used cans for wallpaper. And for every diehard, there's a cynic and a dirt digger. In fact, most people who cheer for celebrities simultaneously joke about it. Internet followers of Ariel—the full-figured cartoon protagonist of Disney's *The Little Mermaid*—formed a group called Arielholics Anonymous to treat their "dangerous addiction." The website reads: "Do you have urges to rub warm olive oil over Ariel? Did you need to take out a loan to pay for your expenditures on Ariel merchandise? . . . then you need help fast!"

Several Harry Potter fan sites have quizzes to sort out the "part time Potter fans" from the truly "obsessed." One fan, whose result indicated that she was 105 percent obsessed, wrote, "Im 12 and i need therapy! lol."

Fans of Mentos have written at length about the company's campy commercials, analyzing them for hidden meanings, staking out obscure details behind their creation, and sharing "Real-life Mento Moments." A lengthy Mentos FAQ—complete with company history, jingle lyrics, "Flavor Considerations," eating instructions, fan fiction, and loads of minutiae—is available on one of several Mentos websites.

Warm olive oil . . . ?

Whether these folks are any less obsessed than die-hard "Disneyaniacs," Mac evangelists, or Nike lovers is arguable. They are, however, ironic rather than earnest. You can be obsessed as long as you do it with a self-awareness of being obsessed . . . a response advertising actually encourages. Ads all but beg to be read ironically: the "not believing" is built right in. That sense of detachment flatters us and keeps us watching.

Joshua Gamson is a Yale professor who has written about the way audiences increasingly crave info about the manufacture of fame. "The process is a story in itself," says Gamson. Look at the "behind-the-scenes" TV documentaries, *Entertainment Weekly* stories dissecting product placements, and commercials that make fun of commercials.

The exposure of artifice—rather than turning us away from commercial culture—engages us in other ways. When authenticity is irrelevant, we can see celebrities and ads as prefabricated jokes and remain wholly entertained. Witness all the anti–Paris Hilton, anti–Rachel Ray, and anti-Starbucks blogs and websites. Of course, people focused on hating Paris Hilton and collecting pictures, building websites, and making jokes about hating Paris Hilton—are nonetheless focused on Paris Hilton. Their criticisms don't challenge consumption; they suggest we're not consuming *the right stuff.*

"Everything is in terms of consumption," says Gamson (who, for the record, loves the Spice Girls, hates Disney, and suspects Julia Roberts could turn him straight). What's disturbing, he argues, is not that we use consumption symbols to create and communicate—but the fact that that's all we use. Commercial symbols clearly address real human needs. But the solution they provide to meet them leads on a treadmill to nowhere. How to transcend mere fandom (or prove inspiration)? Be a bigger fan. To stand out from the audience, watch more, collect more, and whatever you do, be visible about it!

Stepping off the treadmill means not simply exposing and countering ads or TV shows but creating real alternatives to commercial culture. For instance? Um, we're still working on that. Meanwhile . . . Jazzercise?   [*Stay Free!* #15, Fall 1998]

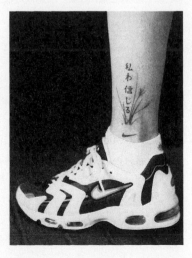

A former drug addict finally found solace through Nike products. The Japanese characters in her tattoo, she explained, mean "to believe in oneself."

Disneyaniacs!

AN INTERVIEW WITH THE LITTLE MERMAID'S BIGGEST FAN

MANY YEARS AGO, while perusing an article in *Disney Magazine*, I decided it'd be fun to interview a die-hard Disney fan. Naturally, the first place I looked was the Internet. Despite Disney's rep for aggressively policing its copyrights, fan websites were chock full of Disney images, sounds, and logos. The most interesting, for me, were those devoted to *The Little Mermaid* and its star, Ariel. Doug Webb, webmaster for *Doug's Ariel Mermaid Homepage*, was one of several Mermaid fans to find his way online. Although his website no longer exists, it was very popular in

its time, and Webb's fan fiction about Ariel and her friends remains online and much loved to date. In this interview, which took place via e-mail in December 1996, Webb discusses how something as seemingly trivial as an animated cartoon has become a central figure in his life.

CARRIE MCLAREN: How many times have you seen *The Little Mermaid*?

DOUG WEBB: About 150. I've seen each TV episode quite a few times too.

Would you say *Little Mermaid* is a children's movie?

Yes. Children see the same qualities in Ariel that many adults do.

Are there other Ariel fans that are as avid as you are?

Many others have been deeply moved by her. The depth to which people are attracted to Ariel depends upon how much they need what she has. Ariel offers a way of life that many of us would like to emulate, if only we could reproduce her personality. I think all of us would like to be happy and innocent and live in a world full of love and clearly marked values. Ariel has affected me so strongly because I see so little of these things in this world. I've also had trouble meeting women, so Ariel fills a need in me to "have someone." Being affected by Ariel is kind of like "getting" religion.

How much Ariel merchandise do you own?

I started collecting *LM* in the fall of 1990, after I saw the video and fell in love with Ariel. I just wanted to have a part of her. It's a way of being with her, to see her in a new way. I've tried to keep up with new merchandise. It's moved me out of my bedroom. I sleep on the living room floor. I want to start an *LM* museum so children can see it all. That's my dream.

How much money would you say you've spent on Ariel?

Over $20,000, and I don't make a lot of money.

There's all sorts of Ariel merchandise, so how do you decide which items to get?

Little Mermaid merchandise began to thin out about two years ago. It's just now starting to reappear, but I can't buy it anymore because I'm saving money to move to Florida and get a job at Walt Disney World (I hope!). Not buying new stuff really hurts, but up until this past summer, I bought everything I could. I even bought the clothes. I like the clothes because they have some really beautiful pics of her on them. I love the Ariel dolls. I got a little colored-glass brooch of her at Walt Disney World that's really beautiful. A shell jewelry box with Ariel on the top. A tea set. There's really so much; I just can't list it all.

How good a job does Disney do with the merchandising?

My only complaint is the sometimes sloppy attention to accuracy on Ariel's face, especially on figures.

Is there a point to be reached where you have enough?

My point has been reached by no more money and no more room in my apartment! If I had more of both, I'd still be buying.

Do you wish Ariel were a real person?

No. A real person could never be as perfect as she is now. She will retain the same personality as long as Disney sees fit to keep her that way. As I've said to others, Ariel and Flounder will be happily exploring shipwrecks long after we're gone.

Do you think Ariel has leadership potential?

Ariel leads without trying. She leads by example. She shows us that goodness and innocence don't have to be put down and laughed at. She shows that decency doesn't have to be hypocritical. Ariel, herself, would not make a good leader. She has a strong will, but not the kind it takes to direct and manipulate others.

Are you attracted to other animated characters? Or other mermaids?

No, I couldn't care less about mermaids. Ariel being a mermaid is just a coincidence.

Do you have friends that are as interested in Ariel as you are?

No one living in my area is a fan. All of the fans that I've met (except for one) I found on the Internet.

When you write other Ariel fans, do you find you have things in common other than Ariel? What sorts of other things?

Many of my fellow fans are very intelligent. I don't know whether this is because they own a computer or what. Many are artists or writers, like myself. Some are a little loony (which gets me worried!). Many are liberal, which is the direct opposite of myself. This just shows Ariel's wide appeal.

Have you done anything unusual related to being an Ariel fan?

Giving my life to an animated character might be considered unusual. I've endured hardships that I would never suffer for most real people.

What's the weirdest thing you've done? Any funny stories you could share?

Lots of stuff to get *LM* goodies. Spent over two hours in a video store waiting for the manager, who told me he had a stand-up display for sale. He never showed up. Visited five Big Lots, all over Nashville, looking for an *LM* shovel. Visited two or three malls, and four or five department stores, numerous smaller stores, through rain, heat, cold, and snow every weekend for six years looking for new merchandise. Bought a computer so I could see the *LM* pages on the Internet. Spent a year making a cross-stitch (my third and last; the others were *LM* too) to send to Jodie Benson [who did the voice of Ariel]. She has it in her living room. Stopped eating seafood—a personal act of devotion, because I love seafood. Gave up watching anything but *LM*. Haven't watched TV in years. Sold everything non-*LM* I own to get more *LM*. Wear an *LM* charm everywhere I go, when I'm not wearing my *LM* shirt (which I wear on the weekends in the mall). Got my picture taken with Ariel at WDW in a pirate costume. Got out of the hospital for a bleeding ulcer and headed to the mall to catch up on *LM* goodies. Borrowed money to bid in the Sotheby's auction of '90. Have a swimming pool in my dining room (no water in it). Go down to WDW and spend all my time buying *LM* and watching *Voyage of LM*. None of this is funny, sorry. It's just a testament to how much Ariel has affected my life.

Would you describe being an Ariel fan as a hobby? What are your other hobbies?

If life is a hobby, then Ariel is a hobby. I like to write *LM*, read *LM*, draw *LM*, and paint *LM*. I'll also admit a fondness for playing Doom. It releases my aggression. :)

Do you prefer to watch alone or in groups?

I've never watched *LM* with others.

Do you think you'll ever get sick of Ariel?

I have times when Ariel isn't in my thoughts. But in six years, she has always been close. As long as she makes me happy, I'll never grow tired of her.   [*Stay Free!* #13, Spring 1997]

Regarding
Media Violence

WHY DO WE HAVE SUCH A TOUGH TIME BELIEVING THAT PEOPLE IMITATE WHAT THEY WATCH?

I N THE FIRST SECTION, I discussed how marketers reach out to potential customers by appealing to their animal instincts. Violence is one of those things, like gooey strawberry pie and naked torsos, which appeal to our primal nature. We may not necessarily *like* seeing violence on TV or in the movies, but we notice it. Violence is a reliable attention-grabber, which is what makes it such a good tool for marketers. While it doesn't exactly put people in a buying mode, and extreme violence may reflect badly on commercial sponsors, violence keeps people watching. In fact, violence is so essential to profit making that it gets TV's defenders to say things that make no sense whatsoever.

To wit: every few years, there is uproar over media violence, and the resulting debate follows a predictable path, framed by zealots. On one side, you've got censors: those who see an immediate, direct causal connection between on-screen violence and the real thing and therefore want to ban television and turn the country into a giant nanny state. This stance is easily shot down by anyone who remembers the First Amendment, so I'll concentrate on the other side: the free-speech absolutists.

These are the people who oppose any and all attempts to regulate media violence, and therefore argue that media violence has no effect whatsoever. Television executives, for example, are quick to deny the influence of media violence, even while they and other media producers practice an unspoken prohibition against portraying suicides. A handful of people throw themselves in front of a New York City subway train every year, but only a tiny fraction of these are ever reported in the media. Why? Because media reports of suicides are widely known to cause more suicides.[1]

Suicide, in other words, is highly suggestible. Suicide isn't the only thing. The entire economy of television hinges on viewers' suggestibility; namely, on the ability of commercials to sell things. This creates an odd paradox: at the same time TV reps insist that violent imagery doesn't influence the audience, they're promising advertisers that other kinds of televised imagery *does*.

Even people who should know better deny that violence has an impact. Media educators can while away days suggesting media violence doesn't affect people, but media literacy is predicated on the idea that media shape reality. The fact that media influence our views on race, gender, politics, and body image are accepted as givens. But somehow, when it comes to violence, the effects aren't "proven."

With the debate defined by extremes—by the censors and the absolutists—there's little room for the reasonable in-between. This much we know: people imitate other people, including people they see on TV. Often those people on TV are doing violent things; and occasionally someone will attempt to copy those acts. Where murders and rapes and capital idiocy are involved, these cases make it into newspaper headlines. We've collected some examples of these in "The Media Made Them Do It" (page 84).

But the vast majority of media-induced actions will never make the AP wire because they are trivial. Mundane. You don't need to take my word for it. A few years ago, I solicited readers of our website for their personal experiences of copying television, and some of my favorite stories follow (page 90).

My point in saying all this is simply to acknowledge an uncomfortable truth. As long as humans remain social creatures, we will continue to copy other social creatures, including those we see on TV. Whether one believes in the censorship schemes proposed by righteous experts is another question entirely. Instead of arguing over whether media violence causes the real thing, they'd be better off looking at the root causes of violent media: a system that churns out content strictly for bucks.

[*Stay Free!* #20, Fall 2002]

The Media Made
Them Do It

AFTER THE 1966 NBC-TV thriller *The Dooms-day Flight* depicted an airplane hijacking, the nation's major airlines reported a dramatic rise in anonymous bomb threats.[1]

. . .

A five-year-old set his baby sister's bed ablaze with a cigarette lighter, killing her and destroying his home. According to the boy's mom, he got the idea from MTV's Beavis and Butt-Head, who play with fire and say things like "Fire is cool."[2] There was a similar case involving three girls in Ohio who, while trying to light their clothes on fire à la Beavis and Butt-Head, ended up burning the house.[3]

. . .

After watching a genie on TV slap someone on both sides of the head, two children in England copied the stunt and suffered perforated eardrums. Other children, in different parts of the country, were also injured in what became known as "the slapping craze."[4]

. . .

After watching the film *Natural Born Killers*, which portrayed serial killers Mickey and Mallory, Nathan Martinez shaved his head and began wearing tinted spectacles like principal psychopath Mickey. Martinez then drove to Salt Lake City and murdered his stepmother and ten-year-old half sister.[5] A similarly inspired Georgia couple, Ronnie Beasley and Angela Crosby, embarked on a crime spree of carjacking, theft, kidnapping, and murder. Beasley shaved his head like Mickey's, and the two lovers called each other Mickey and Mallory.[6]

· · ·

After rugby stars Matthew Ridge and Marc Ellis were shown jumping off a waterfall in a television commercial in England, at least fourteen people died trying to replicate the stunt.[7]

· · ·

There have been numerous cases of kids copying television wrestling. Perhaps the most famous involved fourteen-year-old Lionel Tate, who imitated a popular wrestling move when he bear-hugged a six-year-old girl and threw her on the floor, killing her.[8]

· · ·

Two teenagers from Pennsylvania suffered dire consequences after imitating a stunt from the movie *The Program*. Like the college football hero in the film, the teens tried to prove their mettle by lying down in the middle of a road at night. Unlike the film's star, however, one boy was killed instantly, the other rendered in critical condition. According to one report, about

The "king of the world" scene in *Titanic*—in which Leonardo DiCaprio and Kate Winslet "fly" at the front of the ship—led scores of young people to mimic the stunt. According to *The Daily Telegraph*, the United States Passenger Vessels' Association even issued a *Titanic* Alert, "urging members to close off the bow areas of ships." The alert was no help for a Swedish woman, however, who was presumed drowned after copying the suicide attempt of Kate Winslet's character.

The effect of the film on cruise ships wasn't *all* doom and gloom. Ironically enough, the film inspired more people to go on cruises.[9]

Above: A screen shot from *Titanic*. Right: Photos found on the web by searching for "Titanic" and "king of the world."

thirty kids were playing the "game" a few miles up the road that night.[10]

. . .

After the release of Stanley Kubrick's film *A Clockwork Orange* in England, a number of young men started dressing like the ultraviolent "droogs" in the film. According to *Stanley Kubrick: A Biography*, a sixteen-year-old boy "obsessed" with the movie was convicted after he kicked a sixty-year-old to death. Another sixteen-year-old boy—wearing his media mentor's white overalls, a black bowler hat, and combat boots—"savagely beat a younger child." And a seventeen-year-old Dutch girl was raped by thugs who chanted "Singin' in the Rain."[11]

. . .

After watching a television movie about a woman who burned her abusive husband to death, a man hunted down his estranged wife, doused her with gasoline, and set her ablaze. The man told the police that the *The Burning Bed*, starring Farrah Fawcett, had inspired him to "scare" his wife. Meanwhile, in Quincy, Massachusetts, a similarly inspired wife-beater attacked his spouse, telling her he "wanted to get her before she got him." And in Chicago, a battered wife who watched the show shot her husband.[12]

. . .

After Rob Reiner's 1986 film *Stand by Me* depicted "hooligans leaning out of car windows to whack mailboxes off their posts with baseball bats," kids across the country followed suit.[13]

. . .

So many kids hurt themselves playing Evel Knievel that members of Congress once pressured the networks to stop televising his stunts.[14]

. . .

In the 1970s, an investigation by Senator Gaylord Nelson of Wisconsin found that millions of children turned to pill-popping in response to television commercials.[15]

. . .

After James Dean and Corey Allen played "chicken" by speeding as close as possible to the edge of a cliff in *Rebel Without a Cause* (1955), dozens of teens plummeted to their death trying to imitate that scene. Interestingly enough, when it first marketed *Rebel*, Warner Bros. anticipated the copycat incidents and produced a clip of star James Dean urging kids to "take it easy driving out there. The life you save might be mine." The clip was never used, however, because Mr. Dean was killed when he crashed his Porsche shortly before the movie was released.[16]

The Media Made Me Do It

SOCIOPATHS and the mentally unstable aren't the only ones who imitate the media; everyone copies the things they watch and hear in one way or another. We asked some friends and readers to tell us about their own experiences aping the screen. Here's what they had to say.

When I was in high school, I saw an episode of *Real People* about a boy with no arms. The story showed him using his feet to dress himself, play soccer, and eat at the table. He laughed and held his cutlery between his toes. After watching this, I trained myself to use my toes for all manner of basic tasks normally performed with hands: dialing the phone, lighting cigarettes. In college, I would show off all these feet tricks for my friends. Even today, I still do many things with my feet that others use their hands for.
—*Catherine Sears*

When I was in the eighth grade, I ordered a pizza to my math class after watching Spicoli do it in *Fast Times at Ridgemont High*. When he got to my class, my teacher immediately knew it was for me and flipped out. I think I got detention for a week, but they gave me the pizza back at the end of the day, so I had a nice picnic with some friends as we laughed about the whole thing.

—*Sarah Jacobson*

Mike, someone I knew from the Boston punk scene, was a big guy who was impressed by the movie *Fight Club*. He started a similar club in Cambridge but instead of a bonding experience, it apparently was just guys getting beat up by Mike. Eventually the Cambridge Police broke it up, and the non-Mike participants were reportedly just as happy to have an excuse to stop as they had been to fight in the first place. Meanwhile, Chuck Palahniuk, who wrote the book *Fight Club*, denied knowing that any real fight clubs exist.

—*Rich Mackin*

I can't remember where or when I saw Mary Poppins float down to earth with her magical umbrella, but I do remember desperately searching the house for my own umbrella so I could experience the same graceful descent. I found an umbrella, climbed to the top of the monkey bars in our backyard, and was so confident that the same laws of physics would apply that when I hit the ground with a BANG I reasoned that it must be the wrong type of umbrella and went inside to look for another. Armed with my new umbrella, I plummeted down to earth just as quickly as before. My final attempt involved both umbrellas, which was a big mistake because I had no free arm to help break my fall.

—*Leslie Mello*

In my junior year of high school, I started dressing like Alex from *A Clockwork Orange*. I went to see the movie

nineteen times, and the last eight times I wore my *Clockwork Orange* outfit. I even used to hitchhike in my *Clockwork Orange* outfit.
  —*Jim Rocheleau*

I was one of the few kids in elementary school who didn't have a TV, but my downstairs neighbor let me watch *Happy Days* with him. One day at school, I dropped my notebook and picked it up with my thumbs out, the way I imagined the Fonz would pick up his notebook. "Hey," another kid said to me, "are you trying to pick up your notebook like the Fonz?" I was mortified and hotly denied it. "Of course not," I said. "Don't be stupid, that's just the way I pick up my stuff." He nodded but with a smirk, and walked away.
  —*Rachel Neumann*

I read *A Clockwork Orange* in high school and—though I didn't understand the book at all—thought it would be cool to appropriate the character's slang in my everyday speech. "Droogies" for "friends," "moloko" for milk. Needless to say, this never caught on.
  —*Carrie McLaren*

After seeing *Spider-Man*, I found myself roaming the streets of New York City, pressing my fingers (middle and ring) to the base of my palms. It was strangely comforting—maybe it's an acupressure point?—though I stopped short of aiming my wrists at buildings from which to swing. I am thirty-three years old.
  —*Alexandra Ringe*

As a kid, I was infatuated with *Underdog* and craved the "super energy pill" hidden in Underdog's ring. One afternoon, I climbed the counter and took a bottle of

orange-flavored children's aspirin. Over the next several
hours, I flew through the living room, jumping on and off
the sofa, battling bad guys up and down the stairs, and
strategically downing the orange tabs as crime-fighting
circumstances dictated. By dinnertime, I was barely able to
rise from the sofa. After repeated questioning from my
mom, I showed her the empty bottle. She gave me a glass of
milk, and, upon finishing it, I upchucked my fantasy onto
the floor.

—Dan Cook

—Michael Colton

[*Stay Free!* #20, Fall 2002]

Key Questions

1. Which mental disorder is commonly linked to hallucinations about the media, often manifest in an obsession with subliminal advertising or a perceived broadcast conspiracy?

   a. Obsessive-compulsive disorder.

   b. Schizophrenia.

   c. Sociopathy.

   d. Psychopathy.

2. In what country did the ideal female body shape go from plump to anorexic in a few short years (about 1995 to 1998) with the introduction of American-style television?

   a. The Philippines.

   b. The Fiji Islands.

   c. Namibia.

   d. Paraguay.

3. According to a survey of one thousand Americans by J. Walter Thompson, the time people spend on the Internet is replacing:

   a. Having sex.

   b. Socializing face-to-face.

   c. Physical exercise.

   d. All of the above.

4. Match the tobacco brands to their old slogans:

   a. Eve Cigarettes   i.   "Making smoking safe for smokers"

b. Camels   ii.   "More doctors smoke _____ than any other cigarette"

c. Bonded Tobacco   iii.   "Just what the doctor ordered"

d. L&M   iv.   "The first truly feminine cigarette—almost as pretty as you are"

5. Which of the following fast-food items contains the greatest number of calories (2,900)?

   a. Outback Steakhouse Aussie Cheese Fries with Ranch Dressing.

   b. Chili's Honey Chipotle Crispers with Chipotle Sauce.

   c. Carl's Jr. Double Six Dollar Burger.

   d. On the Border Grande Taco Salad with Taco Beef.

6. Which of the following is NOT an actual fad diet in the last twenty years?

   a. *The Master Cleanse.* Requires subsisting on a mix of water, lemons, cayenne pepper, and maple syrup. Also known as the Lemon Water Detox Diet or the "Beyoncé method."

   b. *The Weight Loss Cure They Don't Want You to Know About.* Based on the book of the same name, this diet advocates injecting oneself with hCG, a hormone found in the urine of pregnant women.

   c. *Blood Type Diet.* Dieters are divided by blood type: those with O blood are "hunters" and get meat; those with A are "cultivators," who should eat mostly vegetarian; B blood is indicative of "nomads," who need dairy; and AB blood is a combination of the two.

    d. *Apple Cider Vinegar Diet.* Recommends swallowing a few teaspoons of vinegar before meals to suppress one's appetite.

    e. None of the above.

7. TRUE or FALSE: Research funded by the National Science Foundation has found that home ionic air "purifiers" emit ozone, better known as smog.

8. What effect did the ABC-TV show *S.W.A.T.* (Special Weapons and Tactics) about a paramilitary-style urban police force have on American culture?

    a. SWAT teams armed with submachine guns and other heavy gear began proliferating in suburban jurisdictions across the country.

    b. Sex shops reported a 400 percent increase in sales of SWAT-themed S&M gear.

    c. Activist groups such as Planned Parenthood and PETA began outfitting demonstrators with more aggressive defensive gear.

    d. It spawned the inner-city game "swatting," played like red rover but with improvised body shields.

Answers

1. B. Fuller Torrey, Peter Lurie, Sidney M. Wolfe, Mary Zdanowicz, "Threats to radio and television personnel in the US by individuals with severe mental illnesses," Washington, DC: Public Citizen's Health Research Group, December 15, 1999. www.citizen.org/publications/release.cfm?ID=6703.

2. B. Erica Goode, "Study Finds TV Alters Fiji Girls' View of Body," *The New York Times*, May 20, 1999, A:17.

3. D. Sharon Gaudin, "Americans Can Go Without Sex Longer Than the Internet, Study Finds," *InformationWeek*, September 21, 2007. www.informationweek.com/news/showArticle.jhtml?articleID=201808208.

4. a. iv; b. ii; c. i; d. iii. www.tvacres.com/tobacco_slogans.htm.

5. A. Chili's Honey Chipotle Crispers has 2,040 calories; Carl's Jr. Double Six Dollar Burger has 1,520; and On the Border Grande Taco Salad has 1,450. Matt Goulding, "The 20 Worst Foods in America," *Men's Health*. www.menshealth.com/20worst/ (accessed April 14, 2008).

6. E. All are actual diets.

7. True. Robert Roy Britt, "Air purifiers can create ozone pollution," MSNBC.com, May 12, 2006. www.msnbc.msn.com/id/12707280.

8. A. Frank Mankiewicz and Joel Swerdlow, *Remote Control: Television and the Manipulation of American Life* (New York: Times Books, 1978), p. 262.

Consumer Culture and Society

3.

IDIOCRACY, MIKE JUDGE'S satirical stab at consumer culture, portrays a dystopia so harrowing that the the film's distributor, Twentieth Century Fox, buried its release. In the movie, "perfectly average" Joe Bauers finds himself transported five hundred years in the future—the year 2505—when an army experiment goes awry. While the new world resembles the old, all signs of intelligent life are missing. Bauers, a mediocre desk jockey, is a genius compared to the people he meets. Humankind, it turns out, has been reduced to its primitive animal drives: sex, food, and crapping. Science is focused on baldness remedies and penis enhancements. Hospital staffers resemble fast-food workers, labeling patients with push-button diagnoses. Lounge chairs are specially designed to allow people to eat and poop at the same time. The legal system operates like reality TV. Courtrooms have the integrity of a middle-school stadium during a pep rally. Anyone who tries to use reason or logic to present his case—or anyone who speaks in complete sentences—gets labeled a "fag."

Meanwhile, in the real world, circa 2006, Procter & Gamble is launching a deodorant for seven-year-old girls that bears the warning "Keep out of reach of children."[1] A customer service rep at Princess Cruises demands a copy of a death certificate to remove someone from its mailing list.[2] Americans spend an estimated 40 percent of their time consuming various media,[3] and yet over 30 percent of them can't name the vice president.[4]

In other words, the year 2505 isn't as far off as it may seem.

One could point to any number of factors contributing to America's collective brain rot, but if we had to boil it all down to one, it would be this: the belief that something is valuable only to the extent that it's profitable. Once you buy into this, all kinds of idiotic notions simply fall in line:

The best way to educate children is to make education a business.

Pharmaceuticals should be sold in the same manner as bath soap or chewing gum.

Eating chocolate is good for your heart.

Counting Oreo cookies helps teach your toddler math.

These claims all reflect a widespread tendency to confuse pecuniary values with other values.

Where did this confusion come from? You can blame any number of forces: the public relations industry, government collusion with corporations; a commercially driven media; or the lazy masses. But there's no need to get conspiratorial. Fact is, all of the money is in idiocy.

Take nursing homes. A "good" nursing home is one where residents are comfortable, content, and receive excellent care. A nursing home that sickens or mistreats patients is a "bad" nursing home, regardless of whether it makes money. This bad nursing home could be a good business, however, because businesses succeed or fail based on how much money they make. Whether a business harms its employees or other people matters only to the extent that it affects this bottom line. This is why Wal-Mart, a company widely accused of abusing its employees, receives raves and awards from the financial sector. (*Fortune* magazine, for example, named Wal-Mart the #1 "Most Admired Company in America" two years in a row.)[5]

There isn't necessarily anything wrong with a nursing home that makes a profit. The problem is that the drive to earn a profit inevitably conflicts with the goal of helping people—and makes it easy to confuse one goal with the other. When profits are involved, feeding tubes replace nurses, pills replace therapists, and "public relations" reps spread the message that the changes are all for the patients' benefit.

In this section, we look at how society and its institutions are shaped—and distorted—by the profit motive. We start by challenging a core tenet of the American economy. In "Shopping for Cancer," Jonathan Rowe shows how the mantra "growth is good" has created a society where medical problems, highway disasters, and housing calamities all merit high praise.

In "L.A. Law" and "The *CSI* Effect," we look at how commercial media and marketing techniques are transforming the legal system.

"How Do Kids Read Commercials?" provides a glimpse of what happens when one of democratic society's key institutions—public schools—are given over to advertisers.

A lot of people hate advertising, but seldom do they get the opportunity to think about precisely how much they hate it and why. The same could be said of those who love ads. In "On Advertising" critics Sut Jhally and James Twitchell debate what's wrong with advertising, saving both groups from having to think up reasons themselves.

We end with two articles on what may at first appear to be trivial linguistic trends but provide a window into how thoroughly and deeply culture shapes us. Leslie Savan's essay "Did Somebody Say Community?" deconstructs Americans' habit of overusing the word "community"—for example, to refer to an "industry" ("the plastics community," "the pharmaceuticals community"). And Chris Boznos's observation about the Volkswagen Bug shows how a consumer product can become so entrenched in the human brain that it literally becomes a unit of measurement.

Shopping for Cancer

WHY ECONOMISTS LOVE BELLYACHES, BEDBUGS, AND BROKEN HOMES

by Jonathan Rowe

I F YOU HAVE BEEN in a car wreck recently, or needed costly medications, or gone through a grueling legal nightmare of a divorce, then congratulations. You have contributed to economic growth, and your life is the kind this thing "the economy" needs more of.

Economics has been called the "dismal science." But beneath its gray exterior is a gauzy romance, a lyric ode to Stuff. It's built into the language. A thing produced is called a "good," for example, no questions asked. The word is more than just a term of art. It suggests the automatic benediction that economics bestows upon expenditures of any kind.

By the same token, an activity for sale is called a "service." Economists see no "dis-services," no market actions that might be better left undone. The bank that gouges you with ATM fees, the lawyer who runs up the bill—such things are "services" so long as someone pays. (If a friend or neighbor fixes your plumbing for free, by contrast, it's not a "service" and so it doesn't count.)

The sum total of these products and activities is called the gross domestic product, or GDP. If the GDP is greater this year than last, then the result is called "growth." There is no bad GDP and no bad growth; economics does not even have a word for such a thing. It does have a word for less growth—i.e., "recession." No matter what is growing—more payments to doctors because of worsening health, more toxic cleanup—so long as there is more of it, the economic mind declares it good.

This purports to be "objective science." In reality it is a rhetorical construct with the value judgments built in, and this rhetoric has been the basis of economic debate in the United States for the last half century at least. True, people have disagreed over how best to promote a rising GDP. Liberals generally have wanted to use government more, conservatives less. But regarding the beneficence of a rising GDP, there has been little debate at all.

If anything, the left traditionally has believed in growth with even greater fervor than the right. It was John Maynard Keynes, after all, who devised the growth-boosting mechanisms called macroeconomic policy—such as government borrowing and spending—to combat the depression of the 1930s. It was Keynesians who embraced these strategies after the war and turned the GDP into a totem. There is no point in seeking a bigger pie to redistribute to the poor, if you don't believe the expanding pie is desirable in the first place.

Today, however, growth worship is starting to unravel across the political spectrum in ways both obvious and subtle. Envi-

The Flu Economy

Believe it or don't but an entire wing of the economy revolves around people getting the flu. During the winter of 2007–2008, when the flu season erupted later than usual, some businesses went into crisis mode. As reported in *The Wall Street Journal*, Walgreen Co. CEO Jeffrey Rein suggested to attendees at a shareholder meeting that if they had to cough, they should " 'go to a movie theater or on a bus' to spread their germs."

"We're really hoping for a very strong flu season," he added.

A Proctor & Gamble rep blamed weak sales of the company's Vicks cold medicine on the relatively healthy masses. "Unfortunately, people have not been getting sick at a rate that we would all like yet," he said (presumably, half-jokingly) on a conference call.

But all was not lost. In February 2008, the flu came back with a vengeance. Sales of cold treatments, bacterial lotions, and tissues rebounded mightily. Cross Country Healthcare reported that orders were up 35%. Admissions at the LifePoint chain of hospitals also rose. David Dill, LifePoint's chief financial offer, told the *Journal* that a strong flu season is very profitable, particularly when children and the elderly get sick: "Young kids coming into the hospital, that's a nice margin for us."[1]

ronmentalists are, of course, the group most commonly associated with skepticism about growth. To be sure, one faction is trying to put green wine into the old bottles of conventional economic thought. If we just make people pay the "true" cost of, say, the gasoline they burn—through the tax system, for example—then the market would do the rest. We would have be-

How Automobiles Create Economic Growth

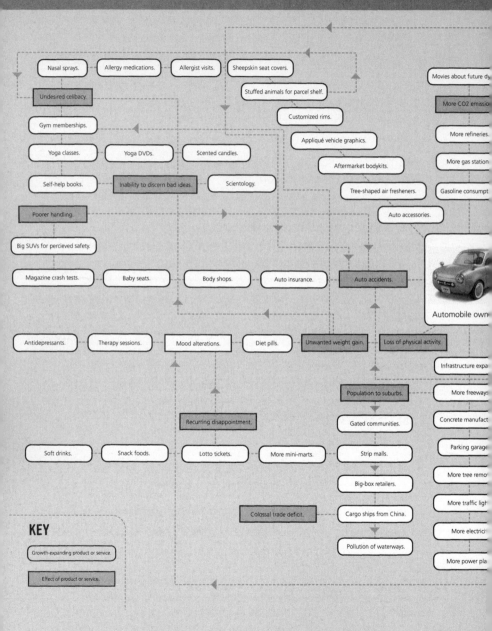

Nasal sprays.

Allergy medications.

Allergist visits.

Sheepskin seat covers.

Movies about future dy

Undesired celibacy.

Stuffed animals for parcel shelf.

More CO2 emissio

Gym memberships.

Customized rims.

More refineries.

Yoga classes.

Yoga DVDs.

Scented candles.

Appliqué vehicle graphics.

More gas station

Self-help books.

Inability to discern bad ideas.

Scientology.

Aftermarket bodykits.

Gasoline consumpt

Tree-shaped air fresheners.

Poorer handling.

Auto accessories.

Big SUVs for percieved safety.

Magazine crash tests.

Baby seats.

Body shops.

Auto insurance.

Auto accidents.

Automobile own

Antidepressants.

Therapy sessions.

Mood alterations.

Diet pills.

Unwanted weight gain.

Loss of physical activity.

Infrastructure expa

Population to suburbs.

More freeways

Recurring disappointment.

Gated communities.

Concrete manufact

Soft drinks.

Snack foods.

Lotto tickets.

More mini-marts.

Strip malls.

Parking garage

Big-box retailers.

More tree remo

Colossal trade deficit.

Cargo ships from China.

More traffic ligh

Pollution of waterways.

More electrici

More power pla

KEY

Growth-expanding product or service.

Effect of product or service.

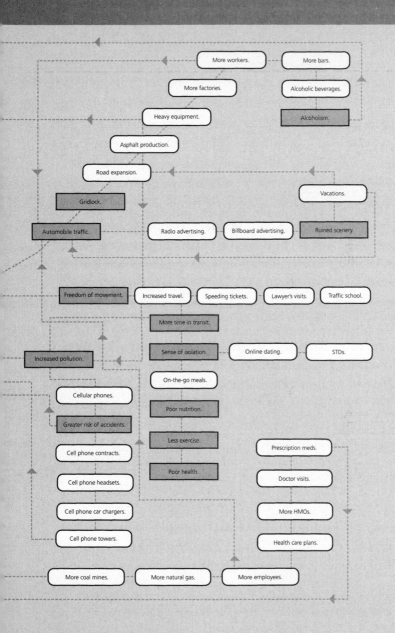

nign, less polluting growth, they say, perhaps even more than now. But the core of the environmental movement remains deeply suspicious of the growth ethos, and probably would be even if the environmental impacts somehow could be lessened.

In the middle are suburbanites who applaud growth in the abstract but don't like the particular manifestations they see around them, such as traffic, sprawl, and crowded schools. On the right, meanwhile, an antigrowth politics is emerging that is practically unnoticed. When social conservatives denounce gambling, pornography, or sex and violence in the media, they are talking about specific instances of the growth that their political leaders rhapsodize on other days. (Honest conservatives acknowledge that growth is the trigger for bigger government, starting with the first traffic light in the once-sleepy town.)

Environmentalists resemble social conservatives in one key respect. They have been moralistic regarding growth, often scolding people for enjoying themselves at the expense of future generations and the earth. Their concern is valid, up to a point: the consumer culture does promote the time horizon of a five-year-old. But politically it is not the most promising line of attack, and conceptually it concedes too much ground. To moralize about consumption is to accept the conventional premise that it really is something chosen—an enjoyable form of self-indulgence that has unfortunate consequences for the earth.

That's "consumption" in the common parlance: the sport-utility vehicle loading up at Wal-Mart, the stuff piling up in the basement and garage. But increasingly that's not what people actually experience, nor is it what the term really means. In economics, consumption refers to everything people spend money on, pleasurable or not. The lawyers' fees for the divorce;

the repair work on the car after it was rear-ended; the cancer treatments for the uncle who was a three-pack-a-day smoker; the stress medications and weight-loss regimens—all these and more count as "consumption." They all boost the GDP.

More and more, consumption consists not of pleasurable things that people choose but rather of things that most people would gladly do without. Much buying today is addictive, for example. Millions of Americans are engaged in a grim daily battle with themselves to eat less, drink less, smoke less—spend less money, period. Yet, economic doctrine declares all such expenditures as growth and progress, without regard to the reality for the people involved. Economists resist this reality of a divided self because it would complicate their models beyond repair. They cling instead to an eighteenth-century model of human psychology—the "rational" and self-interested man—that assumes those complexities away. As David McClelland, the Harvard psychologist, once put it, most economists "haven't even discovered Freud, let alone Abraham Maslow."

Then, too, there's the toll of coercion, machination, and deceit. People don't choose to pay for the corrupt campaign finance system or for bloated executive pay packages. The cost of these is hidden in the prices that we pay at the store. This is compulsory consumption, not choice, and the economy is rife with it today. People don't choose to pay some $40 billion a year in telemarketing fraud. They don't choose to pay 32 percent more for prescription drugs than do people in Canada. ("Free trade" means that corporations are free to buy their labor and materials in other countries, but ordinary Americans aren't equally free to do their shopping there.) For that matter, people don't choose to spend $30 and up for inkjet printer cartridges. The manufacturers design the printers to make money on the cartridges because, as *The Wall Street Journal* put it, that's "where the big profit margins are."

Yet, another kind of consumption that most people would gladly do without arises from the need to deal with the offshoots of growth. Bottled water has become a multibillion-dollar business in the United States partly because people don't trust what comes from the tap. There's a growing market for sound insulation and double-pane windows because the economy produces so much noise. In many cases the economy doesn't solve problems so much as create new ones that require more money to solve. Food is supposed to sustain people; instead it sustains the GDP. The food industry spends billions a year on advertising to entice people to eat food they don't need. Not coincidentally, there's now a $55 billion diet-and-weight-loss industry to help people take off the pounds that inevitably result. When that doesn't work, which is often, there is always the vacuum pump or the knife.

The problem here goes far beyond the old critique of how the consumer culture cultivates feelings of inadequacy, lack, and need so people will buy and buy again. Now this culture actually makes life worse in order to sell solutions that purport to make it better. Traffic shows this syndrome in a finely developed form. First we build sprawling suburbs so people need a car. The resulting long commutes are torture but help build up the GDP. Americans spend some $5 billion a year on gasoline alone. As the price of gas increases, this growth sector will expand. Commerce deplores a vacuum, and the exasperating hours in the car have spawned a booming subeconomy of relaxation tapes, cell phones, even special bibs. Billboards have 800 numbers so commuters can shop while they stew. Talk radio thrives on traffic-bound commuters, which accounts for some of its contentious, get-out-of-my-face tone. The traffic also helps sustain a $130 billion-a-year car wreck industry.

The health implications also are good for growth. Los Angeles, which has the worst traffic in the nation, also leads—if that's the word—in hospital admissions due to respiratory ailments. The resulting medical bills go into the GDP. And while Americans sit in traffic, they aren't walking or getting exercise.

C. Everett Koop, the former surgeon general, has estimated that some 70 percent of the nation's medical expenses are lifestyle induced. Yet the same lifestyle that promotes disease also produces a rising GDP. (Keynes observed that traditional virtues like thrift are bad for growth; now it appears that health is bad for growth too.) We literally are growing ourselves sick, and this puts a grim new twist on the economic doctrine of "complementary goods," which describes the way new products tend to spawn a host of others. The automobile gave rise to carwash franchises, drive-in restaurants, fuzz busters, tire dumps, and so forth. Television produced an antenna industry, VCRs, soap opera magazines, ad infinitum. The industry presents this phenomenon as the wondrous perpetual motion machine of the market: goods beget more goods. But the machine is producing complementary ills and collateral damages as well.

A pesticide plant in Richmond, California, is owned by a transnational corporation that also makes the breast cancer drug tamoxifen. Many researchers believe that pesticides, and the toxins created in the production of them, play a role in breast cancer. "It's a pretty good deal," a local physician told the *East Bay Express*, a Bay Area weekly. "First you cause the cancer, then you profit from curing it." Both the alleged cause and cure make the GDP go up, and this syndrome has become a central dynamic of growth in the United States today.

Mainstream economists would argue that this is all beside the point. If people didn't have to spend money on such things as commuting or medical costs, they'd simply spend it on something else, they say. Growth would be the same or even greater, so the actual content of growth should be of little concern to those who promote it. That view holds sway in the nation's policy councils; as a result, we try continually to grow our way out of problems, when increasingly we are growing our way in.

To the extent conventional economics has raised an eyebrow at growth, it has done so mainly through the concept of "externalities." These are negative side effects suffered by those not party to a transaction between a buyer and a seller. Man buys car, car pollutes air, others suffer that "externality." As the language implies, anything outside the original transaction is deemed secondary, a subordinate reality, and therefore easily overlooked. The effects upon buyer and seller—the "internalities," one might say—are assumed to be good. Externalities, however, are starting to overwhelm internalities. A single Jet Ski can cause more misery for the people who reside by a lake than it gives pleasure to the person riding it.

More important, and as just discussed, internalities themselves are coming into question, and with them the assumption of choice, which is the moral linchpin of market thought. If people choose what they buy, as market theory posits, then—externalities aside—the sum total of all their buying must be the greatest good of all. That's the ideology behind the GDP. But if people don't always choose, then the model falls apart. The practical implications are obvious. If growth consists increasingly of problems rather than solutions, scolding people for consuming too much is barking up the wrong tree. It is possible to talk instead about ridding our lives of what we don't want as well as forsaking what we do want—or think we want.

Politically this is a more promising path. But to where? The economy may be turning into a kind of round-robin of difficulty and affliction, but we are all tied to the game. The sickness industry employs a lot of people, as do ad agencies and trash haulers. The fastest-growing occupations in the country include debt collectors and prison guards. What would we do without our dysfunctions? The problem is especially acute for those at the bottom of the income scale who have not shared much in the apparent prosperity. For them, a bigger piece of a bad pie might be better than none. This is the economic conundrum of our age. No one can articulate a complete answer, but it helps to see that much growth today is really an optical illusion created by accounting tricks. The real economy—the one that sustains us—has diminished. All that has grown is the need to buy commoditized substitutes for things we used to have for free.   [*Stay Free!* #19, Spring 2002]

L.A. Law: How Hollywood Is Shaping Our Legal System

by Julie Scelfo

S ITTING ON his office couch beneath a poster of Andy Warhol's tomato soup can on a shopping bag, Richard Sherwin looks calm. Despite the fact that his book *When Law Goes Pop: The Vanishing Line Between Law and Popular Culture* (Chicago: University of Chicago, 2002) details how media images impact real verdicts, Sherwin is convinced the American justice system isn't unraveling—just yet. On a drizzly evening in November, I met with the full-time law professor at New York Law School to discuss the links between truth, justice, and the movies.

JULIE SCELFO: Was there a specific incident that inspired you to write about media's influence on the law?

RICHARD SHERWIN: I showed my students Errol Morris's documentary, *The Thin Blue Line*. It uses the real parties in a real capital murder case: the defendant Randall Dale Adams, the real judge, the real attorneys, and the real witnesses. I would ask my students to spot all of the procedural errors that we've studied. They loved it. But as I watched the film a few more times, I began to notice all the fictional material and manipulative devices that Morris was using: reenactments, film overlays, Philip Glass's hypnotic score . . . which is interesting because Morris's film prompted a review of the case. Randall Dale Adams was ultimately released from prison.

The film prompted his release?

The film was the catalyst that reopened the case. If Errol Morris had not made that film, odds are Randall Dale Adams would not have been released.

Legal stories have long dominated not just television but film and theater. How come? What is it about law that's so appealing?

For one thing, it's dramatic. The adversarial structure sets up a natural tension, like the *Perry Mason* formula, the great climax of revelation on the stand: "AHA! *This* is the guilty person!" Also, law tends to incorporate the most violent and extreme kinds of behavior. This naturally appeals to our prurient interests and voyeurism.

It's not every day that there's an O. J. Simpson trial. Do you think jurors go into the court now expecting the same level of drama that they get from television and the media?

I haven't done a scientific study, but what people see about law in the media is highly distorted. Court TV bills itself as a window onto the law, "justice without scripts." But of course it's not, it's television. If you track the kinds of trials that appear on Court TV, they follow the same dramatic formulas that succeed everywhere on TV. They're disproportionately violent, usually murders or gruesome sex crimes.

I think television tends to dissuade viewers from either reflecting on what they're seeing or even absorbing very much content. And the danger I perceive is that when you take the aesthetics of TV entertainment into the courtroom, you're taking the same formulas for emotional provocation and sensation and gratification that you see on the screen. And that's a form of persuasion that tends to nullify deliberation.

I have nothing against entertainment and I love popular culture, but I worry when the law becomes synonymous with entertainment so that if you don't entertain, you're not convincing.

Do you think the law has become commodified?

There's no question that it has. Law has always had a presence on TV and film, but now on top of that we have things like Court TV, *Divorce Court*, and *Power of Attorney*, where real attorneys become celebrities in their own right. These so-called real-life television depictions of the law become even more insidious in a way because people who watch them are internalizing a sense of what law really is.

Are you saying the impressions viewers get from TV have an impact on the judgments they make when serving as a juror?

Absolutely. It's like a feedback loop: People who learn about the law through the media form certain expectations about how the law works and they bring those expectations into the courtroom. Trial lawyers need to meet people's expectations, so they tend to emulate the form of communication people are used to.

What are some examples of how lawyers have modified their practices to adapt to the jury's expectations?

One of the key shifts is the introduction of visual communication. The typical courtroom these days, more often than not, is lined with television monitors. It's a normal part of our lives to get information from the screen. Avi Stachenfeld, in Oakland, California, was one of the earliest attorney-filmmakers to provide visuals for lawyers. He said he knew he was onto something when he noticed that most people in a courtroom who were faced with the choice of looking at action live or looking at it on a monitor preferred to watch the monitor.

The way some people will bring TVs to football games?

That's right. And jurors in modern courtrooms often have their own monitors. Depositions are being viewed on the screen. Distance testifying via closed-circuit hookup is increasingly common. And if you're going to operate on the screen, you have to abide by the norms of behavior that we're all used to.

In the book you call it "media logic."

Think about politics today. That's a good example of where law is headed. What do we see? Very rapid-paced visual images using the same techniques of persuasion advertisers have been using for years. The quick sound bite. The fast-cutting images.

In a _Wall Street Journal_ article, one lawyer explained that he puts his lawyers through voice lessons so they can take depositions in the same tone that an anchorman uses.

Right. I've heard judges tell me that when _L.A. Law_ was at its peak, they not only expected lawyers to dress that way, they expected two-and-a-half-minute summations. You know, "Let's make this peppy." But what happens when you put stuff on the screen? You abide by the aesthetics of the screen, you have to make things work using visual production values, and that changes everything. It changes politics, it changes journalism, it changes law.

Any good examples?

There was a really big lawsuit in Texas that involved a claim of insider trading. A Texas company was suing Kidder, Peabody, a New York investment banking firm, because they thought every time an analyst came out to visit the company in Texas, he would go back with information that would result in a spike of stock increases. So the Texas company felt they had to spend a lot more money for the takeover than they would have had the information not been exploited.

The question was: How do you make this kind of circumstantial case palpable to a jury? Stachenfeld used a digital map of the United States, with Texas disproportionately enlarged. It was illustrated with the Texas flag, which is inordinately loved in Texas, where the case was being tried. So you have this large state flag at the center of the map, then there's a very small state at the northeast end: New York. All of a sudden the faces of the Kidder, Peabody team come flying out of New York, with Mike Milken dead center. Then we see what looks like the Texas flag sweeping around New York like a lasso. And what do you know? It's just like a popular salsa commercial that was playing all over TV at the time, that makes fun of a cook who tries to palm off inauthentic New York salsa on some cowboys.

What Avi was doing here was creating association—the familiar "us/them" antagonism: Texas against New York.

So Avi used visuals to create an emotional response?

Yes, inevitably the video elicits an emotional response that is operating on a subconscious level. There's a famous video that was offered in lieu of an oral summation in a case involving Price Waterhouse. The video was used by the plaintiff, who was suing Price Waterhouse for negligence. The video was trying to say, "We lost a lot of money because Price Waterhouse failed to notice warning signs at the bank they were auditing." So the visual started off with an image of the *Titanic* leaving port, using original documentary footage. The *Titanic* sank because of negligence. Throughout the video, the plaintiff's lawyers crosscut between images of the *Titanic* and the warning signs that Price Waterhouse accountants ignored. And what's interesting is that while the summation starts with documentary footage, it then cuts to a feature film made in England in 1957 called *A Night to Remember*. So now you see the captain pocketing warnings, you see water cascading into the lower decks, and at one point this serious narrator will say, "Inexperienced auditors were being used just as in the *Titanic*," and they'd flash to sailors scurrying out of the lower decks. This was in Arizona.

And the judge permitted this tape to be used in court?

He did, although they got into trouble later, on appeal. But at the trial, the judge told the lawyers that since this case involved lots of numbers, he invited them to do something that would keep the jurors awake. So I guess he couldn't very well preclude the video since it accomplished exactly what he wanted. In fact, I think that the jury award in that case was something like $350 million. So these are very powerful tools.

In a famous case involving negligence, lawyers crafted a video that compared Price Waterhouse's actions to the sinking of the *Titanic*.

In the American legal system, lawyers are supposed to rely on legal arguments, not emotions. What happens with trials based on these types of methods, as opposed to oral arguments based on substance?

The biggest fear associated with visual persuasion is that rational deliberation is being short-circuited by a more emotional form of judgment. The fear is that certain forms of prejudice which might not work through an oral presentation can work visually because visual images are so overdetermined. Floating around somewhere in the subterranean depths of the image are useful associations. One of the things I'd like to accomplish with the book is to educate judges about the complexity of visual imagery so they can deal with the dangers of prejudice more effectively.

Are judges reading the book?

I'm in touch with judges, and they are eager to get input because they're seeing more and more visuals in court, like surveillance videos that have been edited. Think about the Rodney King case, where you had a prosecutor who was absolutely convinced that it was an open-and-shut case based on the video that showed King being beaten by the police. Little did he realize that by reediting the images, the attorneys defending the L.A. police officers, in the first criminal case, totally changed the story.

How did they edit the video?

The defense team slowed it down, so you saw frame-by-frame sequences that softened the violence. But even more devastating to the prosecution was a re-pacing of the images in coordination with the defense theory. The defense theory was that Rodney King was in control and that if he had assumed the prone position as instructed, none of this would have happened. The only reason he was struck, went the argument, was that he resisted arrest. And what the images showed in this slowed-down form was Rodney King rising up and a baton coming down.

In that order?

In that order. When King's limb would go down, the baton would go back and then another limb would rise up and another baton would come down. And this was what the jurors saw. In other words, they read causation into the imagery. The defense orchestrated the tape so that jurors would infer causation.

Which is counterintuitive. One would think the videotape would have caused the jury to leap to the conclusion that the officers who beat King were guilty.

The prosecutor constantly urged the jury to watch the tape, without saying anything more. "Just watch the tape." But what he didn't realize was the other side had colonized the meaning of the images by telling the story in a different way, so that when people watched the videotape they read it through the prism of the defense's story. The prosecutor offered no narrative of his own, so this was the only story the jury had available. Cognitive psychologists have shown that the way people reach judgments in legal cases is by telling a story about what happened. Lawyers win cases by telling the best story—the one that captures the most evidence, the one that makes the most sense, the one that's the most com-

The *CSI* Effect

Standing before a jury in Peoria, Ill., prosecutor Jodi Hoos presented her smoking gun: saliva from the defendant—a gang member accused of raping a teen girl—had been found on the girl's breast. The defendant, however, had denied ever touching his victim.

And yet, for the jurors, this evidence—along with credible testimony from the victim, police, and hospital personnel—wasn't enough. Not guilty, they ruled. According to *U.S. News & World Report*, they said the police "should have tested 'debris' found in the victim to see if it matched soil from the park."

Call it the "*CSI* Effect." Thanks to jurors accustomed to the high-tech wizardry of *CSI* and similar crime-solving TV shows, verdicts like this one have become common. Expecting loads of scientific evidence and clear-cut resolutions, jurors have upped the ante for prosecutors across the U.S.

Never mind that blood is found at only 5 percent of murder scenes, that real-life DNA tests are prohibitively expensive and time-consuming, and that much of the science on *CSI* is pure hokum. Because people come to the courtroom with certain expectations, prosecutors feel a need to acknowledge those expectations. As a result, more and more are relying on visuals and entertainment devices to win over jurors.

CSI has had another effect as well: it gives criminals tips for committing crimes. A number of murderers have washed in bleach after making their kill, in imitation of television crime-dodgers. Fortunately, this sort of influence is relatively rare. As a Los Angeles criminologist told *U.S. News*, "[The majority of] our killings involve gang bangers who for the most part are pretty stupid."

—*U.S. News & World Report*, April 17, 2005

pelling. And if you don't tell a story, if the other side is telling a story and you are simply giving fragments of an argument, you will have a much harder time capturing the belief of the jury.

Do you view the use of visual technology as a triumph?

I'm a big advocate of the adversarial system, but only if it's really working. If a lawyer or a judge is insufficiently literate in a medium, such as the visual medium, then the use of that medium might not be subjected to cross-examination. And if it's not being tested in that way, then the adversarial system isn't really working.

What can people do to try to stop this?

Cultivate more critical reflection, learn skills for interpreting what you're seeing. Also, of course, there has to be a willingness to go beyond the surface pull of images. One thing that is true about the postmodern era is that trying to distinguish between fiction and reality, or between fantasy and reality, is getting harder . . .

So you're saying that there has to be some reality somewhere.

I'm not saying there needs to be some reality in the familiar sense of some provable objective thing. But there are meanings and values and beliefs that we can affirm even while knowing how they're constructed. You can watch a movie and enjoy it, go to a class, have it dissected, watch it again, and enjoy it even more. Eventually you need to affirm some sort of meaning. Eventually. A steady diet of disenchantment is insufficiently nourishing to have a good life. We need to make clear what our beliefs are and to affirm them, and what are values are and to affirm them.

How would you respond to critics who say, "Well, you're saying society's coming apart, that law and media and entertainment and reality are all getting jumbled up, but really it's always been like that. People have always turned to fiction and fantasy to understand their own lives and to interpret their own lives."

I agree. But we have to know how these different things are operating. The question is not: Can we eradicate fiction from our lives? The more important question is: When fictional interpretations have real-life consequences in politics and law, how are they affecting life around us? We shouldn't simply indulge in the self-delusion that since it's only fiction, or only an image, let's just go along for the ride because it's a nice sensation. I'm not against sensorial buzzes, but I wouldn't want to have someone's life in a capital murder case depend upon it.

[*Stay Free!* #18, Spring 2001]

How Do Kids Read Commercials?

by Roy Fox

D EBBIE, a ninth-grader, explains why she thinks star athletes make the television commercials that she watches on Channel One, an in-school news broadcast. "I think it's stupid. I don't know why athletes do that—pay all that money for all them ignorant commercials for themselves. Guess it makes everyone like 'em more and like their team more."

For two years, I talked with some two hundred kids in rural Missouri schools about these MTV-like ads, which peddle products ranging from Reebok athletic shoes to Sega video games to Snickers candy bars during a twelve-minute episode.

After hearing Debbie's response, I decided to ask the same question of other small groups of students. Kids at my morning focus group brainstormed reasons why they believed star athletes would make commercials for companies like Nike. They came up with the following:

- Because it motivates them to play better.

- Because it's a reward for doing excellent work.

- Because it helps their team.

- Because it elevates their status and reputation among their peers.

- Because athletes are sponsored by different companies.

Talking further with these students, I realized they did not realize that commercials were designed to sell products or services. Amazingly, most kids saw commercials as aiming for the very opposite: they thought athletes paid for these advertisements in order to bolster their egos and their team's reputation. As one high school senior said, "If you're good at what you do, you need to be recognized for it."

Of the students I talked with, most embraced commercials—trusted them, viewed advertisers' motives in a positive, even warm light. One of these students, Heather, became frustrated because she couldn't better articulate why she and her friends believed that the kids in a Pepsi commercial were not paid actors: "Well . . . I know that I'd be terribly disappointed if the kids in that commercial turned out to be paid actors: they're just real kids off the street, like us . . ."

In fact, students often "blurred" or mistook commercials for public service announcements, confusing a series of Pepsi commercials titled "It's like this" with public service announcements on drunken driving and practicing tolerance. Mindy, for example, described her favorite "public service ad" as follows: "This commercial is mostly about inner-city kids, about how one got shot and stuff. Ya know, it's like this."

It's not an accident that Pepsi's "It's like this" advertisements are designed to look like documentary-style public service announcements. One ad's rapid-fire editing and its swinging, seemingly random camera angles communicate a knockabout day at the beach, with kids cavorting with pals. Interspersed with the black-and-white and muted color shots of kids talking directly into the camera about their problems are several close-ups of bright red, white, and blue Pepsi cans.

Students' confusion between the two genres and their insistence on the ad characters' authenticity demonstrate just how

From 1993 to 1995, educator Roy Fox talked with over 200 kids in rural Missouri about the commercials they watched every day as part of an in-school news program, Channel One. At the time, Channel One broadcasts reached a daily audience of 8 million kids in grades six through twelve, about 40 percent of America's classrooms. It currently reaches six million junior and high school students.

One day Fox heard a ninth-grader named Nathan describe a brand of chewing gum to one of his classmates: "It's that gum that has these little red dots . . ."

Lisa, who sat across the table, interrupted: "No, those are flavor crystals."

Nathan paused and corrected himself—"Oh yeah, flavor crystals"—and continued.

Fox's conversations with the students, which he discusses in this article, were filled with similar anecdotes: of kids unwittingly reciting slogans, believing advertising claims, and misunderstanding commercial motives. Fox found the students to be remarkably uncritical of what appeared on Channel One. The news program was aired during class time, so it must be good for them, right?

Although Fox's research took place well over a decade ago, and although it was limited to rural Missouri, it remains a potent cautionary tale for what happens when schools mix education and advertising.

effective this technique is. Because Channel One also airs public service ads, this blurring seems more than coincidental.

At another school, I talked to twenty-nine students about this Pepsi ad. Of this group, only twelve thought it was a real commercial. Six students thought it was both a news item and a commercial, while four thought it was purely news. Seven students didn't know how to define it. In fact, when my student teacher saw this ad, she couldn't decide if it was a commercial or a news item—and she is a very bright fifty-year-old former editor. One ninth-grader tried to sort it all out for us when he pronounced, "It's not really a commercial—it's just a commercial sponsored by Pepsi."

Most of the nearly 150 students I've talked to about this ad tell me that they could easily be friends with the kids in the commercial because they look and dress and act like them. When I asked, "From whose point of view is this commercial told? Who is telling this story?" Brad replied that "it's not a story," implying no director was constructing the message or calling the shots. Indeed, out of 150 students, only five said the commercial had been fashioned by the Pepsi Corporation, its marketing firm, or producers, directors, and editors.

Like Brad, most of the students said the commercial's point of view was expressed only by the kids who appeared in it. The vast majority felt Pepsi was more concerned with "doing good" than with selling soft drinks:

ME: Do any of you see this commercial as trying to sell Pepsi?

ELLEN: Since that commercial reaches people, it kind of makes them think that Pepsi is a good cause—

CHAD: [Interrupting] And they care.

ELLEN: And they care about people, so they want people to support Pepsi so that they can support the commercials.

Channel One also uses the ancient rhetorical technique of repetition to sell products. Watching the same commercial hundreds of times is an experience that most of us have never had, nor would we want to. But ads on hot rotation are routine in the schools tuned in to Channel One.

In addition to their repetition on the air, ads are, in a sense, rerun every time students mimic parts of them or randomly sing the catchy jingles. Many students told me about a recent football game where home team students in the bleachers chanted in unison, "Got to be, got to be—Dom-in-o's!" This scene echoes a Domino's Pizza ad on Channel One, in which football fans chant the exact same line.

Students also talk about commercials outside of school. Beth, also a ninth-grader, often telephones her friends and tells them which channel to flip to whenever a particularly good commercial airs. Another student, named Jason Smith, signed his name in a yearbook as Shaq Smith, invoking the commercial starring pro basketball phenom Shaquille O'Neal.

At the end of one small-group session, I asked students, "Is there anything else about commercials that we haven't talked about?" "Yes!" they enthused. "We need new commercials!" I was startled by this answer until I realized how logical it was in the context of operant conditioning. Many young people who watch so many commercials, every day for nine months,

News or commercial? A Channel One segment on the "Mazda Design Challenge" at the 2007 Los Angeles Auto Show. Note the pretentious letterboxed wide screen. That's right, kids, you're viewing Art!

The Terrific Tootsie Roll
A Tasty Story

In 1896, Leo Hirschfield invented a candy he called Tootsie Rolls, named for his little girl.

The Tootsie Pop, a lollipop with a Tootsie Roll in the center, was invented in 1931.

American soldiers in World War II ate Tootsie Rolls for "quick energy."

The Tootsie Roll factory moved to Chicago, sometimes called the "windy city."

Soon the Tootsie Roll team grew with new candies called Mason Dots, and Crows and Cella's chocolate covered cherries.

Adding Charms Blow Pops to the team made Tootsie Roll the largest producer of lollipops in the world.

A drum roll, please! Welcome Junior Mints, Sugar Daddy, Sugar Babies and Charleston Chew.

It's 1996! Happy 100th Birthday, Tootsie Roll! You're 100 years old this year. Blow out your candles.

In 2000, Fluffy Stuff cotton candy and Andes Candies joined the Tootsie Roll team to welcome the new millennium!

A Skill-Building Program

Marketing in classrooms begins as soon as school does. Companies such as Youth Marketing International—which bills itself to teachers as Young Minds Inspired—design educational materials for corporate clients targeting kids as young as three. As the head of YMI has said, "The younger the kids, the more positive the response." The above exercise appears in the "Tootsie Roll—A Tasty Story," one of several teaching kits available free on the company's YouthMedia.com website.

with some repeated endlessly, develop a craving for new commercials.

After working with these kids for two years, I shouldn't be surprised by anything, but some things still do. A ninth-grader named Susie, for example, dreamed about a McDonald's commercial. In both the dream and the ad, french fries starred. If you consider how deeply commercials appear to penetrate students' psyches, it's little wonder that they pervade their language and thinking.

If such commercials strike deep, they can also strike fast. One day I joined students in watching a thirty-second ad featuring San Antonio Spurs basketball star David Robinson. The students told me the ad was brand-new—they'd never seen it before. Later that day, most of these students reported that this commercial had three parts, which they remembered in the correct sequence: Robinson goes to college and earns his master's degree, Robinson becomes a naval officer, and Robinson twice goes to the Olympics before becoming a professional basketball player. I could remember none of these things, not even immediately after watching the commercial.

Classic Propaganda

The techniques employed in Channel One commercials—repetition, testimonials, bandwagon appeals, transfers of one quality to another, and highly synthesized music and imagery—are classic propaganda techniques. We've long known that such propaganda is most effective in closed environments, where outside stimuli can't interfere with the intended message. And a classroom full of captive students is the perfect controlled environment: no outside distractions to offset the flood of commercials starring "kids just like us."

Advertisers, of course, don't call this propaganda. Instead, they talk of "brand and product loyalties through classroom-centered, peer-powered lifestyle patterning." Techno-market-speak for propaganda.

Whatever they're called, Channel One ads work. Which is why they cost twice—yes, twice—as much as those on prime-time network news.

Monica, a high school senior, demonstrates what advertisers get for their money as she recalls with delight the special effects that prompted her to buy a pair of designer athletic shoes: "I bought some Fila tennis shoes 'cause I seen 'em on a commercial. I mean, they had this basketball player, but I don't know who he was . . . he was jumping. Anyway, the shoes have like, little flaps on the sides of 'em, like little wings. They're Velcro . . . anyway, they come off, and they started flying [giggles]. They flew off of the building, so I had to have them shoes!"

Evan, a diminutive ninth-grader, also buys items he sees for the first time on Channel One. He enlisted the help of his grandmother to save up $160 to buy Michael Jordan Nike basketball shoes. When I asked why, he drawled matter-of-factly, "Saw 'em on a commercial."   [*Stay Free!* #13, Spring 1997]

From the Mouths of Babes

Blurring Commercials with Other Types of Programming

Kids in Fox's study knew that commercials sell things, but when asked how programs and commercials differ, they seldom mentioned selling products. Instead, they'd cite length of time ("programs are really long"). Overall, kids did not regard commercials as fundamentally different from television shows.

 I don't like commercials because they get old so fast. We've seen 'em since the beginning of this year, and we had them last year.

 If commercials get boring and old because you've seem them too many times, how do you solve that problem?

 What I do in class is, if they're the same commercials—the same ol' basic stuff about Haiti or Bosnia or O. J. Simpson— I don't even watch. I just kind of block it out.

Black-and-White Options

Evaluations were rarely based on multiple options.

 [to boy wearing Nike shoes]
Why did you buy those?

 Because I don't like Reebok.

Describing Intended and Obvious Inconsistencies

By far, the majority of kids in the study did not criticize or evaluate commercials except to state vague generalizations (e.g., "I hate commercials"). Any analysis was confined to arguing trivial inconsistencies.

 Let me start with commercials I don't like, especially commercials with animals, like ads for pet food—that cat food and talking parrot commercial. It's like the cats actually understand and listen to a bird telling them not to eat it! Just the fact that the bird talks gets on my nerves. And he has an accent that doesn't even sound right!

 Why don't you like that?

 'Cause it's not what animals do. It's not real life.

 Do you think the makers of this commercial know that it's not like real life?

 Yeah, but it's just stupid, just downright stupid and idiotic, like that Energizer Bunny commercial, which shows the bunny fighting Darth Vader and then the batteries in his laser go out, but the bunny's laser is still goin'.

 And this one is stupid too?

 Yes! Because you know they change the battery in the rabbit! They have to change the battery! I have never found an Energizer battery that has run that long in my entire life, and I've bought lots of those batteries.

Why do you buy Energizer batteries?

 'Cause they last longer than everything else.

Kids tended to deny that commercials had an effect on them.

 I saw Frutopia on a commercial and bought that . . . The commercial's, like, really psychedelic and they have prismatic figures. It's like a kaleidoscope. And the bottle is really cool too.

 Why is the bottle cool?

 It's just real colorful and has weird designs on it. It has bubble letters and little people and it has your brain and world on it.

 Your brain?

 Yes. It shows life and the mind. It's trying to say it's good for your mind and it's good for your body, and good for the earth . . .

 So why is Frutopia good?

I don't know. I don't pay attention to that stuff.

On Advertising

SUT JHALLY VERSUS JAMES TWITCHELL

PEOPLE HAVE DEBATED the effects of advertising on society for over a century, but seldom are those people quite as sharp as Sut Jhally or James Twitchell. Both men consider advertising to be the dominant mouthpiece of our culture, the key storyteller. Both concern themselves not with what advertising is supposed to do—sell stuff—but what it does while doing it (which is to say that, for them, whether a particular ad succeeds or not is largely beside the point). Both argue that advertising works as a form of religion, that it has even supplanted religion as the key institution of our time. And yet Jhally and Twitchell come to opposite conclusions about what all this means. Jhally says advertising is destroying society; Twitchell says it's holding it together.

I asked Sut and James (he goes by Jim, actually) to participate in a sort of laissez-faire debate, mailed them a list of questions, and, arranged a three-way conference call.

Sut Jhally is a professor at the University of Massachusetts–Amherst, where he founded the Media Education Foundation. Author of *Codes of Advertising*, *Dreamworlds I & II*, and *Advertising and the End of the World*. Marxist. Critic. Straight Man. He's a passionate and articulate speaker. James Twitchell teaches at the University of Florida and is author of *Adcult*, *Lead Us into Temptation: The Triumph of American Material-*

ism, *Branded Nation*, and, most recently, *Shopping for God*. Unlike Jhally, Twitchell writes for the lay reader. He's witty, sharp, and prone to pithy aphorisms—not unlike an adman. As a vocal defender of advertising, he's far too likable.

What's your agenda? What are you trying to accomplish?

JHALLY: As a social scientist, I am interested in the question of determination: what structures the world and how we live in it. To understand the modern world requires some perspective on advertising. For me, the function of knowledge is to provide people with tools to see the world in different ways and to be able to act and change the world.

TWITCHELL: I agree with most of that. Advertising is the lingua franca by which we communicate our needs and desires and wants. Not to take it seriously is not to do our job. I was intrigued by advertising first as a scholar of language and literature. I was amazed by how little my students knew about literature compared to advertising. Almost in a flash, I realized I was neglecting this great body of material while the material I was teaching seemed, to them, unimportant. I jumped tracks then and moved from high culture to commercial culture.

JHALLY: So do you use advertising as a way of doing literary analysis?

TWITCHELL: I look at it like this: we've turned our noses up at the material world and pretended it was not really important. Clearly, for most people, most of the time, the material *is* the world. They live in terms of mass-produced objects. How we understand those objects is, to a great degree, what commercial interests decide to say about them. So I'm not just looking at linguistic aspects. I'm interested in why the material world has been so overlooked. Why has it been so denigrated? Why are we convinced that happiness can't come from it? Why do those of us in our fifties warn the generation behind us to stay away from this stuff?

JHALLY: The material world was for many years ignored, but not by Marxists. Marx says capitalism has transformed the material world, and, in that sense, it's a revolutionary society. Marx thought that capitalism has a lot of very literary and progressive things because it blew away the repression of feudalism. The left has often been criticized for not looking at the material world, but they focus almost entirely on production. What they've really left out is culture. Western Marxism has tried to readdress that imbalance. The reason I am interested in advertising, coming out of that tradition, is that advertising links those two things together. It allows us to speak about both the material world and the world of symbolism and culture.

Jim, you were saying that we are always preaching that happiness doesn't come from things and we should be less moralistic. My view is driven by political factors, not moral ones. I think we should ask empirical questions. Does happiness come from things? If it has, what are the costs of that? The evidence is that material things do not deliver the type of happiness that the system says they should deliver.

TWITCHELL: Is there a system that does deliver more happiness? If so, why hasn't it elbowed its way through and pushed this system aside?

JHALLY: The other systems don't exist. I certainly couldn't point to anything based on what is called the Marxian tradition. The Soviet Union was a dungeon. China is not quite the same dungeon but . . . a better system lies in the future. I encourage students to imagine what a system would look like that catered to human needs. That's why we look at advertising. What does advertising stress as a system? What are the values? Advertising doesn't say happiness comes only from things. It says you can get *friendship* through things. You can get *family life* through things. Things are used as a medium. Advertisers are really smart. They've realized since the 1920s that things don't make people happy, that what drives people is a social life.

TWITCHELL: In that case, maybe they are doing what most people want, loading value into things. You may not like the amount of money they make or you may think the process is environmentally wicked, but aren't they delivering what people want and need?

JHALLY: No! Advertisers are delivering images of what people say they want connected to the things advertisers sell. If you want to create a world focused on family, focused on community, focused on friendship, focused on independence, focused on autonomy in work, then capitalism would not be it. In fact, what you have in advertising, I believe, is a vision of socialism. And that vision is used to sell these things. If you wanted to create the world according to the values advertising focuses on, it would look very different. That's where a progressive movement should start. It should take the promises of advertising seriously and say, "Look, if you want this world, what do we have to do to ensure that these values are stressed instead of the values of individualism and greed and materialism?"

TWITCHELL: But advertising doesn't stress greed and materialism.

JHALLY: Well, it's about individual desires.

TWITCHELL: Maybe advertising excludes communal desires because they are not as high on most people's agendas as they are for those of us in our fifties. Maybe most people are not as interested in the things we say we are interested in such as family and community. Maybe they are more interested in individual happiness.

JHALLY: That's a fair question. We can't answer it yet, though, because advertising dominates so much that it leaves little room for alternative visions. My major problem with advertising is not the vision that it gives out; my problem with advertising is its monopolization of the cultural field. The questions you are asking can only be answered when you have a space in the culture where alternative values can be articulated. Then perhaps we can see what people's real values and preferences are because, at that point, they've had some choice. They have the alternative values expressed in as powerful and creative a form as the values that advertisers express.

TWITCHELL: Why aren't there enough people like you in positions of cultural power? Why haven't these people, these silent but passionate people, been able to make their concerns known?

JHALLY: It's the way power operates. Some of us have more power and visibility than others. It depends on what degree your values link up with the people who control the cultural system.

TWITCHELL: Don't we control part of that system, the schools? Why have we done such a poor job?

JHALLY: I don't think we've done a poor job. The academy is the one place where there is independent thinking. That's why the right and business have targeted it. The right complains about how the universities have been taken over by leftists. To some extent, that's nonsense because most academics are fairly innocuous conservatives.

TWITCHELL: They are? Not at the schools I've been at.

JHALLY: There's a visible minority, but most of my colleagues are quite ordinary people. And the tendency is to focus on liberal academics and leave out the larger academic community: the scientists and business schools . . . But when there is a choice, students will choose those ideas. Our ideas are popular on campuses because it is one place where they can be expressed. It is one of the few places where there is competition between ideas.

TWITCHELL: Then why do these ideas lose their steam when students leave the campus?

JHALLY: When people leave school, they have to figure out what they're going to do. They're $50,000 in debt. That's one of the great tricks of American capitalism; to get loyalty is to get people into debt early.

TWITCHELL: So this is the indenture system simply made more modern? You and I have completely different views of the same nest. My view is that these ideas don't really hold sway with our students, only our colleagues.

JHALLY: That's not my experience at all. When people are exposed to this, they have a couple of responses. The main one is "Wow, this is overwhelming. I don't know what to do." So when people ask me what to do, I say that's not my job. Education provides the tools to think and understand the world. It is up to them to figure out what to do with that. Of course, once outside the university, you've got to have some community working in the same ways, otherwise you are indirectly isolated. This is not strictly evil capitalism; this is also the left not building the kinds of institutions that provide people support.

TWITCHELL: Do you feel marginalized?

JHALLY: Sure. To some degree.

TWITCHELL: You have books that have been published.

JHALLY: Do I have as much power as Peter Jennings?

TWITCHELL: No. Should you? Do you have a pretty face? Can you read well?

JHALLY: Should that matter?

TWITCHELL: In television, absolutely.

JHALLY: Well, it matters in a system that's built on television ratings and keeping advertisers happy. But why must debate and media always be along those lines?

TWITCHELL: All these media are driven by the same machinery, the audience that can be delivered to advertisers. So it's skewed away from certain kinds of people who do not consume and it's pushed toward people who are massive consumers. It's pushed away from Sut and myself. We feel—Sut especially feels—marginalized.

JHALLY: Actually, in that sense, I feel targeted.

TWITCHELL: You're not targeted the way an eighteen-year-old is.

JHALLY: I have a lot of disposable income.

TWITCHELL: I'm not concerned about money. The point is, you've already made your brand choices. You probably use the same toothpaste. You're not as interesting to an advertiser as an eighteen-year-old who has not made these choices. We see this when we look around. We see this great dreck of vulgarity that is being pumped out of Hollywood and the television networks and even in books. It's clear that this is not making me feel important, but I sometimes think, well, maybe that's the price you pay in a world where getting Nielsen ratings or getting on the bestseller list is crucial. Now we're back to Peter Jennings. Peter

Jennings's ideas—if those can be called ideas—are more alluring to more people than what Sut and I have to say. We may think our ideas are great, but the prime audience is saying no.

JHALLY: I totally disagree. It doesn't have anything to do with ideas. It's got to do with access. Americans gave away the broadcast system to advertisers in 1934, which meant that everything was going to be dependent on advertising revenues rather than public service.

TWITCHELL: What about PBS?

JHALLY: Public broadcasting is a great idea. I wish we could have it. PBS was always envisioned as entertainment for the elite rather than an alternative to commercial TV. It's possible to do public interest programming and be popular. Look at England. The BBC is driven by a different set of economic logics and produces different types of programs. It's not because the Brits are more artistic. The BBC operates within a system of public service.

TWITCHELL: Is American dreck popular on English television?

JHALLY: Some. But if you're saying public service stuff is not popular, you're wrong.

TWITCHELL: What do you think should be on PBS?

JHALLY: There is a whole slew of independent filmmakers who don't get their work onto television or into Hollywood . . .

TWITCHELL: And there's an audience for this?

In the late 1800s, the Oppenheimer family established a diamond monopoly with its company, De Beers. At the time, diamonds were practically worthless compared to other gems, but De Beers set out to change that by limiting their supply, driving up the price. In the 1930s, with its monopoly firmly established, De Beers turned its focus to marketing. The company gave Hollywood starlets hefty stones, arranged glamorous photo shoots, and

script-doctored movies to include scenes of jewelry shopping. Movie romances would feature the hero gifting a large diamond ring to his lady. Off-screen, actresses did their part by feeding reporters giddy tales of receiving large stones from their men. And De Beers visited high schools to teach girls about the value of diamonds.

In 1947, De Beers's ad agency came up with the massively successful slogan "A diamond is forever," which implied that diamonds don't crack, break, or lose value. They do, but it needn't have mattered. Thanks to clever marketing, the diamond came to symbolize true love and diamond rings became an inseparable part of courtship and marriage. (For a short history of diamond marketing, see Edward Jay Epstein's excellent "Have You Ever Tried to Sell a Diamond?" *Atlantic Monthly*, February 1982, or www.edwardjayepstein.com/diamond.htm.)

—Carrie McLaren and Robin Edgerton

JHALLY: Sure. The question is whether you want to encourage diversity. Let's say it's not popular: So what! Why must popularity drive everything?

TWITCHELL: It's a great idea. But when I hear this argument, I always think: Why are the people saying it so powerless? Why do they always seem to be saying, "We should have this delivered to us?" Why don't they essentially force it through the system? I think it's because if you observe what they consume, you'll see that it's not what they say they want but is really the popular stuff that other people like.

JHALLY: But do you recognize such a thing as power operating in the public sphere? Do you see that some people have more power than others?

TWITCHELL: Here's where we differ. You see it as power coming from outside in. As if these corporate interests are over there doing things to us. I see it in a contrary way. I see a great deal of advertising and commercialism as being the articulated will of consumers rather than the air pumped out by commercial interests. Let's take an example where you seem to hold all the cards. Take De Beers's diamond campaign. What is more ridiculous than the browbeating of men into buying utterly worthless hunks of stone? Here's this company saying that if you want to be successful in courting women, it requires two months of your salary. Isn't this an example, from your point of view, of power from the outside compressing human freedom and desire? Yet, as hideous as it is—and I think it the most hideous of advertising campaigns—there is something in it that speaks deeply to human beings in moments of high anxiety: namely, how to stabilize a frantic period of time. You stabilize it by buying something that all logic tells you is ridiculous and stupid, at a time in your life when you are the least able to afford it. And they're completely worthless. I mean, at least Nike makes good shoes! You would say, "Boy, I rest my case," but I say, "Is there any other explanation?" The explanation, I think, is the need to make ceremony, to fetishize moments of great anxiety.

JHALLY: Sure, I agree with all of that. Advertising caters to deep human needs. People's relationship with objects is what defines us as human beings. The diamond example illustrates the power of advertising, but it's ultimately about how many goods are sold, which I don't think is a good way of measuring. Advertising can be powerful even if it never sells a product. The De Beers campaign means something to people who may never buy a diamond because it gives a particular vision of what love and courtship are about. I use this example in my class and people become outraged. In fact, I've had students say, "I'm never going to buy a diamond. They've tricked me!" This is how advertising works, by reaching deep-seated human needs. I don't call this manipulation. Capitalism works because in one sense it talks about real needs that drive people.

TWITCHELL: It's doing the work of religion.

JHALLY: Partly, yes. But it takes real needs and desires and says they are only satisfied by purchasing products. So what's real about advertising is its appeals. What's false about advertising is the answers it provides to those appeals.

TWITCHELL: But why not through objects?

JHALLY: We can argue about this in terms of moralistic standards, but I prefer an empirical question: "Do people become happier when they have more things?" There's quite a bit of literature on this, and it shows that more things do not bring you more happiness. Although things are connected to happiness, it is always in a relative state. It is always in terms of what *other* people have at that time. I think you can make a fine argument for a system of production that says, "We are going to make the most number of people the most happy, and we will do this more and more over time." But capitalism is not that system. If you really wanted to make more people happy— which I think should be the goal of a political movement— then what is it that actually makes people happy? What institutions will cater to those things?

TWITCHELL: I'm with you. We agree. But I'm going to be Johnny One-Note and ask: What are those things? I'm very suspicious of those things and how powerful they really are. The great con game when we had very few things was the promised pie in the sky—a life after death. Now we've moved all those promises down here into this world. I don't know if this works or not. But who cares whether it works. We *believe* it works. We think things make us happy. My personal view is probably .0001 percent of that is true.

JHALLY: I want to go back to your question: What are those things? Those things aren't what *I* say they are. The social scientific literature reveals that what people talk about is social things. They want good family life . . .

TWITCHELL: Yeah, I never listen to what people *say*. I always listen to what people *do*.

JHALLY: That's a strange line for a democrat to be taking [laughs].

TWITCHELL: Here's my idea for an independent film. I want to set a camera on the head of my colleagues. And then I want to see what they do when they're left alone, to study the difference between saying and doing. It seems to me that reaching into the wallet is a much more powerful articulation of desire and belief than delivering the lecture. Whatever this stuff is in advertising, it's incredibly powerful. It's pushed all these other things aside. Literature, art, religion. It's eating everybody's lunch. Maybe that's because most people most of the time want that for lunch.

JHALLY: Or maybe it's that the environment within which people make decisions is so dominated by one very narrow segment of the population. That's where the issue of power comes in.

TWITCHELL: Could it also be because, in part, consuming resolves what most people consider to be their concerns?

JHALLY: I go back to Marx on this, who said, "People make their own history [or meaning] . . . but not in conditions of their own choosing." If you only look at the "conditions not of their own choosing," then all you focus on is power and manipulation. If you only look at "people make their own meanings," then all you see is individual freedom and choice. If you only look at one or the other, you get a distorted view. Advertising is the conditions not of your own choosing because it has dominated everything. If you give me a monopoly I can sell you anything. That's what De Beers did.

TWITCHELL: You seem to see advertising as a trick. I see the trickery not as them pulling a trick on us, but us actively collaborating in this process. Like the audience observing the magician, we know the lady is not being sawed in half. We can't quite understand how it works, but we suspend disbelief and give ourselves over to it. Even though we know that the claims of Alka-Seltzer are not true, we give ourselves over to it.

JHALLY: I agree. Advertising is an active process of creating meaning in which people and advertisers interact. But that is not devoid of power. Again, people make their own messages and meanings, but not in conditions of their own choosing. Jim always wants to stress the first part.

TWITCHELL: Yes, I do.

JHALLY: I stress both. If you don't have the second part, then you don't have the context within which things are taking place. You have abstract analysis, literary analysis.

TWITCHELL: Sut, where do you see power existing in a religious world? If power in the consumer world is with the producer or corporation . . .

JHALLY: In the religious world, power comes from the church.

TWITCHELL: I see the power more from the congregation than behind the pulpit. And the analogy with advertising is a valid one: consumers travel through ads looking for meaning and purpose; so, too, the congregation forces the pastor to behave in certain ways. You say the power is with the Vatican or Madison Avenue, whereas the power really is in the supermarket aisle or church pew.

JHALLY: I think power is in both places. You can't just look at one or the other.   [*Stay Free!* #16, Summer 1999]

Did Somebody Say "Community"?

by Leslie Savan

I N T H E P O L L I N G community," the Republican pollster Tony Fabrizio said during the '96 elections, "we have a saying: 'The trend is your friend.'" And the friendliest trend rolling through speech patterns today is the discovery of "communities" where previously there were only interests or professions. Places like Fabrizio's imaginary Pollstertown now dot the map of America, as any group of more than two individuals consecrates itself as a community.

"It's time to get UFO investigations out of the UFO community," a true believer asserted on a Fox TV show about [Twentieth Century Fox's] *Independence Day*. According to the *Dallas Morning News*, "the stock-car racing community wrapped its arms around car owner Rick Hendrick" at NASCAR's annual awards banquet (he had recently been indicted on federal charges). An Emmy award winner thanked "all of you in the television community out there." One member of that community, Peter Jennings, described Christopher Reeve at the Democratic National Convention as an icon of "the paralyzed community."

Real communities in the traditional sense may be struggling to survive, but "community," the word, is booming, cheerfully riding any modifier that waddles its way, as in these recent sightings: "the eco-design community," "the S&M community," "the creative community," "the transplant community," "the hockey community," "the legal community," "the criminal community," and, from the nonplace where this kind of thinking seems to be the default drive, "the online community," "the networked community," and "the virtual community."

Clearly, the Internet has popularized the idea of nonphysical communities, pushing cup-of-sugar-borrowing, town-meeting/ decision-making neighborhoods to the definition. But there's a more fundamental emotional shift in the meaning of the word as well, away from describing an inclusive, indiscriminate mix of people (the sort of community served by the United Way) to something more about personal choice. As a Sausalito interior designer told the design monthly *Metropolis* (which devoted its November issue to answering "What is community?"), "The communities that have some importance to me are communities of intellect or spirit. They are the design community, the artistic community, the psychologically aware community, the health-conscious community, the nonviolent community, the ecologically sound community."

If this busy guy ever gets to New York, he's got to check out a certain Chelsea restaurant: it's called Community.

Almost everybody who isn't a member of the misanthropic community seems to be oversold on the sweets of togetherness. But most of the world's users tend to fall into three, uh, categories: first, minorities, like gays, blacks, and Jews, who may or may not have a cohesive group identity but who, by virtue of their contrast to the majority, have the most natural claim to being at least a community in name. Second, people who share an interest or occupation ("the advertising community," "the cultural community"), who aren't a community by the usual standards but apparently feel girded by the label. And finally, anyone who wants to invoke some form of social consensus, no matter how imaginary. (As Elaine does in a *Seinfeld* episode: Worried what people will think if they discover she dumped a man after he had a stroke, she frets, "I'll be ostracized by the community!" Jerry: "Community? There's a community? All this time, I've been living in a community. I had no idea.")

Identity politics has surely contributed to community's rise, and the word, with its emphasis on collective rather than individual virtue, does serve as a righteous liberal retort to the right's family values. But community isn't limited to a specific PC left. "When *Firing Line* began," William F. Buckley Jr. said on radio a while ago, "conservatives were a very isolated community." And, of course, community is unfettered capitalism's favorite humanizing device: the business community, the investment community, and the financial community are among the worst abusers.

Like so many values, community is on everyone's lips just as it seems to be disappearing. The enormous social upheavals of the past few generations—globalization, suburbanization, television technologies that collapse times and space—have all forced the notion of community to shift from one grounded in a physical closeness that fostered mutual concerns and responsibilities to . . . what? "My definition of community has two components," says Amitai Etzioni, the "guru" of communitarianism, the movement that focuses on balancing rights and responsibilities among individuals and groups, which President Clinton made famous during his 1992 campaign. (Etzioni acknowledges community's overuse: "We've not only noticed it, but we're the culprits.") "The first element," he says, "is a bonding, not one on one, but a group of people to each other. The second is a shared set of values and culture: it's much more than interests."

He doesn't find all self-named communities spurious: "Bankers may not be a strong community, but they are more than an interest group: they often know each other personally, they hang around the same country club. But people who have only a narrowly defined group interest—people who sell office equipment or lobby Congress, for example, when they share no bond, just shared greed—they're not community."

Robert Putnam, the Harvard government professor who wrote "Bowling Alone," an essay on the decline of civic participation in America, says he's "ambivalent to the word community. The word has become so vague and banal and meaningless, I try to use another term: 'social capital,' which means social networks of connectedness, of reciprocity and trust. But if I say 'social capital' before a group of Rotarians, their eyes glaze over." The old community cornerstones, "the PTA, bowling leagues, Sunday schools," Putnam says, "no longer fit the way we live . . . but as a people, we don't seem to want to give up this word for something we long for: a sense of warm, cuddly connectedness to people with whom we share things in common."

And as boomers face their mortality, "we're going to hear a lot more about community," he adds. "In a certain sense, there's a market out there for people who have ideas on how to connect." The success of the Saturn car company, for instance, is due largely to its decision to market community, complete with "reunions" for Saturn owners—who, of course, have never previously met.

But why can't the damn word at least be slowed down, maybe by substituting other nouns that used to work well enough and that, depending on the context, can actually be more descriptive: network, industry, circle, field, movement, association, public, constituency? In fact, why not go for broke and state the entity—investors, artists, scientists—without any appendage? Obviously, community softens and bestows respect on racial and ethnic words that, standing alone, could too easily be turned into slurs. On the other hand, community makes it awfully easy to feign a respect that isn't there (an exercise common on TV and radio talk shows). The reason everyone wants to be a part of a community, rather than an association or a movement, goes beyond respect: the bright and rounded word lends an instant halo effect. Anything it touches seems valiant; whatever the endeavor, it is noble.

Whether community is vanishing or merely evolving, fear of its loss is what keeps us chanting the word. The word provides comfort: it's a prayer or wishful thinking, as if we could yak it into being.

You idiot! You unplugged the community!!

Community's quasireligious overtones may reflect an authentic yearning, but too often we're reaching less for spiritual kin than self-amplification: we want to see our individual selves turned into a multitude—a thousand other people who cherish *The X-Files*, do eco-design, or make a killing in online investments. We're not alone; our identity is validated. But since community is generally a good thing, why niggle over how the word is used? Sometimes magical thinking really works. The writer Robert Atkins recently edited an issue on community for the online journal *TalkBack!* He began by zinging those who "prattle about virtual community as if sex-chat rooms . . . constitute community." But looking back on the project, he now says he "can see the value of adhering to some ideas even if we don't quite believe in them, like Santa. Maybe the fact we say 'community' all the time is an important wake-up call that it's an endangered phenomenon."

Maybe. But if past habits are any clue, we're far more likely to continue to choose a verbal hologram over the real thing. Who wants to do anything if you can merely say it? You don't have to join local organizations, do volunteer work, or even vote because you're already part of the creative community, the Channel 13 community, or—who knows?—the polling community.

You've done your duty by pronouncing the word.

[*Stay Free!* #15, Fall 1998]

A Vehicle for Comparison

THE VOLKSWAGEN AS A MEASURE OF ALL THINGS

by Chris Boznos

"E. coli . . . moves its whole length in two nanoseconds. If it were the size of a Volkswagen, it would be going four times the speed of light."[1]

THE VW BUG, with its nearly immutable design, has been driven all over the world and all over the movies for the better part of a century. You'd be hard-pressed to find someone who couldn't pick its shape out of a lineup or, more realistically, a weedy Southern California backyard. On the web, phrases describing objects as about the size of a Volkswagen have achieved nearly pornographic levels of popularity.[2] Of course, it's not the only product used as a reference for scale: comparisons with Buicks and

747s are popular too. Big Macs make a showing.[3] None of them, however, can compete with the sheer number or variety[4] of comparisons made to the VW.[5] The Bug is the standard. It is the measure of things. It is the ruler itself.

Science writers make the most use of the vehicle, deeming everything in or from space, made or conceived by man or God to be about the size of a Volkswagen.[6] The VW-size Mars Global Surveyor looks down at the planet with cameras capable of resolving VW-size objects[7] such as the "nearly" VW-size Spirit and Opportunity,[8] which, I should note, captured images of VW-size rocks[9] in their travels. For a time, you could experience the thrill of the VW-size International Space Station capsule[10] as projected by the advanced VW-size IMAX projector.[11]

But, as seen in the box on page 162, writers on every topic compare their subject to the Volkswagen.[12] I even get the impression that some authors feel the examination of a subject would be incomplete without a Bug comparison, even when that reference seems inappropriate.[13] This phenomenon manifests itself most plainly when a writer, struggling with an object impossibly out of line with the VW's scale, makes do by referring to only a portion of the vehicle, turning the Bug into a divisible unit of measure. You probably already know that a manatee is about half the size[14] of a VW, but did you know that a mounted bison head is also 50 percent its size?[15] Well, it is. Find those references helpful? All right, but is "half the size of a VW glove box" really a known quantity?[16] Is "the size of a VW bucket seat" especially useful, as opposed to some other bucket seat?[17]

Other writers prefer to switch to the weight of their subject in the pursuit of some equilibrium with the Bug: "The USS *Wisconsin* was one of four ships having huge 16-inch guns,

Extinct giant armadillos with spiked, clublike defensive tails[18] • A target that you can hit from twenty feet even when you can't hit "beans"[19] • A 720-pound pig[20] • Hitler's enormous "Columbus Globe" designed for the New Reich Chancellery[21] • King Kong's artificial heart from the 1986 film "King Kong Lives"[22] • Nomad, a robot designed for identifying meteorites in the Antarctic[23] • The power brick for the Xbox 360 Elite[24] • The "best general description" of a Japanese maple, with the caveat that it will reach that description "but slowly"[25] • Leatherback turtles once considered to be sea monsters[26] • An eerie and gargantuan grouper[27] • The projection of a dime with a new document reader[28] • A DJ's rig in a Polish restaurant in New York[29] • Fictional, and presumably radio-active, giant seventies sci-fi tarantulas[30] • Solar-powered green-house units designed for the potential terraforming of Mars[31] • A blue whale's heart[32] • The testicles of Paul Bunyan's famous blue ox, Babe[33] • A red balloon on which a woman must stand in her dream[34] • The death wish on the shoulder of a fictional and exiled Yakuza boss[35] • The root ball of an oak tree wedged against the roof of Wayne and Norma Murry's Texarkana home[36] • The cooking-oil-disposal unit of the restaurant responsible for inventing the fried pickle chip[37] • A "humming blue box" used for treatment of human waste at oil-drilling sites[38] • A computer disk drive circa 1968[39] • A CAD workstation circa 1979[40] • Loudspeakers placed at a depth of two hundred feet and dangerous to marine life[41] • The head of Russian pugilist Nikolai Valuev[42] • A theoretical pile of brush[43] • Potentially dangerous deorbiting iridium satellites[44] • A knoll preceding a rock garden that "single-handedly justifies the money spent on a full suspension" mountain bike[45] • Artichokelike treetops found on "an extinct African volcano"[46] • A lava rock within the [tidal] pools of the Big Island of Hawaii[47] • A glacierlike mound of methane hydrates surrounded by clam beds[48] • Walruses that require fifty-four kilograms of clams each day[49] • The atomic bomb dropped on Hiroshima[50] • A boil sprouting on your back that gives rise to your dermatologist's concern[51] • The mole on Lincoln's Mount Rushmore face, as described by Lincoln himself in a one-man play about the president[52] • The tempting steak that "your friend wolfs down" even though she's fifteen pounds lighter and a dress size smaller[53] • A supersize nest of yellow jackets possibly containing over one hundred thousand of the insects[54] • "Serious" bodybuilders[55] • An overpriced one-bedroom apartment[56] • The bentwood lobster traps used by Algonquin Indians that, by design, allow younger lobsters to escape[57] • The Weasel, a small World War II–era German tank[58] • The world's largest conventional bomb, the "daisy cutter"[59] • The Galileo probe[60] • The deadly Audrey II from the musical *Little Shop of Horrors*[61] • A "space mollusk"[62] • The upcoming Mars Science Laboratory[63] • Many of the thousands of unplotted minor planets in our solar system capable of causing "considerable damage" to the Earth on impact[64] • A proposed meteorite prior to exploding above northwest Indiana that created a debris field eighty miles long[65] • Debris from the Mir space station[66] • An unidentified orange sphere flying over Farmers Branch, Texas, on June 1, 1972[67] large enough to launch a shell the weight of a VW Beetle 23 miles!"[68] But these weight comparisons prove less common, presumably because a limited number of people can heft the weight of a VW in their head as they would, say, a bowling ball. Moreover, the advantages of the vehicle's unchanging design no longer apply because the Volkswagen's weight is contingent on payload and fuel status.

So what does all this mean? Should we attribute the extraordinarily persistent desire to describe objects in VW terms solely to the popularity of the vehicle? Is it the snowballing popularity of the metaphor itself? Is it simply lazy writing? Or is something more going on? Maybe we're missing a unit of measure. Maybe the volume in question is particularly useful for description and the Volkswagen filled a void.[69] If so, why not take what has already become a de facto standard of measurement and bestow upon it the status of a formal scientific unit, the Vw?[70] After all, it's no less arbitrary than our current measures, both metric and English, and has already proven to be enormously relatable. Besides, if we do need a volume unit the size of a VW, why not use the friendly Bug as the standard—unless, of course, you would prefer to refer to "a couple of mounted bison heads."   [*Stay Free!* #23, Fall 2004]

Notes

1. www.cc.gatech.edu/fac/mark.guzdial/squeak/oopsla.html.

2. A Google search turns up thousands of references to objects the size of a VW or Volkswagen. Interestingly, these are not always references to the ubiquitous Bug, but include comparisons with the far less common Rabbit, VW Bus, and Golf. Consider if there is something special about the Volkswagen brand itself. Are a disproportionate number of "writer types" familiar with or fond of Volkswagens? One could argue that, for at least the past thirty years, individuals (from the cultures responsible for disseminating the VW metaphor) driving VWs have been the more artistic or free-spirited of their societies, and so in theory more likely to write creatively. Moreover, the references

the author found to VW-size spliffs may support the notion that a majority of VW com-
parers are from a liberal subculture. The author found no references to "tax cuts twice
the size of a Volkswagen" or "VW-size moral traditions upon which the fabric of our culture depends." (Conservatives reading this, please insert theories about liberal bias in the
media here.)

3. For example, a ribosome magnified by a factor of 10,000,000 would be the size of
a Big Mac. bass.bio.uci.edu/~hudel/bs99a/lecture21/index.html.

4. Other objects and products of reference are limited in their comparative function. For example, the Buick and the football field are used only to describe objects as
large. In contrast, writers use Volkswagens as a purely scientific frame of reference and to
describe objects as too small as well as too large, i.e., a runner's multifunction wrist-
watch. www.msss.com/mars_images/moc/oct_2000_sampler/polar_site/.

5. Some of the most interesting VW size references involve a convergence of the
Volkswagen with one of these other popular objects of comparison. For example, an article on *AccessAtlanta.com* instructs that you should "keep a look out for a Big Mac the
size of a Volkswagen Bug" while touring the city.

6. My space aficionado friend asserts that many satellites and spacecraft probably
share the VW size because of the commonality of the delivery vehicle cargo bays. (Why
the cargo bays would be the size of a VW was not explained.)

7. pr.caltech.edu/periodicals/EandS/articles/Mars%20Global%20Surveyor.pdf.

8. I should note that this reference is actually quite inaccurate, the actual size of the
rovers being much closer to that of a golf cart. www.thenewatlantis.com/archive/2/soa/
mars.htm.

9. www.msss.com/mars_images/moc/2006/07/20/.

10. www.cinemareview.com/production.asp?prodid=3296.

11. www.thehenryford.org/imax/about.asp.

12. As the mass of material became clear, the author realized a proper examination
of this subject would require substantial research and that he might not be interested
in doing said research. Pretending that the popularity of the VW metaphor involved
some nefarious cover-up, the truth of which he must pursue as implicitly commissioned by the children of the world, he was able to not only complete the article but day-
dream about two-fisted interrogations of the conspirators, from which he derived mild
pleasure.

13. Some subjects even appear to require it. With hundreds of Google references to
the size of a blue whale's heart being that of a Volkswagen, I think I would have to be either a genius or a fool to attempt describing it any other way.

14. ruby.fgcu.edu/courses/sstans/81469/s06litint.html.

15. www.sptimes.com/2003/03/02/Travel/Everything_under_the_.shtml.

16. In reference to "showers on the old smokeboats." www.olgoat.com/substuff/
dex159.htm.

17. In reference to spoons found in an Italian restaurant: www.metroactive.com/
papers/metro/02.20.03/dining-0308.html.

18. www.utc.edu/Faculty/Timothy-Gaudin/gaudin_educ_resint.html.

19. groups.google.com/groups?q=%22size+of+a+volkswagen%22&hl=en&lr=&ie=
UTF-8&oe=UTF-8&selm=9am50g%24763%241%40xring.cs.umd.edu&rnum=6.

20. www.abqjournal.com/venue/personalities/99276trends10-19-03.htm.

21. www.chicagotribune.com/features/lifestyle/chi-1107hitler_fillnov07,1,6332029.story
?ctrack=1&cset=true.

22. fathom.lib.uchicago.edu/2/21701757/.

23. news.bbc.co.uk/1/hi/sci/tech/609905.stm.

24. www.cnet.com/xbox-360/.

25. www.worldplants.com/laceleaf.htm.

26. www.spaceforspecies.ca/track_real_species/leatherback_turtle/about/.

27. www.ms-starship.com/journal/mar00/23.htm.

28. www.piercelaw.edu/courtroom.htm.

29. query.nytimes.com/gst/fullpage.html?res=950DE3DD1E3FF935A2575BC0A9669
C8B63.

30. www.cheftalk.com/content/display.cfm?articleid=3&type=article.

31. www.geocities.com/fra_nl/.

32. A blue whale's tongue is, by the way, about the size and weight of a full-grown
African elephant. www.can-do.com/uci/ssi2000/mammalsinternet/tsld002.html.

33. www-cs-students.stanford.edu/~mpearson/google-sandals.html.

34. www.hominoid.org/skr100702.htm.

35. www.time.com/time/asia/features/heroes/takeshi.html.

36. www.usatoday.com/weather/news/2000/wice1229.htm.

37. www.louisvillehotbytes.com/genny.shtml.

38. www.pbs.org/frontlineworld/fellows/peru0803/nf1.html.

39. www.linuxjournal.com/article.php?sid=4324.

40. According to the Lumagraph website, the CAD workstation in question was also
"almost as noisy" as a VW. www.lumagraph.net/about.htm.

41. www.lightparty.com/Energy/WhalesToNavy-LessNoise.html.

42. www.msnbc.msn.com/id/10467839/.

43. www.star-telegram.com/news/columnists/amie_streater/story/208732.html.

44. www.nationaldefensemagazine.org/issues/2000/Jun/Navy_Agency.htm.

45. www.mtbmind.com/scott.htm.

46. gorp.away.com/gorp/activity/climb/africa_berger2.htm.

47. www.kahumoku.com/mccabe.htm.

48. www.geotimes.org/dec02/NN_hydrates.html.

49. www.calacademy.org/calwild/2002fall/stories/whiskers.html.

50. www.sfgate.com/cgi-bin/article.cgi?file=/c/a/2002/12/15/IN223977.DTL&type
=printable.

51. starbulletin.com/2003/10/19/features/memminger.html.

52. reviewplays.com/abe_lincoln.htm.

53. www.honoluluclub.com/lifedesigns.php?ID=3.

54. www.cleburnenews.com/news/2006/cn-local-0721-0-6g21j4708.htm.

55. www.donramon.net/articles/articles_level2_086.htm.

56. www.tenant.net/Alerts/Guide/press/nyt/bh061397.html.

57. www.sx2.com/choices12.html.

58. leoweekly.com/?q=issue/frontpage/4099.

59. www.nd.edu/~techrev/Archive/Spring2002/a8.html.

60. www.engin.umich.edu/alumni/engineer/00SS/jupiter.html.

61. www.adirondacktravel.com/mtco/archive/2002.html.

62. From the sci-fi book *Forge of the Elders*. www.hazlitt.org/bookofthemonth/fboty 2000.html.

63. www.aerospaceguide.net/mars/science_laboratory.html.

64. www.atscope.com.au/astrometry.html.

65. www.nwitimes.com/articles/2003/03/28/news/region_and_state/dd7b4e9acdf5e04 c86256cf70013e895.txt.

66. www.keynews.org/archives/a_miralpha.htm.

67. www.nuforc.org/webreports/ndxe197206.html.

68. In other references to battleship guns, the projectile weight and distance traveled differs but the VW remains a constant: "The U.S.S. *Missouri* . . . has the impressive might of a cannon [capable of] pinpoint[ing] its 2,100 lb. projectile (the weight of a VW Bug automobile) 21 miles." members.tripod.com/~ButlerC/NEBerkIndex/NAdamsIndex/SB600PeteBergeron/SB600.htm.

69. Is it possible that human social or scientific development has been hamstrung in the past because of the lack of such an appropriate volume unit? Philosophers suggest that without the vocabulary to express an idea, individuals have a difficult time conceiving of that idea. Technologically, the pace of human invention certainly has accelerated since the Bug's inception, in 1938.

70. Consider these hypothetical usages: "Office space for rent! 7.5 Vw. Ample underground parking available," or "The largest brewery on the East Coast, its fermentation tanks can hold up to nearly 1/2 kVw [kilovolkswagen] of refreshment."

Key Questions

1. Early in the twentieth century, when Bayer owned the trademark to Heroin, the drug was promoted for relief of which of the following?

   a. Toothaches.

   b. Respiratory ailments.

   c. Nausea.

   d. Rheumatism.

2. Which of the following entertainments were not available at the U.S. launch of a major antidepressant?

   a. A live orchestra performing "Get Happy," followed by Depeche Mode's "People Are People."

   b. At the national aquarium, a "Stingray Feeding and Presentation for Special Guests and Their Families."

   c. Gigantic photos of the Grand Canyon.

   d. A wall of bricks, each labeled with the name of a competing drug, which was shot down by rainbow lasers in the form of the new product's logo, while the orchestra played Pink Floyd's "The Wall" and dancers wearing helmets and holding pickaxes did a jig.

3. Which of the following practices are regularly used in police investigations but primarily for public relations—i.e., because citizens educated by cop shows expect it?

   a. Dust for fingerprints.

   b. Show the victim mug shots.

   c. Show the victim lineups of potential culprits.

   d. All of the above.

4. According to Western International Media's "Nag Factor" report, which type of parents are the most common?

   a. Indulgers, who give their kids everything they want.

   b. Kids' Pals, who want to have fun like their offspring.

   c. Conflicted, who buy out of guilt and contain a high proportion of single or divorced parents.

   d. Bare Necessities, who have the highest median household income, yet are the least likely to give in to kids' pleas.

5. Which of the following sales points have NOT appeared in ads for Navegar TEC-9 and other assault weapons?

   a. "Excellent resistance to fingerprints."

   b. Silencers are easy to attach.

   c. An image featuring the smoking target of a human being being shot dozens of times in the head and heart.

   d. Slogans including "Only your imagination limits your fun" and "As tough as your toughest customer."

   e. None of the above.

6. Asked to defend his company's marketing of junk food to kids, including a *Shrek 2* promotion, a representative of Hostess Twinkies responded by saying:

   a. "Hostess is not a kids' brand."

   b. The *Shrek 2* campaign wasn't targeting kids because the movie "appeals to all ages."

   c. "Fifty-three percent of households that purchase Twinkies have no children."

   d. All of the above.

7. About seven hundred Ohio children who were three years and younger received mental-health drugs through Medicaid in July 2004. Which of the following drugs were the least commonly prescribed?

   a. Antihistamines used as sedatives.

   b. Antipsychotics.

   c. Antianxiety agents.

   d. Antidepressants.

   e. Valium.

8. In 2003, employees at Wal-Mart and McDonald's with limited-benefit health insurance paid how much annually for a *maximum* of $1,000 coverage per year.

   a. At least $100.

   b. At least $275.

   c. At least $400.

   d. At least $500.

9. Due to drastic government budget cuts, schools in Alberta, Canada, have implemented which controversial effort to raise funds:

   a. Casino night.

   b. "Gentleman's" clubs.

   c. Student-teacher boxing.

   d. Seniors' swimsuit calendar.

10. TRUE or FALSE: Toyota opted to build a new plant in Canada instead of the United States because American workers are too uneducated and illiterate.

Answers

1. B. The drug was recommended as a sedative to quiet coughs and noisy infants.

2. A. Tears for Fears's "Everybody Wants to Rule the World" was played after "Get Happy," not the Depeche Mode song. Andrew Solomon, *Noonday Demon: An Atlas of Depression* (New York: Scribner, 2001), pp. 395–96.

3. D. Frank Mankiewicz and Joel Swerdlow, *Remote Control:*

Television and the Manipulation of American Life (New York: Times Books, 1978), p. 256.

4. A. David Clark Scott, "Of Pleas and Purchases," *Christian Science Monitor*, August 18, 1998, p. B1.

5. E. Frank M. Pitre, "Assault Weapons: The Case Against the TEC-9," Burlingame, California, Consumer Attorneys of California Annual Seminar, 1996. www.cpsmlaw.com/publications/assault.shtml.

6. D. Janet Adamy, "Snack Foods' New Marketing Sweet Spot: Grown-Ups," *The Wall Street Journal*, April 12, 2005, p. B1.

7. B. Encarnacion Pyle, *Columbus Dispatch*, April 25, 2005. www.dispatch.com/live/contentbe/dispatch/2005/04/25/20050425-A1-00.html.

8. D. Chat Terhune, "Fast-Growing Health Plan Has a Catch: $1,000-a-Year Cap," *The Wall Street Journal*, May 14, 2003. online.wsj.com/article/SB105285938790553200.html.

9. A.

10. True. Steve Erwin, "Toyota to Build 100,000 Vehicles per Year in Woodstock, Ontario," CBC News, July 3, 2005.

Behind
the Scenes

4.

GREW UP in the no-man's-land of Clearwater,
Florida. My high school was the typical suburban
horror show: big and soulless, with a popular crowd oriented
around sports, beach life, and beer parties. This was in the mid-
1980s, when a lot of great music was being made in the country, but you would never have known it living in Clearwater.
Radio was geared to overproduced pablum, the audio equivalent of car commercials. I never quite understood why. Somehow, though, I got the idea that there was better music out
there and ended up choosing my college, UNC–Chapel Hill,
based largely on the fact that it had a student radio station that
played stuff you couldn't find scanning the radio dial in Clearwater.

In 1991, while I was working at WXYC, Nirvana's *Never-
mind* hit platinum and, seemingly overnight, the music industry started paying attention to "alternative" music and stations
like ours. Chapel Hill became an overhyped music mecca, after
Seattle and Athens. Reps from the major labels would call constantly to track records, promote upcoming live dates, and of-

fer freebies to the "jocks." Around this time I took a trip to the dark side: I became a paid college rep for Sony Music. It was then, while working as an insider, that I began thinking seriously about marketing's effect on culture.

My mission at Sony was to "work" Sony bands at WXYC. The thought of trying to bribe my friends with shitty records was a joke, so I decided to take the joke further by producing a fake zine, *Sonyland*, using my Sony allowance. By "fake zine" I mean that *Sonyland* parodied the obvious and pathetic attempts by major labels to co-opt underground music. *Sonyland* was a photocopied, sloppy newsletter that hamfistedly promoted the label with scrawled headlines shouting "Corporate rock rules!" interspersed between swipes at other major labels. My friends and other local indie rockers loved it; many had no idea that it was actually funded by Sony: they thought the whole thing was a joke. I thought it could get me fired.

But *Sonyland* didn't get me fired. My bosses loved—LOVED— it. The head of college reps, one of the biggest tools I'd ever met, called me to say, "*Sonyland* is so fucking great! Genius!!"

Terrifying, maybe. But *genius*?! I hadn't realized it at the time, but a lot of young people who worked in marketing were, like me, learning to apply their ironic sensibilities to sell things. Advertising to my so-called Generation X, in fact, became defined by the same kind of reflexive, self-deprecating style written into the pages of *Sonyland*. While I didn't quite understand why this was all happening or how it worked, I was starting to see how the forces that shaped the music industry were similar to those influencing other aspects of culture. The record companies bribed DJs with free CDs and drinks, label reps formed "friendships" in order to move product and influence bands, and much of what ended up on the college charts as a result was total crap.

In this section, we peer into this hidden side of the media machine: places and processes that the normal person never sees or ponders but that influence our daily lives. In "My Very Special Trip to the Nike Store," actor and comedian David Cross recounts his visit to Nike's "celebrity" store, where the rich and famous can pick up Nike wear for free. In "How to Tell You're a *Details* Reader," we review the peculiar language of magazine media kits. As it turns out, a magazine's *real* customers aren't readers but, rather, advertisers. Alan Benson surveys the celebration-as-stealth-ad, from National Bosses' Day to Bladder Health Week, in "I'm Dreaming of a White National Cheese Day: The Selling of the American Calendar." Finally, in "Shopping Spies" we study the marketers who secretly study shoppers. These stealth researchers follow unwitting customers around in stores and sometimes ask them for advice. Who knows, the next time a kindly old man asks you about hair cream, he could be trying to download your brain.

My Very Special Trip to the Nike Store

by David Cross

THERE'S A LITTLE mom-and-pop store where I live (the quaint hamlet of Hollywood, California) that gives away free shoes. It's true! It's called the Nike Store, and they'll give you free clothing . . . well, not you, but me.

Now, I've got plenty of money. I do not need free shoes, and hopefully never will. Still, I went to the Nike Store. In fact, I called them and arranged an appointment. And it wasn't for research purposes. When it comes right down to it, I just wanted the free shit.

I was getting ready to leave L.A. for a week in the Nike-friendly township of Aspen, Colorado, for the annual Comedy and Executive Write-off Vacation Fest. I try to participate every year because I enjoy paying twenty-five dollars for a hamburger and listening to wealthy white people bitch about comedians. All the more reason to stock up on minimally used winter wear.

I called the nice lady (who shall remain referred to as "the nice lady," 'cause she was) whose sole job is to corral a seemingly never-ending stream of real-life, honest-to-gosh celebrities through the maze of logo-embossed Nike swag. I told her who I was and what I did. It turned out that I had showed up on a television set occasionally. And that, ladies and gentlemen of the jury, is the only criterion for getting free clothing and accessories, hand spun by the gnarled, malnourished, immature hands of children unfortunate enough to be born into a poverty-stricken country whose government's ethics jibe perfectly with our government's. But I digress.

For some reason, the Nike Store is located in an industrial park near the airport (but there's good soul food nearby, so there). To make the experience of getting free clothing even more enjoyable, the store is designed to resemble the interior of a fancy-pants professional basketball arena, albeit one filled with jock wear. The playful quality of the store seemed to wash any misgivings I had down the Nike drain and straight into hell, where they will remain.

I was escorted (or es-"courted," ha-ha!) around the showroom by the nice lady. She walked around pointing out various shoes here or a sweatshirt there and would say, "This is nice. What about this?" My response became limited to a few "Yeah's" or "Sure's," all the while stocking up enough Nike clothing to barter my way through an impending race war.

I turned down very little that was offered. I remember being suddenly honest when presented with a couple of turtlenecks with the Nike Swoosh prominently displayed on the turtle of the neck part. "I wouldn't ever wear those, no, thanks . . . Oh, okay." I got the feeling that not too many people turned stuff down. Would Shaq have taken them? (Note to self: Call Sha-quille O'Neal—ask about Nike turtleneck.) Well, the end result of all of this was not only walking out of there with a new friend—someone that I will forevermore refer to as a "nice lady"—but with bags of clothing that, as of this day, are scattered about the United States in various Goodwills, in ex-girlfriends' closets, and on the feet of several colleagues.

So remember, next time you see newly arrived immigrants, eyes wide open, fearful and intimidated by our great Market-place, look down at their feet. Are they wearing a fancy pair of high-tech sneakers? They are? Oh, those are from the Nike Store. I gave them away.   **[*Stay Free!* #23, Fall 2004]**

How to Tell You're a *Details* Reader

(AND OTHER SECRETS OF MAGAZINE ADVERTISING)

I ONCE WORKED at an indie record label, and among my responsibilities was advertising. When one of our bands had a new release coming out, it was my job to select the magazines in which we'd promote it. To "help" me with this decision, the salespeople who work for magazines did any number of things. Bigger mags tried to bribe me with free lunches and dinners, which wasn't too terrible (although I would have preferred it if they had just given me the money). Or they offered to drop by for an office visit and give the sales pitch. (I invariably declined.)

The other option was to do away with the face-to-face altogether and let the media kit make the pitch. Magazines of all sizes employ some variation of a media kit, which is the promotional material they use to attract advertisers like me. Small publications usually keep it to a page of ad rates, while bigger magazines tend to have bigger and more complicated kits—kits so complicated that, in fact, I had no idea what most of the stuff meant.

All kits, however, share a single purpose: to provide a solid argument for getting my ad money. The surprising part is that this generally has nothing to do with the content of the magazine. I wasn't being asked to advertise in *Details* because it's well-written, informative, or interesting, but because it reaches and influences the right audience. Magazine content is beside the point, a means to an end. The audience is what matters, the audience is what's for sale.

As a mere reader of magazines, you probably aren't aware that most of them are hip, influential, cutting-edge, and important to an entire generation. At least, that's what the media kits say:

> *Spin*: "The voice of a generation."

> *Vice*: "Each generation has a small-run, intensely hip magazine that proves influential far beyond its circulation numbers . . . *Vice* is this generation's model" (quoting *Advertising Age*).

> *Vibe*: "Speaks to a whole generation of young men and women whose lives defy categorizing."

Spin subscribers average 3.7 trips a month to record stores

80% of *Maxim* readers wear fragrance at least once a week

66% of *Esquire* readers spend more than half their income on outerware

99.4% of *Details* adults do NOT read *Blender*

74% of *Alternative Press* readers regularly go to malls

33.8% of *Wired* readers plan to buy a suit over $400 in the next 12 months

40% of *Blender* readers smoke

12% of *Rolling Stone* readers have listened to Internet radio in the last 30 days

According to media kits, *Vibe*'s readers aren't the only ones who defy categorization. Just about every mag has its own way of saying "Stereotypes are bad; our readers are all different and unique." Supposedly the only thing that unites readers—other than them all being "influential" consumers (see next page)—is their devotion to the magazine in question.

But maybe the magazines are joking about their readers. This would explain why the parts about defying categorization are followed by pages and pages of charts, percentages, and decimal points categorizing readers. (No two psychographics are alike!)

65% of *Wig* readers call themselves artists

63% of *Interview* readers "have more self-confidence and style" than others their age; 92% love new and different things (the other 8% are unconscious)

98% of *Film Threat* readers wear hip clothes

Too bad publishers don't make their magazines as interesting as their math. (If I start reading *Film Threat*, are my clothes more likely to be hip?) Granted, I'm no numbers whiz, but publishers' stats seem impossibly off. *Spin* readers are buying 7.5 CDs a month. Yeah, right.

From the *Esquire* media kit, which confirms that intelligent, sophisticated men ought to know about topless hotties in tiny, tiny hot pants. Sometimes they ought to know about them several times a day, vigorously.

All Things Influential

Apparently, if you just read the magazine, you're not following the rules. Magazines are for consumers, not readers. Magazines don't make money selling magazines; subscriptions and vendor sales don't even come close to covering costs. Magazines usually make over 50 percent of their income from advertising—that is, from selling their audiences, their targeted markets.

Marketers constantly survey, poll, and interview readers to see how much they're consuming. Some of this audience research has a secondary purpose, such as helping the editors "give readers what they want." Others offer incentives: answer a few questions, win some prize. Lifestyle magazines such as *Details*, *Paper*, and *Wired* recruit readers to serve as marketing consultants, answering questions for the magazine's advertisers in exchange for free goods and other perks. Once they've collected the data, magazines compile and transform it into something that proves how influential they are. They set trends and cut edges. Their readers are the first to try new products and encourage their friends to do the same. As an early MTV trade ad says, "Buy this 28-year-old and get all his friends for free." Or, as the media kits put it:

> *Paper* is "the ideal 'tastemaker' readership based in America's largest and most cutting-edge single city market, New York, as well as strategic trendsetting markets across the country."

> *Jane* is "built for the 20-something woman who is the ultimate front-row influencer."

> *GQ* "reaches millions of leading men each month. These men are trendsetters; they are hip, affluent, and above all influential."

What I want to know is: If magazine readers are so influential, what are they doing filling out marketing surveys? Don't they have anything better to do? Shouldn't they be out influencing?

"General, Yet Specific"

You'd think the most likely people to be able to cut through the b.s. would be ad buyers. But whoever puts these things together believes ad buyers can't read. Media kits contradict themselves all over the place. Pronouncements like these are eerily common:

> **Maxim**: We're "general, yet specific . . . [Our reader] is not interested in fashion, he's interested in clothes. He's a man who has arrived, but is still going places."

> **Spin**: "We are cutting-edge, but avoid the hypnotic trap of being trendy."

> **Surface**: "A spotlight for today's 'avant-guardians'" and yet "*Surface*'s cover stories are the superheroes of our media age, icons like Grace Jones, Nina Hagen and Debbie Harry . . . official slogan: the subculture is surfacing."

Using imagery to reach these sorts of oppositional contradictions is a cliché in advertising. When you consider that media kits function as advertisements for magazines, I guess this isn't so surprising; it's even less so considering how the line between editorial and advertising is getting pretty impossible to find.

Advertorials

The downside of passing up lunches and office visits was that I didn't get to have the sales rep offer editorial coverage. These sorts of deals aren't in media kits—they're, you know, unethical—

Coked Out
of Your Magazine

While working as the ad buyer at Matador Records, I received this memo from a friend of mine at *Spin* magazine. Dated March 6, 1998, the memo was from McCann Erickson, then Coca-Cola's ad agency, and it was sent to magazines that Coca-Cola advertised in at the time.

So, according to Coke's guidelines, the best place to run their ads is at least six pages outside of any possibly interesting magazine.

The purpose of this letter is to clarify the positioning clause that is included on Coca-Cola Company insertion orders.

The positioning clause has been revised to state, "Any Coca-Cola advertising that faces less than full editorial and/or inappropriate editorial matter will be subject to a full makegood." The Coca-Cola Company requires that all insertions [advertisements] are placed adjacent to editorial that is consistent with each brand's marketing strategy/positioning. In general, we believe that positive and upbeat editorial provides a compatible environment in which to communicate the brand's message.

We consider the following subjects to be inappropriate and require that our ads are not placed adjacent to articles discussing the following issues:

- Hard News
- Sex related issues
- Drugs (Prescription or illegal)
- Medicine (e.g. chronic illnesses such as cancer, diabetes, AIDS, etc.)
- Health (e.g. mental or physical medical conditions)
- Negative Diet Information (bulimia, anorexia, quick weight loss, etc.)
- Food
- Political issues
- Environmental issues
- Articles containing vulgar language
- Religion

If you have a positioning question or if an ad needs to be moved due to inappropriate editorial, you must contact the AOR immediately and provide positioning options. If an appropriate positioning option is not available, we reserve the right to omit our ad from that issue.

The Coca-Cola Company also requires a minimum of 6 pages separation between competitive advertising (any non-alcoholic beverage, including water, juice, coffee, milk). If there is more than one Coca-Cola brand running in an issue of your magazine, we require 6 pages of separation.

Christine Maggiore
McCann Erickson

but magazine editorial is for sale along with ad space. In exchange for financial favors, the mag will put an agreed-upon artist on the cover, for example. I can't even begin to count the phone chats with ad reps that relied on the assumption that I should advertise band X because the mag covered them. Even legit mags do this kind of thing. You'd be surprised.

Or then maybe you wouldn't, especially once you consider the number of magazines launched by Madison Avenue types. This is something media kits are up front about: *Plazma* was founded by former creatives at Wieden+Kennedy, supposedly one of the hippest ad agencies (they work with Nike); the men's mag *P.O.V.* was started by a couple of guys from *Forbes* "looking for a younger, cooler mag"; and the soft-porn men's "zine" *Hollywood Highball* was the brainchild of Steven Grasse, CEO of a marketing agency that helps companies like R. J. Reynolds, Coca-Cola, and MTV target young people. These magazines ultimately failed, but editorial and advertising has only grown more incestuous.

In a few years we'll all think back to the golden days when the issue of advertiser influence was a matter of censorship: *Rolling Stone* canceling an article that pisses off Subaru, or whatever. What we've got now is a situation where advertiser money doesn't merely censor content, it dictates and defines acceptable content in the first place. This is one of the reasons that music magazines—like other specialty publications—have transformed into so-called lifestyle mags. It's hard to name a mass music mag that doesn't regularly feature fashion spreads, trend reports, tech columns, and consumer tips (*Rolling Stone*'s guide to cameras, *Spin*'s guide to makeup for men). It's not as if the *Spin* editors are actually thinking: "Hey, let's get some skinny models, an expensive car, and take pictures of them frolicking with PowerBooks in the desert: readers love that!"

A Rag for Every Bag

For most niche magazines, the editorial content and the staples are pretty much of equal value in accomplishing their primary goal: holding a bunch of ads together. For every conceivable consumer segment, there's a niche magazine selling to it. Here are a few to watch out for.

merican Gentrifier
Brooklyn Edition Winter 2005

10 VIOLENT CRIMES YOU
CAN LIVE WITH

LOCAL DELIS NOW
STOCKING BRIE

BED STUY: STILL
TOO BLACK?

PLUS: WHEN TO
START THE KIDS ON
ANTIDEPRESSANTS

TROPHY WIFE
June 2005

NOW WITH
MORE ADS!

¡Limpia lo, pendeja!
Essential Spanish for all your needs

Exclusive Male Lifespan Chart
Stop guessing!

Do You Look Interested?
Take our Quiz!

Ten Recipes +L

modern
phobiac

Phones:
Is it finally time to fear them?

Get scared for winter:
8 new must-fears

Environmental Disease:
Why you have it

BONUS! There may be
spiders in this magazine!

choking victim
what's in YOUR throat?

Little Meatballs:
this year's must-lodge

Eat Fast, Gag Quick!
And other Hot Tips!

Clutching your throat—
too 'obvious'?

Features often aren't designed to inform or even to entertain, but to sell gear.

Fortunately, magazines have other ways of making money besides selling editorial content: "ancillary revenues." These include things like brand extensions: Spin Radio, The Source clothing, Rolling Stone Rock and Roll Bowl and New Music Tour, Paper Promotions, Playboy cigars.

So What Have We Learned?

Magazines, particularly lifestyle magazines, aren't designed for readers. That's not to say they can't be appreciated for what they do offer: an occasional great article, photos of scantily clad models, and free fragrance strips. In fact, understanding and questioning the way magazines work makes it possible to appreciate the content even more.

As an advertiser, however, I found it unfortunate that I needed to spend a bunch of money advertising in magazines, whether people actually read those magazines or not. If I had my way, we would have bypassed magazines altogether. You know, cut out the middleman: take the several thousands of dollars it costs for a Pavement ad in *Details* and just pay people to buy the record. I bet we'd have received a greater return on our investment that way. But then, what do I know. I'm no influential.

[Originally published by Carrie McLaren
in *Escandalo!*, the Matador Records Newsletter, #6, 1997]

THE AFFLUENCERS.
(ALL ACCESSORIES INCLUDED)

NOW AVAILABLE AT BRAVO!

Bluetooth earpiece:
Part communication tool,
part design statement.

Rock t-shirt:
Bought online, but he still digs the band.

Linen blazer:
Learned to "make it work" by watching
PROJECT RUNWAY.

Movie tickets:
Seven tickets for opening night,
two tickets for date night.

Latest cell phone:
Loaded with contacts, recent vacation
wallpapers, favorite band ringtones and
latest video downloads.

Financial newspaper:
Subscriber at home, reads in transit,
trades online.

Key ring:
Two cars, one home, one summer share –
too many to keep track of.

Credit cards:
Most recently used at the mall for
lunch and shopping.

TV's Most Affluent + Most Influential + Most Engaged Viewers = THE AFFLUENCERS

watch what happens when you buy  **watch what happens**

bravotv.com

**What's true for magazines is true for cable channels as well:
they're designed to sell audiences to advertisers.
This ad for Bravo ran in the trade magazine *Brandweek*.**

I'm Dreaming of a White National Cheese Day

by Alan Benson

FTER THE French Revolution, while the guillotine was still busy parting aristocrats from their heads, a cadre of professors, intellectuals, and radical antimonarchists came up with a new decimal calendar that sliced the year up into twelve thirty-day months of three ten-day "decades." This new calendar signaled a break with monarchist tradition and was seen as a more scientific way of keeping time. The calendar also signaled a break with simplicity, since each day had its own name. Not like "Tuesday, April 15" or "Monday, November 23," but like "Eggplant" or "Manure." Granted, it's a bit more catchy and a hell of a

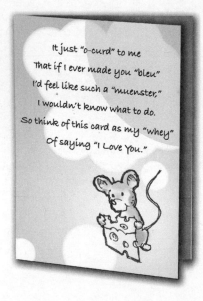

It just "o-curd" to me
That if I ever made you "bleu"
I'd feel like such a "muenster,"
I wouldn't know what to do.
So think of this card as my "whey"
Of saying "I Love You."

lot more specific, but would you want "Birthdate: Manure" on your driver's license?

The French gave up on their calendar in 1806, and calendar makers around the globe heaved a sigh of relief, happy that this foolishness was behind them.

Or was it? Fast forward to twenty-first-century America, and we find that every day, every week, and every month has its own name. Only instead of "Eggplant" and "Thermidor," we have "Moon Day," "National Chemistry Week," "National Peanut Butter Lovers' Month," and even "National Mustard Day." And every one of these holidays has a sponsor, a person or group who has spent the money convincing Congress (or calendar makers) to establish a holiday, no matter how spurious.

It's easy to figure out the sponsor of some of these:

National Senior Health and Fitness Day—The Mature Market Resource Center

National History Day—The History Channel

National Milk Week—The National Fluid Milk Processor (or, conceivably, some well-funded cow)

National Private Investigators' Day— *PI Magazine*, the National Association of Investigative Specialists, and several state PI associations

Others are a bit harder to decipher:

National Chemistry Week—the defense industry? A cabal of science geeks?

National Blueberry Month—the muffin man?

National Courtesy Month—Miss Manners?

And that's not even including the unholy trinity of Hallmark-inspired consumerism: Mother's Day, Father's Day, and Saint Valentine's Day (yeah yeah yeah, I know it's a real Catholic holiday, but would people be buying reams of cards, tons of chocolates, and gallons of perfume if Valentine had switched duties with, say, Saint Sithney, patron saint of mad dogs, or Martin de Porres, patron saint of race relations?).

Love mustard? So does Mount Horeb Mustard Museum. They deemed August 3 to be National Mustard Day. Crazy about pickles? May brings International Pickle Week. Old tennis shoes? March 20 is Rotten Sneaker Day. Dairy products, cleanliness, and politics? On a good year, Cheese Day, Clear Off Your Desk Day, and Presidential Inauguration Day all fall on January 20. Astronomy Day? Take your pick: various calendars claim it's either April 19 or May 13.

The proliferation of holidays has made for some strange bedfellows. Not only is February American Heart Month and National Boost-Your-Self-Esteem Month, it's also National Canned Food Month. So if your self-esteem's in the pits, at least you can bury your sorrows in salty snack foods, safe in the knowledge that National Diet Month, January, is almost a year away. A good binge might even keep you until October (National Pizza Month, National Pasta Month, National Dessert Month).

Why? Why is there a fascination with giving each day, week, and month a name? Is it really possible that we have learned nothing at all from France's mistakes? How did this ridiculous obfuscation of the calendar happen?

Holidays, for one thing, make good PR. They're stealth ads, basically. They appear to be on the up-and-up while providing a news hook for story-hungry journalists.

For example, when faced with the difficult task of promoting an anti-incontinence device, the Contigen Bard Collagen Implant, PR firm Hill & Knowlton invented Bladder Health Week. Hill & Knowlton's client, Bard, teamed up with the Bladder Health Council of the American Foundation for Urologic Disease to help promote the festivities. "We realized we could not move the needle on an issue of this magnitude alone. The Bladder Health Council provided the credibility and visibility that helped us achieve the objectives of the campaign," Bard marketing director Rhett Frye told *O'Dwyer's PR Report*. In other words, the BHC's involvement made it look like less of a craven grab for bucks.

Hill & Knowlton provided camera-ready ads, press releases, radio ads, community education ideas, and a public service announcement featuring former *Partridge Family* mom Shirley Jones (whose star has fallen farther then we thought).

O'Dwyer's reported that the effort resulted in a stunning 182 print stories and 63 broadcast stories. (One imagines the lower broadcast number probably has a lot to do with the fact that it's hard to find acceptable images for an incontinence story.) The newsletter also reports that more than one thousand health-care providers conducted special Bladder Health Week events.

For its troubles, Bard was amply rewarded. *O'Dwyer's* reports that the Bladder Health Council "awarded Bard its Presidential Award for the program, the first company to receive the award." Interestingly enough, the other awardees included Jones, Bob Dole, Stan Musial, Abigail Van Buren, Lou Gossett Jr., and former Carmel-by-the-Sea mayor Clint Eastwood. (*O'Dwyer's* did not mention whether incontinence was a requirement for receiving the award.)

Another example: The American Numismatic Association, sponsors of National Coin Week, has some ideas of how to get involved in their cause on their website. The group's education director, James Taylor, talks about coin fans' attempts to raise awareness of rare coins:

Michael Fay and Alex, his nine-year-old son, salted Alex's suburban New York school lunch cash register with more than four hundred rarely seen but low-value coins so each student would receive one coin. Parents were notified in advance so they, too, could become involved in their child's "discovery."

And, more likely, so that they wouldn't go berserk and complain to the school.

Not only does a holiday help rally the troops, it's a clever way of getting the media on your side. A random story about peanut butter isn't all that appealing to your average assignment editor, but a weekly list of recipes all throughout National Peanut Butter Month: hey, that's news!

Lee Apparel has taken this idea to its logical but devious extreme: linking a spurious holiday with a noble cause. The company's Lee Denim Day, October 25, is a financial benefit for breast cancer research and a PR gold mine for the company. On

Lee Denim Day, workers who donate $5 to breast cancer re-
search get permission to wear jeans to work. Lee jeans, natch.

There's also a more sinister way to get prime consumers—
kids—involved in these "holidays": you can subvert the schools.
In *Giving Kids the Business,* Alex Molnar recounts how Lifetime
Learning System used teachers as
potato-chip pimps during Feb-
ruary, which is both National
Potato Lover's Month and Snack
Food Month.

The promotion came packed
in an envelope marked "Open
immediately! Free educational
program focusing on math, social science, and language arts
skills enclosed." Inside, the teachers found "Count Your Chips,"
a thinly veiled marketing piece for the National Potato Board
and the Snack Food Association. "Count Your Chips" encouraged kids to compute the number of chips eaten by Americans
each year, explore the history of potato chips, and investigate
people's favorite flavors. Who would have thought cramming
Pringles down your gullet was educational?

Molnar's book also includes information about other LLS
projects, including a collaboration with General Mills on the
"Gushers [fruit snacks] Wonders of the World." And no, there
is no level to which these goons will not stoop.

So how does one go about getting a National Whatever Day?
There are three basic ways. Michael Moore did a bit about this
phenomenon on *TV Nation* in the 1990s. They contracted a
lobbying firm whose specialty was in big-business negotiations
(there are several firms who specialize in such services) to get

an official *TV Nation* Day declared. The palms were greased, Congress voted it in, and the now-canceled show was given an official holiday. The cost? Five thousand dollars: small change for the pork, milk, or beef lobbies.

More appealing causes—anti-drug efforts, anti-birth-defects groups—can get around the need for lobbyists by handling the negotiations themselves. Get a couple of senators on your side, and whaddaya know? The Great American Smokeout goes national.

Of course, there is an alternative. Why involve Congress at all? If you want a holiday, declare it. There's nothing anyone can do about it. After all, Thanksgiving was celebrated for decades before it became a national holiday.

The fact is, the government has no trademark on the word "national," although the word gives the ring of truth to an otherwise unbelievable holiday. There's no law that says National Consume or Die Day has to be declared by Congress. Heck, there's nothing stopping us from declaring June to be National Consume or Die Awareness Month.

Of course, if you're going to go about it this way, it helps to have friends. More specifically, it helps to have friends like the huge marketing firm Porter Novelli. Porter Novelli transformed February, traditionally a slow month in snack-food sales, into National Snack Food Month. Coincidentally, two of the firm's bigger clients are the Snack Food Association and the National Potato Promotion Board, who generously agreed to sponsor the month. In a press release, Porter Novelli described its success: "Supermarket Sales of Snack Foods Jump by as Much as 386 Percent During National Snack Food Month."

Three hundred and eighty-six percent! In America, the land of deep-fried, chocolate-coated, heavily salted snacks! If only National Long Live Lefties Day (June 10) had such a backer.

And hey, if you're lucky, a pol will retroactively declare your chosen day National Whatever Day. So c'mon; who's up for some rousing Denim Day carols?

[*Stay Free!* #13, Spring 1997]

A short (believe it or not) list of holidays

JANUARY
National Hobby Month
Prune Breakfast Month
National Soup Month
Diet Month
National Book Blitz Month
National Eye Health Care Month
National Hot Tea Month
National Volunteer Blood Donor Month
National Bowling Week
National Pizza Week
Mozart Week

4 • Trivia Day
7 • Panama Canal Day
16 • National Nothing Day
20 • Cheese Day
20 • Clear Off Your Desk Day
21 • National Hugging Day
23 • National Handwriting Day,
    National Pie Day
25 • School Nurse Day
29 • Common Sense Day

FEBRUARY
National Dental Month
Chocolate Lover's Month
National Cherry Month
American Heart Month
Canned Food Month
American History Month
Creative Romance Month
Human Relations Month
National Boost Your Self-Esteem Month

National Snack Food Month
National Pencil Week
International Friendship Week
Boy Scout Week
National Youth Fitness Week
National Crime Prevention Week

1 • National Freedom Day
5 • National Weatherman's Day
11 • National Inventor's Day

MARCH
National Nutrition Month
National Peanut Month
Music in Our Schools Month
Youth Art Month
American Red Cross Month
Mental Retardation Month
National Women's History Month
National Feminine
    Improvement Month
National Physical Education Week
Woman's History Week
Foreign Language Week
Save Your Vision Week
Procrastination Week
Girl Scout Week
Daffodil Week
National Wildlife Week
National Poison Prevention Week
Mathematical Education Week
Drug and Alcohol Awareness Week
Newspapers in Education Week
National Bubble Gum Week

8 • International Women's Day
20 • Rotten Sneaker Day
21 • National Energy Education Day
21 • National Agriculture Day
22 • National Goof-Off Day
23 • Liberty Day, World Meteorological Day
26 • Global Understanding Day
29 • Vietnam Veterans Day

APRIL
Pets Are Wonderful Month
Community Service Month
American Cancer Society Month
National Garden Month
Thai Heritage Month
Stress Awareness Month
National Soyfoods Month
National STDs Education and Awareness Month
Prevention of Cruelty to Animals Month
National Science and Technology Week
National Laugh Week
National Library Week
National Coin Week
Bike Safety Week

2 • International Children's Book Day
7 • World Health Day, Metric Day
19 • Astronomy Day
20 • Food Day
22 • Earth Day
25 • Arbor Day

MAY
American Lung Association Clean Air Campaign
Better Hearing and Speech Month
Mental Health Month
Allergy/Asthma Awareness Month
National Good Car Keeping Month
National Strawberry Month

National Physical Fitness and Sports Month
National High Blood Pressure Month
Arthritis Month
Better Sleep Month
Correct Posture Month
Older Americans Month
National Barbecue Month
National Bike Month
National Mine Month
Music Appreciation Week
International Pickle Week
National Family Week
Teacher Appreciation Week
National Photo Week
Be Kind to Animals Week
National Transportation Week
All-American Buckle-Up Week

1 • Law Day
3 • Holocaust Remembrance Day
3 • International Tuba Day
8 • International Red Cross Day
12 • Limerick Day (Edward Lear's birthday)
13 • Astronomy Day, Native American Day
16 • Biographers' Day
18 • International Museum Day
21 • Armed Forces Day
25 • National Missing Children Day

JUNE
Diary Month
National Flag Month
National Little League Baseball Week
Tennis Week
Family Day

5 • World Environment Day
6 • Doughnut Day
7 • Daniel Boone Day, Freedom of Press Day
8 • Architect's Day (Frank Lloyd Wright's birthday)

JULY

National Flag Week
Freedom Week
Special Recreation Week
Captive Nations Week
Space Week

3 • Stay Out of the Sun Day
11 • Cheer Up the Lonely Day,
     World Population Day
12 • Video Games Day
17 • National Ice Cream Day
20 • Moon Day
24 • Pioneer Day
28 • Singing Telegram Day

AUGUST

National Smile Week
National Clown Week
Aviation Week
Nisei Week
Be Kind to Humankind Week

1 • Friendship Day
3 • National Mustard Day
4 • Coast Guard Day
6 • Crop Day
7 • Peace Day,
    American Family Day
10 • Middle Children's Day
11 • Daughters' Day
12 • Indian Day
13 • International
     Left-handers Day
14 • Liberty Tree Day
15 • National Relaxation Day
16 • Joke Day
18 • Bad Poetry Day
19 • National Aviation Day
25 • Kiss and Make Up Day
26 • Women's Equality Day
26 • Susan B. Anthony Day
28 • Dream Day

SEPTEMBER

Better Breakfast Month
Emergency Care Month
National Sight Saving Month
National Piano Month
Self-Improvement Month
Women of Achievement Month
National Hispanic Month
National Courtesy Month
National School Bus Safety Week
American Newspaper Week
National Courtesy Week
National Grandparents' Day

8 • International Literacy Day
10 • Popcorn Day
16 • World Peace Day
17 • Citizenship Day
19 • Talk Like a Pirate Day
20 • International Day of Peace
21 • World Gratitude Day
24 • Good Neighbor Day
26 • Native American Day
27 • Ancestor Appreciation Day

OCTOBER

Country Music Month
Family History Month
Hispanic Heritage Month
National AIDS Awareness Month
National Book Fair Month
National Car Care Month
National Cosmetology Month
National Depression Education and
    Awareness Month
National Dessert Month
National Seafood Month
Polish American Heritage Month
Vegetarian Awareness Month
National Collegiate Alcohol Awareness
    Month
Gourmet Adventures Month
Popcorn Poppin' Month

Pasta Month
Pretzel Month
Pizza Month
Computer Learning Month
National Apple Month
National Stamp Collecting Month
National Footwear Week
National 4-H Week
National Possum Week
National Fire Prevention Week
National School Lunch Week
Clean Air Week
Energy Awareness Week
National Social Studies Week

3 • Child Health Day
4 • World Day for Animals
6 • Universal Children's Day
6 • German American Day
9 • Leif Erikson Day
11 • International Newspaper
   Carrier's Day
15 • National Poetry Day,
   National Grouch Day
16 • National Bosses' Day
16 • Dictionary Day (Daniel Webster's
   birthday)
21 • World Food Day
24 • United Nations Day
25 • National Denim Day
31 • National Magic Day, UNICEF Day

NOVEMBER
Aviation Month
Good Nutrition Month
National Epilepsy Month

Latin American Month
Hunger Awareness Month
National Diabetes Awareness Month
National Red Ribbon Month (anti–drunk
   driving)
National Stamp Collecting Month
American Education Week
National Children's Book Week
National Family Week
National Cat Week
National Geography Week

6 • Basketball Day
21 • World Hello Day

DECEMBER
Universal Human Rights Month

1• World AIDS Day
10 • Human Rights Day (Nobel Peace
   Prize awarded)
12 • Poinsettia Day
15 • Bill of Rights Day
17 • Aviation Day (Wright Brothers' first
   flight)
22 • International Arbor Day

Shopping Spies

WHY IS THAT MAN STARING AT ME?

ANDY GREENFIELD, president of Greenfield Marketing Consultants, is setting the scene for me:

"You're standing at the salad bar, Carrie, so I sidle up next to you. You're looking at the chicken and broccoli, and I mumble something like, 'Gee, I was thinking of having that chicken and broccoli,' and you say something like, 'Look, that broccoli is kinda wilted.' Then we sorta go along and I see you dip the ladle into the macaroni and cheese and I say, 'Gee, what's the story with that?' You might say, 'Man, I love the cheese. It looks fresh and hot and steeeeamy . . .'"

Andy sounds like he's salivating. For a second, I feel like the star of my own commercial. An unappetizing, dreamlike, and (thank God) transient moment where roles are reversed: I'm not the audience—the marketing guy is.

This is how Andy conducts his business: buddying up to people in public and secretly tapping their unconscious. Greenfield has coined a term for his research: studying "naked behavior." Other marketers call this work "ethnography" or "anthropology." Regardless of the term, the work is part of the ever-burgeoning field of qualitative research. With qualitative research, the consumer isn't just a number, she's a complex set of attitudes, lifestyle preferences, and values.

"In an ideal world, I'd actually be in your head," says Green-field, "and I'd understand that what Carrie is looking for in a deodorant is something a little bigger with a better grip on it." He continues, "What we're doing is enabling manufacturers to better meet the real needs of the consumer."

Funny how such a studied observer of consumer behavior could overlook a pretty basic truth: any company spending that much money, time, and energy on my psyche must not have a product worth buying. That is, my so-called needs bear such intense scrutiny only when the differences between deodorants don't matter. The products may all be more or less the same, Greenfield might as well say, but people still aren't!

The primary tools of qualitative research have typically been in-depth interviews or focus groups. Trouble is, the tools aren't working. For one thing, humans overreport good behavior and underreport bad. Moms will report giving Junior fruit and whole wheat for lunch when they actually doled out Doritos and Coke. Often interviewees don't even realize they're fudging. Outside of focus groups, these issues aren't things they think about much. And that's another problem: focus groups measure conscious rather than decisive unconscious responses.

Further complicating matters, people have grown familiar with the concept of focus groups, and that makes their responses difficult to gauge. As marketers say, focus groups aren't the real world.

Paco Underhill is, like Greenfield, a market researcher. Underhill's company, Envirosell, uses hidden video cameras to study shopping behavior. To pick up subtleties, undercover researchers trail individual customers in stores, taking note of facial expressions and nuances. Later, a second researcher will approach the customers and ask them for a brief interview. Do these shoppers ever catch on?

"If a researcher has any indication they are upsetting someone, they are simply to turn around and walk away." Underhill says.

In other words, yes, but, he assures me, "Our intention is not to disturb people."

Naturally, Envirosell doesn't want to *disturb* people. The goal is to conduct research without subjects even *noticing*.

Although media attention hasn't exactly kept them invisible, a burgeoning breed of "cool hunters" operate under similar principles. These marketers don't just study the cool kids, they hang out, videotape, and parrot the cool kids. This kind of research is becoming de rigueur among corporations targeting youth, who are considered to be too cynical and too media savvy (or numb) to be reached by any other means.

According to Underhill, consumer resistance varies not so much by age as by region and zip code. Educated and wealthy New Yorkers are less willing than a blue-collar worker in the South to, say, speak to a researcher. The purchasing power of blue-collar workers is limited, however. Therein lies a catch-22: The people marketers most want to reach are also the hardest to reach.

In a way, marketers are their own worst enemy. The more a technique is used, the less effective it becomes. The most desirable consumers have had so many marketers vying for their attention, they've adjusted their behavior accordingly. They're less likely to talk to telemarketers, fill out surveys, or give out personal data. Call it consumer revenge or simply savvy, but that response helps drive a perpetual tug-of-war between buyer and seller.

But consumer revenge has a side effect: adapting means tuning out. People avoid certain aisles in the grocery store when their kids are in tow, zap television commercials, screen out telemarketing calls.

But what happens when the boundaries of time and place are erased? When anyone, anywhere, at any time, could be studying you to make a buck? When consumer savvy means mistrusting everyone?

Underhill has an "ethical problem with practices that invade privacy."

"I could call someone up right now and get your bank and credit balance, your driving record, grades in school, and almost no one is addressing that," he says.

Marketers often defend themselves from critics by pointing to a bigger bad guy. Although in this case, Underhill must've missed the *Time* and *Newsweek* cover stories, multiple *New York Times* reports, and just about the bulk of privacy scaremongering. While discussion of privacy issues focuses almost entirely on identity theft, "unobtrusive" research by the likes of Underhill and Greenfield slips by under the cloak of anonymity. These people don't necessarily need your name or address (at least not for now; not until their techniques become the new standard and it's time to push further), they just need your brain. And since focus groups aren't the real world, they're working damn hard to make the real world a focus group.

[*Stay Free!* #15, Fall 1998]

Coca-Cola and the Case of the Disappearing Water Glass

"When we're done, tap water will be relegated to showers and washing dishes."
—Gatorade chief Susan Wellington[1]

"The biggest enemy is tap water."
—Robert S. Morrison, vice chairman of PepsiCo, 2000

"You want us to put water on the crops . . . ?!? Water?!? Like out the toilet?!? [sic]"
—*Idiocracy*

IN THE FIRST few years of the twenty-first century, restaurants throughout the U.S. stopped doing something they had been doing for decades: filling water glasses once customers sat down at a table. Water glasses had been a standard part of the table dressing, like flatware and napkins. So why were they suddenly nowhere in sight?

The main reason is that regional water shortages made all that water seem wasteful. Several municipalities (New York City, Colorado Springs) actually made it illegal for restaurants to serve customers water, except upon request.[2]

But conservation wasn't the only factor in the disappearing water glass. Behind the scenes, soft-drink manufacturers had been targeting tap water as an impediment to increased sales. Perhaps the most ambitious on this count was Coca-Cola. Coke's marketing execs had a revelation in the 1990s: instead of trying to increase its market share, Coke started focusing on "stomach share." Coke had already saturated global retail, restaurants, and other outlets where beverages are sold; the human body was its only "undeveloped market."[3] Since the average person drinks sixty-four fluid ounces of liquid per day, Coke's goal became to make sure as many of those ounces as possible were Coke products.

Enter H_2NO. In the 1990s, Coke launched a program to help restaurateurs such as The Olive Garden discourage customers from drinking tap water. The crux of the plan revolved around upselling: when customers requested water, waitstaffs were trained to suggest more profitable beverages instead. (The Olive Garden took the plan one step further and offered an employee incentive contest.)

But perhaps we should just let Coke explain the program itself. Before PR types truly understood the nature of the Internet, Coke's reps described H_2NO as one of its "Success Stories" on the web. When the story was discovered by civilians in 2001, Coke took the web pages down out of concern that, according to a *New York Times* story, they "might be misinterpreted by customers."[4]

Success Stories

The Olive Garden® Targets Tap Water & WINS

The Situation

Water. It's necessary to sustain life, but to many Casual Dining restaurant chains it contributes to a dull dining experience for the customer. Many customers choose tap water not because they enjoy it, but because it is what they always have drunk in the past. In response, some restaurant chains are implementing programs to help train crews to sell alternative choices to tap water, like soft drinks and non-carbonated beverages, with the goal of increasing overall guest satisfaction. Because of its own successful campaign against water, The Olive Garden® has recently sent a powerful message to the entire restaurant industry - less water and more beverage choices mean happier customers.

The Plan

Olive Garden restaurants, like many other Casual Dining locations, were facing a high water incidence rate. They wanted their restaurant crews to emphasize the broad array of alternative beverage selections available, with the hope of reducing tap water incidence. Olive Garden's goal was to influence customers to abandon their default choice of tap water and experience other beverage choices to improve their dining experience.

The Olive Garden asked Coca-Cola USA-Fountain (CCUSA-Fountain) to help them create their beverage plan. CCUSA-Fountain stepped up to the plate and suggested a tap water reduction program named H2NO.

These web pages were taken from Coke's website in 2001. (After the site was discovered by civilians, Coke promptly took it down.)

Success Stories

Satisfying Your Customers with Beverage Choices (continued)

The Plan Details

H2NO is a crew education kit containing information about beverage suggestive selling techniques (a technique used when a server suggests a profitable beverage in place of water to the customer during the ordering process). It matched perfectly with what Olive Garden had envisioned. Restaurant managers and servers use the kit to emphasize the wide range of beverage selections available, including soft drinks, non-carbonated beverages and alcohol. As a side effect, overall check averages should increase, and remember, increased check averages mean higher profits for the restaurant and more cash in servers' pockets.

Olive Garden restaurants embraced the program and even took it to a higher level. H2NO was incorporated into the restaurant chain's schedule of monthly skill sessions where sales managers (store managers) led the crew through training exercises. In addition, The Olive Garden developed an employee incentive contest linked to H2NO with CCUSA-Fountain called "Just Say No to H2O."

Olive Garden sales managers set beverage sale store goals and server goals in connection with the contest. All restaurants that reached the combined goal had a chance to win an all-expense paid trip for servers and the management team to Atlanta, Georgia. Other prize packages containing Coca-Cola merchandise were awarded.

The Win

When the contest was completed, almost all participating restaurants realized significant increases in beverage sales and reduced levels of tap water incidence - a strong indication that Olive Garden restaurants succeeded in enhancing the customer's dining experience. And perhaps most importantly, Olive Garden expects to see this trend continue as the skills learned become part of the crew's everyday interaction with restaurant customers.

<< Previous Page

Key Questions

1. When Coors was cited in June 1990 for killing more than ten thousand fish by pumping hazardous wastes into Clear Creek in Colorado, how did the company try to reassure stockholders?

   a. Claimed that the fish were only "trash fish" and that the stream "was not a prime fishing stream."

   b. Said that "hazardous" is a relative term and that many fish were still alive.

   c. Announced that Charlton Heston was coming out to visit the Clear Creek plant.

   d. Promised that Coors would find a new place to dump mercury, lead, and cadmium waste.

2. As reported in *The Wall Street Journal*, the 2004 showcase home for Pardee Homes, a builder of McMansions in Los Angeles, featured a girl's "hideaway karaoke room," a boy's playroom with a plasma TV, a "home management center with a divided countertop instead of a family room, and a separate room for the dog." TRUE OR FALSE: According to the company's chief executive, "We call this the ultimate home for families who hate each other."

3. Which of the following was NOT included in Merck training materials as a sample of how drug reps should transition from small talk to sales pitches when taking doctors out to eat?

   a. *Physician says:* "What a nice restaurant! I hear that the food is wonderful."

Possible rep response: "You're right, it is. I'd only arrange the best for you. I'm sure you feel the same way about your patients. When you decide to prescribe an anti-hypertensive, what characteristics make one product stand out from another?"

b. *Physician says:* "I love coming to this restaurant. It has a great menu."

Possible rep response: "That's one of the reasons I chose this place. You can get boiled lobster or a venison steak. Speaking of a great menu, what concerns you about the HMOs you're dealing with, limiting your choices when choosing a specific drug therapy for a patient?"

c. *Physician says:* "What a great football game yesterday. Did you see how effective Drew Bledsoe was in the fourth quarter? That guy is amazing."

Possible rep response: "Bledsoe is effective on so many levels. He's a leader, you feel safe with him carrying the ball, and he's a proven winner. You know who else that sounds like? Zocor, a market leader with an eight-year safety record, proven to save the lives of your patients. Physician, what concerns do you have about Zocor leading your team in the fight against congenital heart disease?"

d. *Physician says:* "So, what plans do you have for the holidays?"

Possible rep response: "Well, my wife and I are going to visit my grandmother. It should be a lot of fun, though I feel so bad for her. She really has advanced osteoporosis and can't travel at all. She wasn't on any treatment plan for the longest time. Physician, what do you think the reasons are that some physicians don't do much about osteoporosis until it's in its advanced stages and nearly too late?"

e. None of the above; all were included.

4. In 2005, the Pharmaceutical Research and Manufacturers of America (PhRMA) secretly commissioned a novel to scare the public out of buying drugs from Canada. According to one of the writers hired, PhRMA wanted the novel to:

a. Center on greedy Muslim terrorists who distributed counterfeit drugs through Canadian pharmacies.

b. Avoid complicated plot twists that would "confuse" women.

c. Make the protagonists periodically argue against the "evils" of drug importation.

d. All of the above.

5. In 1996, the Democratic National Committee came out with a plan for taking back talk radio. What was the key instructive?

a. Candidates should "sound dumb," adopting Andy Griffith–like mannerisms before "unloading" on talk show hosts with fact and figures.

b. Candidates were briefed on animal psychology, with lessons on dominance, submission, and the "pack mentality."

c. Candidates should attack key Republican personalities with evidence of their lies and hypocrisy.

d. Candidates should hire talking animals.

6. What was the key complaint addressed by a new contract for Disney World employees hired to dress as Mickey, Minnie, and other Disney characters?

   a. The plastic in the costumes contained dioxins, toxic chemicals linked to cancer, thyroid disorders, and severe, persistent acne.

   b. Employees were required to wear their costumes at all times, including on the drive to work, which, they argued, was demeaning.

   c. Workers were required to wear Disney undergarments, and these undergarments were dirty, spreading lice and scabies.

   d. The costume heads were in some cases over twelve pounds, causing back pain and other injuries.

7. According to the latest estimates in February 2008, how much does it cost the U.S. government to make $80 million worth of pennies?

   a. $44 million.

   b. $80 million.

   c. $96 million.

   d. $134 million.

8. Prosper, Inc., a corporate coaching company based in Utah, has used which method of torture to motivate employees?

   a. Waterboarding.

   b. Electric shock.

   c. Whipping.

   d. Foot roasting.

Answers

1. A. Robert J. Burgess, *Silver Bullets: A Soldier's Story of How Coors Bombed in the Beer Wars* (New York: St. Martin's Press, 1993), p. 138.

2. False, sort of. The actual quote was "We call this the ultimate home for families who *don't want anything to do with one another*" (italics added). June Fletcher, "New Floor Plans Provide Peace, Quiet and Privacy," *The Wall Street Journal*, April 7, 2004.

3. E. "A Spoonful of Sugar," *Harper's*, July 2005, pp. 16–17.

4. D. www.thekarasikconspiracy.com/backstory.htm.

5. A.

6. C. Steven Greenhouse, "Pact for Mickey and Minnie," *The New York Times*, June 8, 2001. query.nytimes.com/gst/fullpage.html?res=9C06E5D9163EF93BA35755C0A9679 C8B63.

7. D. Morley Safer, "Should We Make Cents?" *60 Minutes*, February 10, 2008. www.cbsnews.com/stories/2008/02/07/60minutes/main3801455.shtml.

8. A. Erin Alberty, "Employee's Suit: Company Used Waterboarding to Motivate Workers," *The Salt Lake Tribune*, February 27, 2008. www.sltrib.com/ci_8385103.

Down the
Memory Hole

5.

EVERYONE KNOWS the history part should go at the beginning, but that just makes it easier to forget. And in a consumer culture, history is already all too easy to ignore. History is a nuisance to the marketing machine, in part because it teaches us that things can be different. It shows us the consequences of our actions.

Everyone carries around little bottles of water these days, and it's difficult for some of us to imagine life without them. But those of us who *remember* the pre-Evian era know that survival wasn't hard, for two reasons: water fountains were commonplace, and restaurants and take-out joints served water gratis. As we discussed in the fourth section, soft-drink manufacturers such as Coke and Pepsi made a concerted effort to combat this "competition," and as a result, we're stuck paying for it.

Cell phones are another example. If you're old enough to remember life without your mobile, you can remember pay phones that worked—and peers who didn't assume that once you left home or the office, you were easily reached. The rise of these products actually changed the environments in which they were used. For anyone unfamiliar with this past, however, cell phones seem normal, natural, and irreversible—in the same way, perhaps, that seeing Martin Luther King Jr. selling Internet gear seems natural.

In this section, we'll show how true, warts-and-all history can pose a counterpoint to the idiocracy by helping us to see how the past shapes the present.

A 2001 advertisement for Alcatel intended to sell its "communication networks"

Grave Revisionism: Advertising Resurrects the Dead

Research by Jeff Hyslop

EVERYONE from Albert Einstein to Mahatma Gandhi has been given new life selling products. No doubt many of the exhumed, having achieved fame through the old-fashioned method of *doing* rather than *promoting*, are rolling over in their graves. By the time Madison Avenue gets through with them, we may have a tough time recognizing them. "Hm, was Einstein the one who sold computers or french fries?"

Here are a few quotes we've collected by some of the greatest social thinkers mangled by advertising below.

Albert Einstein

"The trite objects of human efforts— possessions, outward

success, luxury—have always seemed to me contemptible."
(*Used in ads for Apple Computers; Nikon cameras; Coca-*
Cola; an unnamed hair-loss product; many others)

Aldous Huxley

"Popular philosophy . . . is now molded by the writers of
advertising copy, whose one idea is to persuade everybody
to be as extroverted and uninhibitedly greedy as possible,
since of course it is only the possessive, the restless, the
distracted, who spend money on the things that advertisers
want to sell." (*Bass Ale*)

Martin Luther King Jr.

"The profit motive, when it is the basis of an economic
system, encourages a cutthroat competition and selfish
ambition that inspires men to be more concerned about
making a living than making a life." (*Coca-Cola; Coors;*
Sears, Roebuck & Co.; AT&T; Alcatel; numerous others)

Malcolm X

"Show me a capitalist and I'll show you a bloodsucker."
(*X cigarettes; "X" clothing line*)

Ralph Waldo Emerson

"For me, commerce is of trivial import; love, faith, truth of
character, the aspiration of man, these are sacred."
(*American General Corp.*)

Che Guevara

"In culture, capitalism has given all that it had to give and
all that remains of it is the foretaste of a bad-smelling
corpse; in art, its present decadence." (*Che Beer; Swatch*
watches; Renault Mégane)

John Lennon
"Money doesn't matter, it never did.
Money is just another trap . . . It makes
you sexy and intelligent and talented in a
flash, poof! And it's a lie." (*Apple
Computer; One2One*)

Mohandas Gandhi
"What is a man if he is not a thief who openly charges as
much as he can for the goods he sells?" (*Apple Computer;
Telecom Italia*)

Henry David Thoreau

"Trade curses everything it handles; and though you trade in messages from Heaven, the whole curse of trade attaches to the business." (*Jeep*)

Famous dead rock star Kurt Cobain loathed corporate culture and consumerism almost as much as he loathed himself, and is fondly remembered for showing up to a *Rolling Stone* cover shoot wearing a shirt that said "CORPORATE MAGAZINES STILL SUCK." In 2007, with Cobain presumably safely in the past, agency Saatchi & Saatchi resurrected his image for a Dr. Martens advert. The ad was immediately withdrawn, however, thanks to howls of protest from Cobain's fans.

Attn: Advertisers

Since advertisers like dead people so much, we decided to come up with a list of people they *should* use in commercials. Unlike the folks above, these guys probably would have loved to pitch products.

Joseph McCarthy (1908–1957)

Joseph McCarthy did the advertising industry a huge favor, however inadvertently, by igniting the 1950s Communist witch hunt that purged Hollywood of talent. Those who lost their jobs were welcomed to Madison Avenue, where—unlike films or movies—their work appeared anonymously.

Adding to his natural business appeal, McCarthy attacked
public housing as a Communist plot. McCarthy was
paunchy, pasty, and balding, but he did lure viewers to
TV screens.

Edward Bernays (1891–1995)

The godfather of corporate PR found his calling with
Damaged Goods, a play about the dangers of venereal
disease. Bernays was the nephew of Sigmund Freud and,
like his uncle, probed the depths of the human psyche.
Bernays, however, saw his mission as uplifting the moronic
majority (on behalf of corporate sponsors), and this
perspective colored everything he did, from promoting
mass persuasion techniques to affectionately nicknaming
his house servant "Dumb Jack."

H. H. Holmes (1861–1896)

Nineteenth-century psychopath Holmes amassed a fortune
through insurance fraud and drugstore management. He
then bought a hundred-room mansion equipped with gas
chambers, trapdoors, acid vats, lime pits, fake walls, and
secret entrances. During the 1893 World's Fair he rented
rooms to visitors, who, after being forced to sign over their
savings, were tortured, gassed, dismembered, skinned, and
thrown down an elevator shaft (not necessarily in that
order). As one of the first American serial killers, Holmes
would assuredly have loved the media attention an
endorsement deal could offer.

Francis Galton (1822–1911)

A leading intellectual of his day, Galton helped pioneer
modern statistics. He is, however, less known for his
creative math (including a statistical test of the efficacy of

prayer) than for his devotion to eugenics, his method of genetically improving humans through science. Galton advocated the regulation of marriage and family size according to the heredity of parents. Although support for eugenics began to wane in the U.S. in the 1930s, some of Galton's ideas became a real hit in Germany.

Ernest Borgnine (1917–?)

Although Ernest Borgnine is not yet dead, he *did* star in *BASEketball*.   [*Stay Free!* #17, Summer 2000]

Subliminal Seduction

HOW DID THE UPROAR OVER SUBLIMINAL MANIPULATION AFFECT THE AD INDUSTRY?

I N THE ANNALS of advertising, few strategies are more notorious than subliminal persuasion. If you asked your average Joe to name the advertising practices he objected to, somewhere after spam and before tampon commercials he'd probably mention subliminals.

The public uproar over subliminals took place over two key periods. The first, in the late 1950s, focused on marketer James Vicary's claims that he had inserted split-second, invisible ad messages into movies. In the 1970s, Wilson Bryan Key rekindled the frenzy with his book *Subliminal Seduction*, which pur-

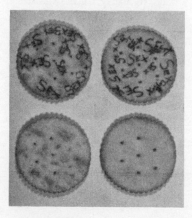

In *Media Sexploitation*, Wilson Bryan Key claimed that Ritz crackers were secretly emblazoned with the word "SEX." Evildoers at Nabisco, he speculated, must have embedded the word into the dough molds.

ported to reveal that ads for liquor and other everyday products were riddled with hidden skulls and humping donkeys.

Experts have long since debunked the subliminal hoaxes, and many people with more than a passing knowledge of advertising know not to take this nonsense seriously, but I can't help but be fascinated with the subliminal myth, particularly as a critique of advertising. Of all the people who have criticized advertising over the years, the men who popularized subliminal advertising seem to have gotten the most mileage. Books on the topic (Key's as well as Vance Packard's *The Hidden Persuaders*) were bestsellers, and their ideas circulated far more widely than other social critiques. In the late 1950s and again in the 1970s, the outcry over subliminals even inspired legislators to draft laws banning the practice.

Although Packard and Key had very different approaches— Packard backed his claims with industry sources, while Key essentially made things up—both authors tapped into deeply entrenched Cold War–era fears of brainwashing and mind control. Two decades may have separated the subliminal scares, but the same fear was evoked: secret, hidden messages in advertising manipulating an unwitting public into buying things they don't need.

But how did the advertising industry deal with all this conspiratorial talk? Advertising has long proved itself adept at co-opting critiques of consumer culture. In the case of subliminal advertising, though, the industry didn't need to co-opt its critics, because the criticism was ambiguous and misguided at the outset. The effort to expose advertiser manipulation ironically benefited the ad industry, at least in the short term. How and why that happened brings us to the story at hand.

———

In 1957, *Hidden Persuaders* detailed the "strange and rather exotic" techniques of motivational research, exposing the marriage of psychology and advertising. While we now take it for granted that professional persuaders are hired to reach us through our emotions, this idea caused quite a stir in the late fifties. Packard became a media sensation, and his book topped the bestseller list, remaining there for a year.

Packard never used the word "subliminal" in his book, but he made passing reference to a newspaper article featuring a New Jersey cinema that flashed split-second ads during regular screenings. These ads—exhortations to "Eat Popcorn" and "Drink Coca-Cola"—were invisible to the naked eye but supposedly influenced viewers' subconscious. To his chagrin, Packard couldn't verify what happened at the theater. When he contacted the newspaper that had run the story, a spokesman told him that "although the facts we published are well attested, the authorities in question are unwilling to come any further into the open."

James Vicary, a motivational researcher mentioned several times in Packard's book, smelled gold. Hoping to ride the *Hidden Persuaders* hype, Vicary stepped forward and took credit for a practice he called "subliminal" projection. Clearly, he wasn't one to hide from publicity, and so it's unlikely that he was the authority the newspaper contacted. Nonetheless, he churned out press releases claiming that he flashed hidden messages during films—an effort to promote his consultancy business. To add credibility to his claims of manipulating unwitting viewers, Vicary cited studies he conducted that showed subliminal advertising had increased popcorn sales by precisely 57.5 percent, and Coca-Cola sales by 18.1 percent. The ploy worked. The press homed in on Vicary's subliminal scheme. *The New*

Yorker, *Newsday*, and the *Saturday Review*, among others, deplored the subconscious sell (the most alarming invention since the atomic bomb, according to *Newsday*). Representative William Dawson of Utah said subliminal advertising was "made to order for the establishment and maintenance of a totalitarian government if put to political purposes." The National Association of Radio and Television Broadcasters banned the use of subliminals by its members. And the New York State Senate unanimously passed a bill outlawing the technique.

Such vitriol made Vicary a rich man. Far from shunning the controversial new practice, corporations clamored for his services. Movie theaters and television and radio stations across the country began trying out subliminals. Television stations in Maine, Los Angeles, and Canada ran subliminal spots. Radio station WAAF in Chicago sold subaudible advertising time, after testing whispered messages like "Drink 7 Up" and "Buy Oklahoma Oil."

The more cautious promised to use subliminals as a "public service tool." Radio station WCCO in Minneapolis ran "phantom" messages warning of "slippery roads" during icy weather, "mail cards now" at Christmas, and "Ike Tonight" when President Eisenhower was scheduled to speak. Precon Process and Equipment, another company that sprang up to hawk subliminal services, told *The Wall Street Journal* that it was seeking financial backing to study whether or not subconscious projection could teach kids their multiplication tables. The U.S. Army also jumped on the bandwagon, directing its Human Factors Research Division to examine if the process could be used for education.

Before long, however, media professionals grew suspicious, questioning whether the tactic actually worked. To resolve the matter, the FCC held a demonstration in January 1958, limited to government officials and the press. At that session, the phrase "Eat Popcorn" was flashed at five-second intervals during a television program. When no one found themselves unexpectedly craving popcorn, the dignitaries seemed placated. The only reported response was that of Senator Charles E. Potter: "I think I want a hot dog."

Gradually, people in advertising stopped pumping money into subliminal snake oil, and by June 1958, James Vicary's Subliminal Projection Company had closed up shop. Corporate advertisers, presumably ashamed of having been fooled, stopped talking about subliminal advertising, except to deny ever having used it.

Almost two decades after the first subliminal sensation, Canadian professor Wilson Bryan Key stormed the press with *Subliminal Seduction: Ad Media's Manipulation of a Not So Innocent*

Wilson Bryan Key described this Gilbey's Gin ad at length in *Subliminal Seduction*: "Subtle shadows on each side could be interpreted as lips—vaginal lips, of course. At the top of the opening is a drop of water which could represent the clitoris. If the scene were put into a story line, this still-open vagina is where the discharged penis has just been . . ."

America (1973). Unlike Packard, Key had little use for nuance or subtlety, and his book hammered home a single premise: that sinister hidden "embeds" lurk behind everyday commercial messages. Unintelligible to the conscious mind, embeds were said to ride the fast lane to the id, luring unwitting consumers with appeals to their primal instincts. The word "sex," according to Key, was emblazoned on everything from baby-doll ads to Las Vegas travel guides. In a single whiskey ad, Key found a volcano, a mouse, a skull, scorpions, three wolf faces, the head of a rat, a lizard, a shark, a white bird, various masks, fish, a swan, a cat, and dozens of "sex's." The "carefully calculated banality" of soap commercials and beer ads was said to prevent members of the public (with the exception of Key, of course) from seeing media images for what they really were.

Like *Hidden Persuaders*, *Subliminal Seduction* ignited a media frenzy. Government officials, religious leaders, and important people everywhere spoke out against the conspiracy. Politicians introduced legislation, and government agencies established policies against subliminal selling.

Controversies over subliminal campaigns erupted throughout the 1970s and 1980s. During this period, Key wrote three more books with the same premise (*The Clam-Plate Orgy*, *Media Sexploitation*, *Age of Manipulation*), spreading the word about embeds ever more widely. In doing so, he not only earned himself millions of dollars in royalties and lecture fees, he also accomplished what he considered a social mission: increasing public awareness of subliminal persuasion.

By 1989, however, Key seemed to have grown uncharacteristically apprehensive. Perhaps he suspected that his efforts had helped the advertising industry as much as they harmed it. Key prefaced his fourth and final book, *Age of Manipulation*, with an "Author's Warning." Readers, he observed, could make prac-

tical use of the book in two ways. First, they could use it to defend themselves against "exploitation by picture and word
symbols." But, he noted with dismay, readers "preoccupied
only with media-propagated self-indulgence" would use the
book to "prepare them for profitable careers in advertising and
public relations."

It's hard to draw conclusions from Key's observation, because he was something of a crackpot. Yet his concerns about
the ways people used his books were partly justified. Advertising educators used them in class, PR specialists studied them,
and entrepreneurs read them in the search for new opportunities. Although none did so in quite the way that Key imagined,
they nonetheless took advantage of the subliminal controversy.

New Woman magazine, for example, created a system called
"subliminal synergism," which it claimed made more readers
look at its ads. Placing an ad's dominant colors behind the
headline of an adjacent editorial page would prompt readers to
move their eyes from the article to the ad, *New Woman* told potential advertisers.

Copywriter and audio guru Shelly Palmer made a name for
himself by employing "subliminal" frequencies in broadcast
commercials. Although the FCC bars TV commercials from
depicting the consumption of alcoholic beverages and airing
the sounds of a "gambling environment," Palmer touted his
subtle sound waves—of crackling ice and clanging bells—as a
way for clients such as Bally's and Seagram's to avoid government restrictions.

But Key's books did not quite do for subliminals what Vicary's effort did. Most advertisers who read Key's books were re-
luctant to try subliminals—not because they thought the tactic
was unethical, but because studies showed it didn't work. Admen mocked the supposedly widespread practice as ridicu-

lously inefficient while contending that no one in advertising actually used it. Why bother *hiding* naked breasts and rippled torsos, they reasoned, when you could *show* them? For admen in the seventies, subliminal advertising was not a social threat but—worse!—a waste of money. (Just to be sure it was a waste of money, Madison Avenue continually tested subliminals' effectiveness long after the technique was considered unethical.)

Advertisers' responses to Key's books were, then, a product of well-founded skepticism. But even if few in the ad industry took Key seriously, his books were a boon for the business—just in unintentional ways.

In overstating the power of subliminal influences, *Subliminal Seduction* inspired an audience to use the selling technique on themselves. The book inadvertently created a market for subliminal media, mostly self-help tapes consisting of music, over which "affirmations" had been recorded at a low-decibel level. Listeners could not hear the messages but were supposedly subliminally influenced—as one subliminal publisher put it, like "a dog whistle going straight into your brain." There was no evidence that this worked; it more than likely did not. Nonetheless, tens of thousands of consumers bought subliminal tapes and, later, videos and computer software. Originally sold only through direct mail, subliminal products began cropping up in retail stores by the late 1980s. At their peak, cassette sales alone brought in an estimated $50 million annually.

Unlike the subliminal media Key criticized, self-help subliminals were voluntarily embraced. Consumers wanted to be subconsciously influenced in a manner they considered desirable. It just so happened that the qualities consumers desired were those promoted by the market. *Prosperity/Living the Dream* was typical, inspiring listeners with messages like "I attract money," and "I deserve the good life." Kids' tapes (or, rather, self-help tapes for parents) were also popular. *Positive Thoughts for Children* offered the sounds of a seashore and, somewhere in there, the assurance "I am loved." *I Am a Great Reader* was designed for tots and even, for consumers with particularly active imaginations, fetuses. The owner of a self-help store in Salt Lake City told a reporter for the *Bergen (NJ) Record* that pregnant women listen to such tapes because "kids come out more intelligent and walk sooner."

Other winners in the subliminal gold mine included *Freedom from Acne, Winning at the Track*, and *I Am a Genius.*

Institutions bought into the subliminal cure as well. South Point Prison in Utah used one called "Pedophilia" to quell criminal impulses. Sound Threshold Systems sold subliminal anti-theft systems to stores. Department stores and grocery store chains would play messages like "Stealing is dishonest" under background Muzak.

Could a vagina be hidden behind the couple in this L&M cigarettes
advertisement? Yes!—according to Key in *Media Sexploitation*. In several books,
Key argued—and purported to illustrate—that sexual Imagery is routinely
hidden in display advertising. Yet he had little to say about the sexual
undertones that people could actually *see*—in this case,
the sultry couple with cigarettes dangling, cheek to cheek.

Whatever their particular message, subliminal tapes offered easy answers to a host of modern problems. Although the mainstream press usually traced the tapes' roots to get-rich-quick schemes and mail-order scams, the underlying message of these tapes was the same as that of any TV commercial. In a world where the right fragrance brings true love, household cleansers cure fatigue, and carbonated beverages solidify family ties, the subliminal pitch fits right in: buy this and your problems will be solved; listen mindlessly and you'll be cured.

Outside of self-help, subliminal media was comparatively scarce. Yet, as any self-respecting marketer knows, scarcity can mean novelty. This brings us to another way the subliminal controversy served what it attacked: "subliminal" became a marketing gimmick. Time Warner promoted a video game, Endorfun, by touting the subaudible messages programmed into the background ("I am powerful," "I am at peace"). The game tanked, but not before receiving widespread press coverage. Around the same time, computer companies began using subliminals in screen savers and other software.

A 1959 public-opinion study found that half of the respondents who professed awareness of subliminal advertising considered the form unethical, yet most of them said they would still watch a TV program that used subliminals. After all, people were curious about them. Numerous spoofs cropped up, mocking the uproar over subliminals as much ado about nothing. Not long after the first subliminal brouhaha, several radio stations began broadcasting subaudible messages such as "TV's a bore" and "Isn't TV dull?" WAAF in Chicago began offering advertisers subliminal radio commercials: five hundred radio spots no one could hear, the station boasted, for only $1,000! Around the same time (1959), comedian Stan Freberg produced a TV commercial for Butter-Nut coffee that featured a cartoon man warning viewers that they were watching a subliminal commercial. As he's speaking, the word "subliminal" flashes on-screen while fireworks and elephants trumpeting Butter-Nut parade about in the background, eclipsing his speech. Subliminal? Hardly, and that was the joke. The commercial helped launch Butter-Nut nationally and earned several advertising awards.

In 1990, Seagram's Gin, one of the companies fingered in *Subliminal Seduction*, devoted its "Hidden Pleasures" campaign to subliminal advertising. Ice cubes appeared airbrushed with clearly outlined golfers and tennis players, air bubbles whispered sweet nothings, and fornicating gin bottles cleverly played up the absurdity of such devices. Seagram's, the ads implied, was so sure of its quality that it had no need for such nonsense. Seagram's agency, Ogilvy & Mather, actually commissioned a poll confirming the belief in subliminals in order to promote the "Hidden Pleasures" campaign. Of eight hundred respondents polled, 61 percent believed advertisers used subliminals to manipulate consumers. By promoting these ostensibly negative findings, Ogilvy & Mather correctly sensed that it would earn free media coverage for Seagram's. The apparent taint of public criticism made the campaign seem ballsy. But the risk was strictly illusory: if 61 percent of the public believed in subliminal advertising, Seagram's was shooting for the other 39 percent—for the upscale, cynical adults who "got" the joke. To this audience, the poll results suggested only that 61 percent of respondents were buffoons. The ads flattered the audience, who kindly returned the favor. Seagram's sales increased noticeably after the spoof campaign.

Criticism of subliminal advertising benefited sellers in yet another way. By suggesting that the only kind of advertising manipulation was subliminal manipulation, the controversy deterred more meaningful discussions of advertising's influence. The advertising industry couldn't have asked for a better straw man. Once the idea of subliminal advertising could be revealed as bogus, advertising manipulation could be considered fictitious too. A 1989 *New York* magazine article mocking subliminal-phobia was typical of the "enlightened" response to the subliminal critics: "People don't walk around in a semi-trance; buying is a rational, cognitive process."

But as any marketer knows, buying is not simply a rational, cognitive process. Despite his shortcomings, Key was quite correct on this count. The power of advertising, he argued, lay in controlling cultural symbols, in linking virility to hard liquor and soap to safety. Such subtle twists of meaning, he argued, shape the cultural environment and, in doing so, influence

In 1986, the American Association of Advertising Agencies (AAAA) launched a perfunctory campaign to debunk the subliminal myth and to counteract "misperceptions which are sullying advertising's reputation." Alas, Key never quit. According to the author–cum–conspiracy theorist, the ad contains "a collection of grotesque faces, animals, a shark . . . and an erect penis."

PEOPLE HAVE BEEN TRYING TO FIND THE BREASTS IN THESE ICE CUBES SINCE 1957.

ADVERTISING

people's subconscious. Many scholars of advertising would agree. Indeed, there is a great deal of truth to Key's statement that "It's what you don't see that sells you"—so long as that claim is read figuratively. It was Key's bizarre, literal interpretations that made it difficult to take anything he wrote seriously. When Key got it wrong, he got it *really* wrong. The title of his third book (*The Clam-Plate Orgy*), for example, was inspired by the following incident:

> After a University of California lecture in San Diego, several students and I dined in a nearby Howard Johnson's restaurant. Our heated talk, which had begun at the university, continued as we squeezed ourselves into the booth. As we chatted, several students casually glanced through menus. When the waitress finally materialized, four out of the six of us, including myself, ordered clam plates. Shortly after the waitress had taken the order and disappeared, I incredulously recalled that since childhood I have loathed clams in any form.[1]

Key then suggested to the group that someone had "put something into our heads" to eat clams. Could it be the background music? They listened but couldn't detect anything. After more searching, one student pointed to the place mats on the table. The group began studying them, looking for clues. The place mats featured a plate of fried clams under the headline "Dig Into Our Clam Plate," a fact that inspired little interest in itself. Key noted that the text for the copy was modestly suggestive, describing "a batch of succulent tender clams . . . They always COME . . . out crispy and crunchy . . . piled high and crowded with *creamy* cole slaw."

Nothing illegal, and nothing particularly salacious, Key wrote. But, he added, copy usually only reinforces the imagery. Turning his attention to the image, a plate of fried clams, Key employed an "effective technique of media analysis": he compared the media representation with the actual clams. His analysis ultimately boiled down to this:

The place mat illustration is not a photographic representation of actual clams, of course, but an airbrush painting. It includes nine caricatured human figures as well as a donkey astride a human figure. The donkey seems to be licking the stomach of the figure upon whose lightly shaded face is a long mustache. To the left of the prostrate face-up male figure appears a female figure with a highly piled coiffure. A head can be seen between her legs. Who would believe a sexual orgy, oral sex, and bestiality could be so deftly incorporated into an innocent restaurant placemat?[2]

Key claimed that Howard Johnson's clam plate photo included nine human figures and a donkey.

Who, indeed? Why would anyone attempting to seduce the Howard Johnson's clientele use sex scenes with donkeys? (Why not throw in a few mules? Or puppies, even?) And, more important, why should this donkey orgy explain the clam orders when perfectly reasonable explanations go unsaid? For starters, it is quite natural for a group of people engrossed in conversation to give little thought to ordering. Studying the menu would mean missing out on the discussion, so naturally members of the party would listen to what their peers had ordered and leap at the first thing that sounded appetizing. The cue could have been any number of things, but it is certainly worth noting that place mats (essentially print ads) for clam plates could have themselves—sans stomach-licking donkeys—inspired the orders. Advertisers, after all, have developed quite a number of mechanisms for effecting impulsive, split-second decisions. The calculated use of color, typography, emotional appeals, and graphic devices all do their part in "manipulating" consumers. But Key never really takes such mundane details seriously. It's as if something so pedestrian as a picture and a headline couldn't possibly influence anyone; as if, in order to work, advertising must have nudie pictures and death symbols.

Similar episodes are repeated ad nauseam in Key's books. In *Subliminal Seduction*, Key explains the success of a Bacardi ad by claiming that if a mirror is held above the pictured brandy glass, the mirror image (which is upside down, mind you) reads "u buy." Never mind that the ad itself already implies that message. Similarly, Key takes note of a Virginia Slims ad only for its subliminal cues. Key translates the slogan as "You've *Come* a Long Way Baby" and claims that the model's right hand "could be touching her genitals—likely her clitoral area." In another ad, a shaggy dog (or a polar bear—the author is not sure which) and a woman have sex in a glass of Sprite. Quips Key,

"Bestiality may be illegal throughout most of the world, but, at the symbolic level, it appears to have sold a lot of Sprite." One imagines the man would gaze at a fully nude model, slathered in oil and spread-eagle on a canopy bed, then point out a tattoo on her upper left forearm as suggestive. (He actually goes so far as to claim that men masturbate to *Playboy* not because of the blatantly pornographic photos but because of the subliminal embeds.)

Key's books might have worked as novels; the embeds could have served as metaphors for the power of advertising—a physical manifestation of advertising's unconscious influence. Alas, readers were not so fortunate. Embeds were not considered metaphors for persuasion—they *were* the manipulation. The books were therefore easily positioned as self-help guides, for they simplified both media manipulation and the process of combating it. The books argued that there was a relatively quick and easy way of immunizing oneself against advertising persuasion—namely, spotting subliminal embeds.

Ultimately, the particulars of Key's texts are less important than this self-help mission. Even if no one actually read Key's book, people turned the hunt for ad manipulation into a parlor game. Lessons in subliminal advertising became common at civic groups and schools, where the uninitiated were taught how to spot embeds. (Many of us who were in middle school in the late 1970s can remember classroom exercises devoted to finding skulls in liquor ads and deconstructing fashion spreads.) This practice supposedly made people more discriminating, critical media consumers.

The critique of subliminals—in both the 1950s and the 1970s—rested on the premise that ads are designed for emotional, not intellectual, impact; for the unconscious rather than the conscious. Key bemoaned the fact that people, particularly Americans, refused to acknowledge the power of the unconscious. He hoped to convince readers that advertisements influenced them without their knowledge. But if ads worked emotionally and unconsciously, why urge people to defend themselves rationally and consciously? Well, because there was no way of shutting off natural responses, so defending oneself consciously, through increased awareness, was the only available option—or so critics like Key professed. Paradoxically, by encouraging readers to defend themselves solely through their own know-how, the books actually deterred them from acknowledging advertising's influence. If unconscious influences can be prevented through awareness, why bother taking the unconscious seriously? By claiming that awareness easily foiled manipulation, the books contributed to the popular delusion that *other* people were affected by advertising—not oneself.

Even when one grants that Key had a point, he advocated a dubious form of awareness. Contrary to the "seduction," "sexploitation," and "orgies" implied by his titles, real advertising manipulation isn't particularly sexy, nor is it easy to grasp. You can't find it in a mirror, hidden in the shadows, or having sex with polar bears in ice cubes. So when everyone started hunting for dog heads in Scotch bottles, the reality—that advertiser influence is everyday, ordinary, and infinitely more subtle—became more remote.

Although it was uncertain how analyzing subliminals helped members of the public, it clearly encouraged them to spend more time gazing at ads than they would have otherwise. Hunting for subliminals made advertising intriguing. Even if scrutinizing ads took the guise of criticism, any advertiser with a brain would have preferred that to having his message ignored. At a time when ad clutter was reaching new heights, getting the brand name across was a victory in itself. Studying subliminals also linked ads to those forbidden pleasures that Key claimed were so nefarious. Key's popularity ensured that these brands became *known* forbidden pleasures. Benson & Hedges became the cigarette for "extra-long penises," whereas Kent stood for vaginas (replace the "e" in the name with "u," says Key), masturbation, and "good horny feelings." The Sears catalog was filled with "fascinating perversities." If, as Key argued, such imagery affected people through subliminals, would it not also affect them through criticism and analysis?

The image that comes to mind when reading Key's books is of the author sitting quietly in his library, stark naked and gazing lustfully into magazines, using his sole free hand to wipe sweat off his brow and, every so often, turn the page. At any rate, the vivid scenes Key conjures suggest that he gets a visceral charge out of their recounting. In this sense, he is again reminiscent of Packard in his book *The Status Seekers*. As an astute reader observed, Packard's details of wealthy lifestyles belied the author's true relationship with them. *Status Seekers*'s critical stance, the reader suggested, was but an illusion:

> It seems to me as if you yourself are a little fascinated among all the vast million-dollar figures . . . just like most of the gangster-movies, in spite of the gangster's violent death, provide most youngsters with a feeling that gangsterism is a hell of an exciting way to live.[3]

Where Packard was cautious and genteel in his critique, Key was extreme and lurid. But in both cases the pretense of criticism allowed the authors to have their cake and eat it too: to appear critical while selling loads of books that helped the enemy earn piles of money.

Perhaps Packard and Key secretly craved the very objects they critiqued (Key, it has been claimed, once told a colleague that he wore his hair closely shaved "to make himself look like 'a giant penis.'") Regardless of the authors' inner workings, devoting oneself to exposing wrongdoing requires a strong interest in that wrongdoing. This contradiction, or love/hate relationship, is a fitting corollary to the ways criticism and promotion work hand in hand. Even at the personal level, the line between criticism and appreciation isn't easily drawn.

Although the controversy over subliminals had subsided by the 1990s, the technique itself had not. Ironically, by the time advertisers had found a way to make split-second flashes actually work in a commercial, they were no longer considered subliminal.

In the 1990s, subliminal advertising—or what was formerly known as subliminal—returned. In the revamped lexicon, a subliminal message was now known as a "prime" or "visual drumbeat." These primes were generally quick bursts of images lasting one to three frames and were used in commercials to convey edginess and mood.

The roots of the technique are often traced to Music Television (MTV), which inspired a vogue for rapid-fire editing in the 1980s. MTV aimed to influence viewing less through the content of primes than through the style of editing, a signature for the network. The young audiences that MTV targeted—raised on television, video games, and thirty-second commercials—were said to require extra stimuli to remain attuned. Once the audience adjusted to the quicker pace of images, that pace then came to be the norm, requiring even faster editing.

It wasn't long before MTV's strategy caught on with the networks. A television spot for NBC's *The Pretender* quick-cut a flurry of images: two frames of a sign saying "Wall Street," two frames of a man sitting behind a desk, and two frames of a Greek statue. None of this was apparent when viewed at normal speed. In another ad, for Reebok sneakers and Lady Foot Locker, an exhausted woman collapses after an apparently grueling run. Suddenly a flash of light appears. Although the viewer sees nothing in the flash, slowing the scene down frame by frame reveals an image of the woman standing confidently, comfortably, serenely gazing in the distance.

According to the creators of such ads, quick cuts make the spots more interesting, even mysterious. The general sense is that these image bursts have nothing to do with the subliminals of yore. As one MTV director put it, editors were "just punching images into the [editing] machines, to see how fast we could get them to go." But such aesthetic explanations belie the fact that these images convey textures and moods that reflect favorably on the brand. In other words, they do what any commercial technique purports to do: they help sell products.

In a way, visual drumbeats have less in common with subliminals than other, far more common sales strategies. Like packaging design (which capitalizes on intuitive responses to color, typography, and word choice) and product placement, rapid-fire imagery works by slipping "under the radar." Though by no means guaranteed, these time-worn strategies continue to influence people's subconscious. And they are not alone. It could be argued that most every advertisement is subliminal. The ubiquity of advertisements means that people tune out the vast majority of them, only to experience them unconsciously. Yet, like visual drumbeats, everyday embed-free ads are not considered subliminal. It's as if, in order for something to be considered subliminal, it can't be effective!

In the end, the subliminal scare could be lumped in with JFK assassination lore and the fluoride controversy as a conspiracy theory that assumed mythic proportions because it resonated with the public—a public eager to understand advertising's influence. People, after all, have no idea how advertising truly affects them. A theory that appeared to explain it all, that cast consumers as victims of a secret plot, held tremendous appeal.

Before moving on, I can't help but add one final note of irony: not only did the critique of subliminal advertising serve what it purportedly attacked, but the critique of Key's books backfired as well. One of the reasons the fervor surrounding subliminals lasted as long as it did—and one of the reasons why Key was able to publish essentially the same book four times—stemmed from its critical use in education. As suggested earlier, Key's claims about subliminal advertising were commonly taught by advertising educators, particularly at universities. According to Jack Haberstroh's account of the subliminal controversy, *Ice Cube Sex* (1994), the majority of university professors who taught Key's theories considered them ludicrous. Haberstroh contacted the heads of advertising departments at thirty accredited universities and found that not one of the instructors thought Key's ideas persuasive. These educators taught his work not to promote or refine the use of subliminal advertising but to debunk it.

Haberstroh himself argued that "those of us who teach future advertising professionals have an enormous stake in the public invalidation of Dr. Key's subliminal theories." In a four-thousand-word cover story for *Advertising Age*, Haberstroh urged the industry to join him in loudly denouncing subliminal quackery.

The response from advertising practitioners to Haberstroh's article was overwhelming—overwhelmingly negative. Rather than joining Haberstroh in denouncing Key's work, the majority of letter writers blasted Haberstroh for his naïveté. An adman at a Chicago agency summarized the sentiments of many practitioners in a letter to the editor:

> [Haberstroh's] pleas for ad people to speak out against such charges seems a little misguided. By doing so, we as ad professionals will only add credence to Wilson Bryan Key's silly theories. Even worse, we'll make the public believe we have something to hide.[4]

Jack Elliott Jr., former chairman of the board of Ogilvy & Mather, echoed this charge beautifully:

> The solution to the perpetuation of this myth is not for the advertising world to speak out but for the academic world to shut up! Prof. Haberstroh writes, "I discuss his theories every semester in my large advertising classes." Why, one wonders.[5]

What Haberstroh and his colleagues failed to grasp was obvious to ad professionals: rather than debunking Key's claims, the academics were promoting them. A survey Haberstroh conducted of his own students revealed that even after listening to thorough, point-by-point repudiations of Key's claims, many students nonetheless believed that the use of subliminals was rampant. However, Haberstroh refused to accept any responsibility for helping to spread the subliminal myth.

So Where Are We Now?

In a media class I recently taught, every one of the teen students was familiar with the term "subliminal advertising," if not its historical roots. I go back and forth about whether to blame people such as Wilson Bryan Key for this. I suspect that if the subliminal brouhaha had never happened, the public's concerns about advertising manipulation would not be so grossly misdirected. But even though Key and his cronies disinformed legions of consumers, there's hope yet, and my students illustrate why.

These urban, middle-class teenagers derided advertising for being annoying, incessant, and boring, while proudly sporting Nike logos and Gap sweats. These kids weren't around in the 1970s. They've never heard about flashing popcorn ads or ice cube sex. We never discussed subliminal persuasion in class. But when these students used the term "subliminal advertising," they did so in a way that is quite revealing. For example, one twelfth-grader, Ben, titled a homework assignment focused on alcoholic beverages "Subliminal Advertising." His brief illustrated essay did not examine ice cubes for death symbols or vodka labels for bestiality. Rather, Ben pointed to the phallic shapes of liquor bottles, to a Guinness ad that equated the "power" of drink to sexual performance, to Coors's juxtaposition of a scantily clad female body with a similarly shaped beer bottle. Having never learned the earlier claims about subliminal advertising, Ben defined "subliminal" in a way that actually makes sense: as an adjective for images designed to appeal to us unconsciously, in ways we usually don't recognize or rationally comprehend. Ben was a particularly sharp thinker, but most of the kids who referred to subliminal advertising used the term in this way.

With the coming of a new generation, the definition of "subliminal" has shifted to a more practical meaning. Once a source of dangerously misguided claims, the subliminal myth has given the world a term that may very well help identify advertising tactics it formerly concealed. Vance Packard, at least, would be proud.   [*Stay Free!* #22, Summer 2004]

The Idiot Consumer

ADVERTISERS ONCE DESCRIBED TYPICAL CONSUMERS AS BARNYARD ANIMALS AND MORONS, BUT THEN THEY GOT "SAVVY"

[Generation Y] is the most marketing-savvy group ever . . . They are hip to what marketers are trying to do, and they shun anything that they perceive as overt marketing tactics.
—Cheskin Strategic Consulting

I F YOU, LIKE ME, remember waking up one day to find that you'd been identified as a member of the alienated Generation X, then the quote above will no doubt cause déjà vu. Much of what trend watchers say about today's young people is what they said about my generation. And it's largely what they said about the baby boomers.

Consumers, the line goes, have gotten too smart for advertising. They're tough, and they see through the bullshit. "People are so media savvy now," Thomas Hayo, creative director at Bartle Bogle Hegarty, told *The New York Times*. "The audience is so aware of advertising . . . that you have to be a little more genuine. People are not willing to buy manufactured truth any more." Or as the *Adweek* columnist Barbara Lippert put it in a History Channel special about advertising, today's consumers are no longer naïve.

You don't have to read the trade press or watch advertising

documentaries to get the idea: it's all over the advertisements themselves. Taking a tip from Volkswagen's "Think Small" campaign in the 1960s, companies like Sprite, Geico, and Diesel have used a style of advertising that congratulates the smart (and supposedly advertising-resistant) customer while simultaneously pushing the product.

If any single media outlet could be credited with defining young viewers like me, it was MTV, which catered to advertising that made fun of advertising. Sprite commercials parodied soda commercials, Denis Leary Nike ads assaulted viewers watching Nike ads, and MTV's quirky house spots assured viewers that they were smarter than the crap they were watching.

But while MTV was busy courting me and my peers, it ran a rather revealing campaign in trade publications like *Advertising Age*. The ads pictured a twentysomething slacker coolly lounging in an easy chair, remote in hand, gazing smugly at the camera. The headline, directed at media buyers, read: "Buy this 24-year-old and get all his friends absolutely free." The copy underneath explained that MTV influences the influencers, those hip young things who determine what the masses do. So at the same time MTV was flattering its young audience members, winking at their independence and smarts, it was telling its real customers—advertisers—that the kids were, in fact, sheep.

MTV's trade ad is but one example of a common practice: the advertising industry flatters the public for being smart all the while telling clients that the public is no match for its tactics. This practice is in some ways as old as the ad industry itself. Commercial media and ad agents alike have long made their cash by convincing clients that they influence consumers. But the way advertising professionals talk about their audience has changed considerably. If you go back to the time before

generations were sorted into tidy target markets with catchy
names, you find marketers loudly trumpeting not audience
"savvy" but audience stupidity.

Admen hashed out their view of "human nature" in trade
publications around the turn of the twentieth century, when
the advertising industry was still in its infancy. In the first half
of the nineteenth century, opinion leaders tended to view man
as a rational creature, but increasingly began to see him as an
emotional, illogical mess. By the time the first ad agencies were
established in the late 1800s, admen (and they *were* men, with
very few exceptions) were comparing consumers to barnyard
animals and shut-ins. "Advertisers should never forget that
they are addressing stupid people," advised copywriter Charles
Austin Bates in his 1896 handbook, *Good Advertising*.

After researchers claimed
IQ tests showed that typical
adults were barely literate,
advertisers repeatedly
referred to consumers'
"twelve-year-old minds"
(or, in this case, fourteen).[1]

"The average normal American, broadly speaking, cele-brates his twenty-fifth birthday by shutting shop mentally and refusing to accept any new ideas," remarked the authors of a popular trade book, *What About Advertising?* "He has then the literate capacity of a 12- or 14-year-old child."[2]

William Esty of J. Walter Thompson summed up the views of his agency's experts: "It is futile to try to appeal to masses of people on an intellectual or logical basis."[3]

The monthly edition of *Printers' Ink*—the *Advertising Age* of its day—offered some advice on crafting advertising appeals: "You've got to convince the hogs you have something for them."[4]

The "moron myth," as I call it, hit pay dirt in 1923, when so-cial scientists analyzing the U.S. military's use of IQ tests con-cluded that the average adult had the mind of a seventh-grader. Seemingly overnight, the trade press was filled with blather about "the twelve-year-old mind," and the phrase took on a life of its own. Scholars pointed out serious flaws in the IQ test, but these objections were ignored. Nearly a decade later, William L. Day, an executive of the J. Walter Thompson agency, reflected his colleagues' beliefs when he described the average consumer as a "14-year-old human animal" who displayed in his daily ac-tions "inexplicable whims," a "careless, uncomprehending men-tality," and "crude and often false standards of measurement."[5]

Day, let's keep in mind, was partly responsible for the noto-rious Fleischmann's Yeast campaign to transform the "Soul of Bread" into a cure for everything from constipation and "intes-tinal fatigue" to bowleggedness and poor teeth. In this single campaign, J. Walter Thompson somehow managed to utilize every bad advertising strategy: paid testimonials by European doctors, celebrity endorsements, pictures of comely women coupled with pseudoscientific charts, and false medical claims. This campaign—along with those for Lucky Strike cigarettes,

Listerine, and patent medicines—all played a part in developing advertising for what elites called "the tabloid mind." Mass-market advertising stooped to new lows in the 1920s and 1930s with scare headlines, ludicrous health claims, and maudlin stories about dying babies. Psychiatrists coached repressed spinsters into finding love through "sweeter, purer" breath (Listerine). Children lost friends over "B.O." (Lifebuoy). Ads warned that men without the right underwear might get sick and lose their jobs (Duofold).

Naturally this sort of advertising was a magnet for critics, but for Day and his cohorts, the moron myth provided an easy rationalization. By believing their audiences to be numbskulls, admen like Day could justify tabloid tactics as necessary evils. "This advertising may be crude," admitted the Ruthrauff and Ryan agency in a trade ad, "but the masses are crude."[6]

Many in the industry refused to subscribe to Day's views, however. They wanted to be seen as professionals, not carnival barkers. As social liberals, some had genuinely populist leanings. Yet even these men tended to consider themselves smarter than the average person. (In fact, since the rise of advertising agencies, copywriters had advertised themselves as "brains" and their work as "intelligence." An early advertising trade magazine, for example, was called *Brains*.) They were, after all, part of the white, educated urban class.

To maintain some dignity for themselves and their chosen career, politic ad agents would describe their audience euphemistically. Instead of throwing around terms like "idiots" and "morons," they'd refer to the audience as "intensely human" or "salt of the earth."

The Ruthrauff and Ryan agency illustrated the conscientious adman's dilemma with a series of ads offering its services in *Printers' Ink*. "Who cares about war in Bolivia?" one headline announced, mimicking the voice of the imagined consumer. "I'm worried about my waistline." The ad went on to describe the plight of the working girl, the "ardent lodge worker," and other "flesh and blood human beings."[7]

"To sell them you must know them," claimed another Ruthrauff and Ryan ad. And to show that it knew them, Ruthrauff and Ryan offered up slice-of-life vignettes of American society, at once patronizing and empathetic:

> People. Put them together—scholars and dunces; esthetes and clods; prodigals and nickel-nursers; the shrewd and the dull—and there's your audience, the hundred and twenty million people you want to sell. Most of them aren't very discerning. Few of them grasp ideas with any degree of celerity. Dozens speak correct English; millions wouldn't understand syntax if you blue-printed it. But ALL of them—and all of us— understand purely emotional things . . .[8]

Ruthrauff and Ryan wasn't telling media buyers anything they didn't already know about John Q. Public's "mental auditorium." It was as if the real purpose of the ad was to tell the industry: *Hey, just because we make stupid ads doesn't mean* we're *stupid! We understand how consumers' stupidity works and how to appeal to it.*

Naturally, Ruthrauff and Ryan's advertisements reflected its ethos. Recalling his early years at the agency, the copywriter John Caples described his job as hawking "hair-growers, fat-reducers, dandruff-removers, and books on mental healing and personal magnetism." Caples wrote the definitive Ruthrauff and Ryan appeal, a schlocky but stunningly successful testimonial for the U.S. School of Music, headlined "They Laughed When I Sat Down at the Piano but When I Started to Play!—."

The ad pulled so well that Caples recycled the format again and again, with beauties such as "They Grinned When the Waiter Spoke to Me in French—but Their Laughter Changed to Amazement at My Reply."

Ruthrauff and Ryan's approach wasn't the only way to address the tabloid mind, nor the cleverest. A few advertisers developed a more nuanced method, a form of "reason-why" copy that in some ways foreshadowed the ironic advertising of today. Dating from the nineteenth century, reason-why copy ostensibly armed readers with facts, tossing off technical terms and jargon. Victor Radios advertised features including a "super-efficient Super-Heterodyne circuit," "continuous bandpass variable tone control, impregnated condensers," and a "pentode tube with push-pull amplification." Listerine toothpaste

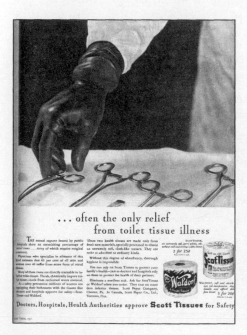

"Tabloid advertising" of the 1920s and 1930s—with its shock headlines and pitiful accounts of unforeseen horror—was widely considered an insult to the average person's intelligence. Many admen themselves complained about it for tarnishing the industy's image.

boasted its "Luster-Foam detergent $C_{14}H_{27}O_5$." Ads for Old Golds claimed cigarettes tested in an "oxygen bomb calorimeter" produced less "BTUs." Westinghouse "Columaire" radios were "built with 8-tube super-heterodyne chassis."[9]

Rather than insulting readers, this form of reason-why advertising slyly flattered them by implying that they were intelligent and discriminating, that they understood technical information and considered it in purchasing decisions. The average person had no idea what a "pentode tube" was, but, some admen argued, it didn't matter.

"Even if people don't understand every word, they get an impression," wrote one *Printers' Ink* contributor. "You may not understand a doctor's description of a case, but his technical lingo conveys the impression that he knows his business."

While appearing to appeal to the rational mind, reason-why in fact aimed for emotion. There was, then, little difference between reason-why and the far-fetched testimonials, medical claims, and other lowest-common-denominator techniques of the period. All played to consumers' passions, fears, and senses. What ad professionals seldom acknowledged was that they used essentially the same strategies to target so-called intelligent audiences as well.

If, in the 1930s, the presence of emotional appeals indicated an audience full of morons, then morons had a lot of company: readers of highbrow magazines such as *The New Yorker*. An Elizabeth Arden Bronze Make-Up advertisement told *New Yorker* readers the sad tale of a woman who prepared for a long-awaited society ball, only to find—horrors!—that her much-loved evening dress revealed her tan line. Dorothy Gray Cosmetics (1933) recounted the saga of "The Lovely Rebel Who Fought for Youth . . . and Won!"[10] Upon discovering the "faint, yet plainly discernible . . . beginning of a double chin," the rebel in question took a trip to Dorothy Gray, banished all signs of age, and lived happily ever after.

The ads in *The New Yorker* and its cohorts *The Atlantic* and *Harper's* were more literary, to be sure. Lines of copy often resembled poetry, complete with historical allusions and four-syllable words. There were no tacky, screaming headlines; ads relied on delicate illustrations and modernist designs to draw readers' eyes. But the underlying strategies were pretty much the same. Considering that these magazines were the very magazines that ad professionals themselves read, it's hard not to see a flaw in the admen's reasoning. They used emotional strategies because they worked. But if emotional ads worked on the very people advertisers considered most intelligent, wouldn't that make everyone a moron?

Why did advertisers cling to the consumer-as-moron fiction? Partly because of run-of-the-mill sexism. Women were widely assumed to be the primary target of consumer advertising, making some 80 percent of all household purchases. Small wonder, then, that the reigning stereotype of women—that they were emotional, impulsive, childish—was the same one applied to consumers.

Ads that targeted women nevertheless tended to flatter them, especially when they appeared in the "class" magazines for educated and affluent adults. Products were touted as suiting "the smart set" or "sophisticated" consumers. The notion that sophistication was something to strive for was itself a product of successful marketing. Up until the 1920s, "sophistication" actually held negative connotations; it meant adulterated or not pure, fake or put on (as in "sophistry"); it was closer to phony than cultured. But in 1923 a popular novel, Gertrude Atherton's *Black Oxen*, helped popularize "sophistication" as meaning "worldly knowledge or refinement." Subsequently, advertisers latched onto the word, and in the process helped marry intelligence to fashion sense. One could speak of a "sophisticated" argument (suggesting complexity and intellectual rigor) as well as "sophisticated" tastes.

In this way, "sophistication" was like that other keynote of advertising, "smart." Like "sophistication," "smart"—which had long denoted elegance and chic—was increasingly used by marketers to mean mental acuity or cleverness. Advertisers spoke of "smart society," "smart styles," "smart coats," "smart frocks," "smart resorts," and the smart people who used them. "Smart to be seen in, smarter to buy," ran a 1930s Studebaker slogan. The different meanings were easily blurred, in part because fashionable people were presumed intelligent, and intelligent people, fashionable.

Unlike today's ads, ads of the 1920s and 1930s tended to portray the product—not the consumer—as smart; a consumer was only smart when she bought the advertised goods. Studebaker's slogan "Smart to be seen in, smarter to buy" illustrates the tendency of advertising in the 1930s to blur the once-popular definition of smart as "fashionable" or "chic" with the modern usage, meaning "intelligent."

This brings us to another reason why advertisers clung to the moron myth. Admen defined intelligence in a way rooted in their class. They considered the upper classes brighter in part because upper-class consumers tended to share the admen's own interests. When the masses didn't respond to ad appeals, admen considered them stupid—even when the flaws of a campaign should have been obvious. For example, writing in *Advertising and Selling*, John Caples—the copywriter who cut his teeth at Ruthrauff and Ryan—complained that the public was too stupid to interpret his advertisements. He blamed people for mistaking an ad he created to sell radios for one selling motorboats, for instance. But Caples's ad featured a large image of a boat! What did he expect? Miracles?

Describing an ad he created for a self-help book, Caples reasoned, "One of the best-known examples of courage is the bulldog. And one of the most striking words for expressing the idea of courage is the word 'grit.'" So he came up with the headline "I'll give you BULLDOG GRIT." When a friend mistook this hack job for a dog-food ad, Caples lambasted his friend's mental laziness and ignorance.[11] (For the record, Caples was no bit player. In its retrospective of the twentieth century, *Advertising Age* ranked him as one of the industry's top twenty talents.)

The moron myth didn't simply reflect elites' biases, it promoted them. The legacies of Calvinism and social Darwinism contributed to a pervasive, self-serving assumption among elites that affluent people were intelligent and vice versa. Rich people, the theory went, got that way because they deserved it; they got that way through some combination of strong character, hard work, God's blessing, and sharp wits. Once again, this is clearly on display in industry publications and trade ads.

Class magazines promoted themselves to advertisers by touting their audience's intelligence and wealth, as if the two naturally belonged together. *Redbook* described its readers as "intelligent, well-to-do families,"[12] while *Time* appealed to "intelligent, alert, modern-minded, well-to-do men and women."[13] *Cosmopolitan* was "*The* class magazine" for "the intelligent people."[14] A *New York Herald Tribune* pitch to potential advertisers erases any distinction between intelligence and wealth:

> You can't do a representative selling job in New York without mass. But one factor that often decides between loss and profit in New York is the ability to reach the greatest number of people whose minds and pocketbooks are open to new ideas. In other words, get intelligent, responsive New Yorkers. . . . Then you reach the mass you need. *Mass* with the added benefit of above-average incomes![15]

The masses, see, weren't very bright, because they didn't open their purses.

An even more blunt *Printers' Ink* campaign contrasted the magazine's base of successful advertising professionals to low-wage earners and working-class people. One ad highlighted the garbled English of an immigrant grocer: "You gotta good proposish," the man is quoted as saying. "I spend maybe five, ten dollars." The lesson, according to *Printers' Ink*: "Nobody gets much business from the man with a low IQ."[16]

Here, *Printers' Ink* puns "IQ," calling it "ideas quotient," but the suggestion that working people are dullards is hard to miss. Another ad in the campaign depicts slack-jawed telephone operator Mazie, who, we're told, has a "low IQ" but "can't help it."[17] Only professionals lucky enough to read *Printers' Ink* can succeed in business: "The more *P.I.*, the higher the IQ."

But perhaps nothing better illustrates the way marketers

measured intelligence than the IQ test itself. The makers of the IQ test touted it as a gauge of "innate intelligence," not of learning. But the early IQ tests relied partly on test takers' familiarity with brand-name goods. For example, here are some of the test's questions:

Crisco is a patent medicine, disinfectant, toothpaste, food product.

The Delco System is used in plumbing, filing, ignition, cataloguing.

A 1930s campaign for *Printers' Ink* typified the view ad industry professionals had of the working public: slack-jawed, stupid, and stuck in the rut of tradition. "Big advertisers," by contrast, "are characterized by the high I.Q." Another ad in this campaign mocked the broken English of immigrant corner grocers.

The Corona is a kind of: phonograph, multigraph, adding machine, typewriter.[18]

The Tide Turneth

"The average mind which the advertising man or woman must convince today is probably the shrewdest purchasing mind in the world. It has been duped by hokum, matured with dearly bought experience and sharpened by adversity."
—*Printers' Ink*, August 20, 1932, p. 57

While the moron myth continued to hold sway up through the early 1930s, it faded midway through the decade with the rise of a consumer-driven attack on advertising. This consumer movement first took root with a spate of popular books criticizing the ad business, the most successful of which were authored by social critic Stuart Chase. In his 1927 bestseller *Your Money's Worth* (cowritten with F. J. Schlink), Chase argued that advertising provided no basis for making rational decisions. He blasted advertisers for supporting the "conscious and deliberate fostering of arrested mental development" instead of using the "unparalleled forces at their disposal" to "raise the level of popular education." In place of advertising, Chase demanded sound facts—and true ones at that—which consumers could reliably base their purchases on.

Chase led the way for groups such as Consumers Research (a forerunner of Consumers Union, which publishes *Consumer Reports*) to win congressional hearings on curbing advertising abuses. And for a period in the mid-1930s, it looked as if this determined group of consumers might actually get results: taxes on advertising, rules on labeling, and stricter definitions of fraud were all on the table. Ultimately, however, their legislative efforts failed to pass and resulted in the mostly worthless Wheeler-Lea Act of 1938.

If the consumer movement failed to achieve its goals, it's at least partly because those goals were misguided. Consumer advocates wanted ads to be rational and to provide facts, and didn't foresee how their attempts to legislate would pan out. Wheeler-Lea, in an attempt to combat fraud, placed greater limits on the kinds of facts that could appear in ads. But in so doing, the legislation had an unintended side effect: it prompted the more legitimate advertisers to skirt regulation by omitting facts entirely. Ironically, ads grew even more indirect and emotional.

Despite its shortcomings, the attack on advertising nonetheless had a tremendous impact on the industry. For one thing, it made the industry gab about moronic consumers and "twelve-year-old minds" politically untenable. Any suggestion that consumers were easily fooled risked playing into the hands of critics. But, interestingly enough, those critics themselves were prone to viewing average consumers as morons. Stuart Chase, for example, sincerely believed the average person incapable of seeing through a sales pitch: "Caught in this net of primitive stimulus and response," he said, "the consumer is stripped of all standards of judgement, his native sense is overwhelmed with psychological reactions which reduce him almost to an automatic idiot."[19]

And Chase was not alone. Like the ad industry professionals, advertising critics tended to come from the educated upper classes and were therefore outside of the masses that they claimed to represent. Naturally, proponents of advertising saw this as an opening, and argued the point to defend advertising: *How can these do-gooders claim to represent consumers? We're the real consumer advocates; we give the people what they want.*

In a speech before the American Association of Advertising Agencies, *Vanity Fair* editor Frank Crowninshield argued that advertising critics like Professor Rex Tugwell aim to tell "50 million women what they can or cannot eat, what they can and cannot wear, what they may or may not drink, and how and how not they may attract the attention of gentlemen."[20] Women who live boring, stay-at-home lives, he said, crave the romance that advertising provides.

Which brings us to another nail in the moron myth's coffin. The 1930s saw the beginning of what would later become the industry's battle cry: *Social critics are elitists! We're on your side, guys!*

In order to accuse their opponents of elitism, though, the industry's defenders had to first clean their own house—or at least wipe the surfaces. Thus, advertising's geniuses no longer talked openly about the limits of John Q. Public's brainpan. To this day, you'll almost never hear a word from the ad industry about consumer stupidity—quite the contrary. Which isn't to say that people who work in the ad industry today are less likely to think of consumers as morons: they're only less likely to say so publicly. Advertisers, you could say, have grown more media savvy.   [*Stay Free!* #24, Summer 2005]

Everything
I Know About Life
I Learned from
Medical Marketing

OKAY, NOT REALLY. But the history of medical advertising has a lot to teach nonetheless.

Medicine is in some ways the very foundation of modern advertising. The forerunners of the Pfizers, Mercks, and Glaxos were the traveling salesmen of the 1800s who hawked what was essentially snake oil. These sellers, including one P. T. Barnum, pioneered the sales techniques that have become well-trod clichés in our day. Gratuitous use of statistics, "used by doctors," testimonials, appeals to patriotism, nature, and politics—all were initially honed by sellers of nineteenth-century medical cure-alls. In fact, even Coke—perhaps the greatest embodiment of American advertising—began its life as a brain tonic.

Medicine was the perfect advertising vehicle in the 1800s for a number of reasons. In a period before widespread mass production, furniture, clothing, and other goods were made by hand, which kept supply low and demand high. Medicine, however, was cheap and easy to bottle. There were no laws regulating it. And unlike, say, carpenters, medicine men didn't need to worry about quality. So the only barrier to making piles of money on it was the seller's creativity; entrepreneurs merely needed a hook for distinguishing their formula from competitors'.

Selling medicine then was like selling a fragrance today: the product was all image. Medicine had no physical properties for the buyer to inspect. There was no way to objectively test or identify ingredients, no medical approval process to pass.

Most remedies were loaded with alcohol and would make patients feel better to the extent that getting drunk is feeling better. A few provided a heartier buzz with opium, cocaine, or heroin. But for the most part, the ingredients in patent medicines were inert and practically interchangeable. If they worked at all, it was by not killing the patient and by exploiting the placebo effect. Which is to say: if they worked at all, it was thanks to advertising.

Advertising promoted the symptoms a particular medicine treated. A drug treated rheumatism because its advertising and packaging said so. Consequently, if a potion didn't sell as a cure for whooping cough, the seller could always change the label and say it cured baldness or fatigue instead.

Today, you can't turn on the TV or open a magazine without seeing the descendants of patent medicine advertising—not just spots promoting pharmaceuticals but all kinds of products. In fact, there's often no difference between ads for meds and those for other products. Most pharma ads could just as well be selling cars, jeans, or carbonated beverages, and vice versa. The product is, like the patent medicines of old, practically interchangeable. Cars that make you sexy and allluring, low-fat cookies that boost self-esteem, mutual funds that cure anxiety—seemingly magical cures surround us. The catch, of course, is that these things, like the old patent medicines, are merely placebos: they're cures only to the extent that we believe they're cures.

For the enlightened patient, this should come as good news. Once you can glimpse some company making ridiculous claims about yeast and intestines or cookies and self-esteem—once you realize that something that's just sugar, flour, and water can make you feel better—it's clear that the solution to many ills, however mysterious, already resides within us.

Originally *How Advertising Can Wreck Your Health*,

[*Stay Free!* #16, Summer 1999]

Medical Advertising Through the Ages

Coca-Cola (circa 1890s)

Developed by a morphine addict who believed it cured morphine addiction, Coca-Cola was initially sold as a "cure for all nervous affections— sick head-ache, neuralgia, hysteria, melancholy, etc." The name was inspired by the coca leaf; and yes, early formulas included a small dose of cocaine.

Bayer (circa 1890s)

Bayer developed and sold heroin around 1900 for a number of uses, including as a nonaddictive substitute for morphine and as a children's cough medication.

Today, independent suppliers and marketers of heroin sell it as a highly effective "lifestyle drug." Regular users swear by the stuff; some love this "wonder drug" so much, they dedicate their lives to its use.

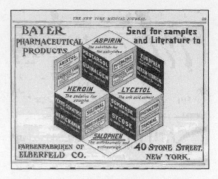

Lysol (1928)

Nowadays, we tend to hide Lysol to stop kids from accidentally drinking it. But back in 1928, women were such badasses that they would actually pour this stuff right into their vaginas. Really. Copy such as "protected her health and youthfulness" and "stayed young with him" is prude code for "sloshes this harsh cleanser up her vag." "Germ" and "organic matter" are euphemisms for "semen." The pamphlet referred to in the ad spelled this out in more detail, suggesting that you could use Lysol as a moment-after contraceptive.

Of course, you *could* use Lysol as a contraceptive, but all it would do is burn and scar your tender parts. In fact, a later ad specifically referred to

Lysol as a poison, one you poured inside yourself with abandon.

Fleischmann's Yeast (1934)

Once a household staple, yeast sales started declining around 1910, when home baking fell out of fashion. J. Walter Thompson, the ad agency for yeast kingpin Fleischmann's, responded by capitalizing on the burgeoning fad for

vitamins, pitching yeast as a source of the nutrients, to be eaten straight from the pack. After vitamin tablets came along in the 1930s, however, yeast eating declined, and so the ad agency repositioned Fleischmann's as a cure for constipation. A cake and a half three times a day supposedly combated "intestinal fatigue." Yeast had no proven laxative effect, and "intestinal fatigue" was pure invention, but sales more than doubled. As one ad exec explained, "Fatigue is universal; we simply have to credit it to the intestines."

Kelp-a-Malt (1934)

Today, Americans seem to have finally conquered the plague of being too skinny, but probably not thanks to Kelp-a-Malt. For one thing, the name "Kelp-a-Malt" provides a mental image that alone keeps people skinny.

Also, notice the claim that Kelp-a-Malt will add "5 LBS. OF SOLID FLESH IN 1 WEEK." Who knows, that five pounds could come out as a dense, solid hump right between your shoulder blades, or maybe a fat, stumpy horn atop your head.

These amazing hyper-dense tablets, we learn, have more "food iodine" (far better than, you know, "furniture iodine") than 1,600 pounds of beef. Sixteen hundred pounds of beef! That's pretty much a whole Volkswagen of beef. Was eating almost a metric ton of beef the other option for young, willowy ladies looking to grow a bit of T&A? The ad goes on to say that the "jumbo sized" tablets are "4 to 5 times the size of ordinary tablets." Oh boy! Gross *and* harder to swallow than a Kennedy half-dollar!

Listerine (1938)

Warner-Lambert, the makers of Listerine, pioneered a now common ad strategy: creating a disease and pitching your product as the cure. Formerly advertised as a surgical antiseptic, a dandruff cleanser, a sore throat treatment, a

guard against
Asian flu, and a
vaginal douche,
Listerine
transformed into
a cure for bad
breath when
Warner-Lambert
decided one was
needed. The
company began
by promoting
"halitosis"—an
obscure medical
term for bad
breath—and sales

skyrocketed. This, despite the fact that Listerine's claims
were pure fiction; there was no evidence that the
disinfectant alleviated bad breath. Listerine wasn't alone, of
course. What Listerine did for halitosis, Absorbine Jr. did
for athlete's foot. (Absorbine Jr. previously treated sore
muscles and insect bites.) Lifebuoy soap gave the world
"B.O."; Phillips' Milk of Magnesia, "acid indigestion"; and
the discovery of vitamins popularized scurvy and led many
advertisers to refer to ever-rampant "vitamin-starvation."

This particular ad is notable for the fact that it focuses
on a woman who visits a psychiatrist because she has bad
breath. Let's imagine that this lovely young lady subsists on
a diet of cat turds studded with garlic salt. Her friends
thought it better to let this woman descend into depression
than to take her aside and gently help her? She doesn't need
a doctor; she needs new friends.

Premarin (circa 1960s)

In the 1960s, when a new batch of psychotropic drugs hit the market, pharmaceutical companies began marketing menopause as a disease, treatable with sedatives and hormones. Robert A. Wilson's bestseller *Feminine Forever* (1966) initiated an era of hormone replacement therapy by touting the wonders of synthetic estrogen as a treatment for the "living decay" of menopause. Wilson's work was largely funded by the pharmaceutical industry: Searle, Upjohn, and Ayerst Laboratories, makers of Premarin.

The whole family likes "Premarin."

Ritalin (1967)

Before hitting the jackpot with attention deficit disorder, CIBA-GEIGY promoted Ritalin as a cure for "tired mother syndrome." Today, the drug (methylphenidate) is instead targeted at the source of those tired mothers: their children.

Valium (1970)

Menopause certainly wasn't the only disease created in the 1960s. The affliction of being a thirtysomething single woman was also

discovered. This ad
for Valium directs
doctors to dose
"unmarrieds with
low self-esteem"—
people like Jan, who
"never found a man
to measure up to

her father." Still, one wonders if Jan should take the pill
herself or give it to men in the hope that it will increase the
"like Jan's father" levels in their blood.

Because no one needs it as much as you do.

Panexa knows all about people like you. No matter what you do or where you go, you're always going to be yourself. Your lifestyle is one of the biggest factors in choosing how to live. Why trust it to anything less? Panexa is proven to provide more medication to those who take it than any other comparable solution. Panexa is the right choice, the safe choice. The only choice. *Visit us on the web at www.panexa.com.*

Ask your doctor for a reason to take it.

Panexa
(ACIDACHROME PROMANGANA

Panexa®
(ACIDACHROME PROMANGANATE)

PANEXA is a prescription drug that should only be taken by patients experiencing at least one of the following disorders: metabolism, binocular vision, digestion (solid and liquid), circulation, menstruation, cognition, osculation, extremes of emotion. For patients with coronary heart condition (CHC) or two separate feet (2SF), the dosage of PANEXA should be doubled to ensure that twice the number of pills are being consumed. PANEXA can also be utilized to decrease the risk of death caused by not taking PANEXA, being beaten to death by ocelots, or death relating from complications arising from seeing too much of the color lavender. Epileptic patients should take care to ensure tight, careful grips on containers of PANEXA, in order to secure their contents in the event of a seizure, caused by PANEXA or otherwise.

WHEN PANEXA SHOULD NOT BE USED

There are no known medical circumstances (based on extensive internal testing) in which PANEXA should not be used. However, PANEXA is not quite as aggressively recommended in the following circumstances:

- PANEXA should not be used as a physical aid to set a broken bone, as in the case of a splint;
- PANEXA should not be used as a substitute for real human relationships; tablets (and gel-coated caplets) are incapable of displaying any real emotion, and would prove dissatisfying as friends or mates;
- PANEXA should not be used to soak up spills or remove stains. This is disrespectful to PANEXA;
- PANEXA should not be resold with the intent of generating a personal profit;
- PANEXA should not be used as a form of motive transport, as it lacks the government regulated (US DOT 1445/88-4557) safety lights and reflectors;
- Women with uteruses should consider avoiding PANEXA or moving to a state or province where the concentration of PANEXA is lesser;
- Do not taunt PANEXA.

WARNINGS

Muscle: In a small number of tested cases (84%) PANEXA was found to cause abdominal wall muscle breakdown coupled with spasmodic activity in lower back/spinal muscles, resulting in most patients violently bending forward like a book slamming shut. While some other drugs promote similar responses (gemfibrozil, fresh cherries, nicotinic acid, cyclosporine, mustard gas, and acetaminophen) PANEXA's reactions are over 48X as powerful and take place with a great deal more panache. Also, PANEXA can contribute to developing inhumanly powerful tongue muscles, capable of licking through steel. Lymphatic System: If, after taking PANEXA for a period of four to six weeks, you still have any functional lymph nodes remaining, double the dosage every two (3) weeks until they are all gone.

IMPORTANT INFORMATION FOR WOMEN

Pregnant women, or women who plan to become pregnant, should avoid taking PANEXA or handling broken tablets. Or intact tablets. Women considering becoming pregnant someday, or who have ever been pregnant, or who have had a pregnant friend or pet, or who have seen other pregnant women, naked or otherwise, should also follow these precautions: Do not handle PANEXA tablets, containers, or related literature. If a PANEXA product nears your field of vision, avert your gaze. Try not to say the word "PANEXA." If you do happen to pronounce the syllables, spit thrice and soak your hands in iodine. If you hear the words spoken, live or via recorded medium, cover your ears and immediately see a specialist to try and staunch the bleeding. Try not to think too hard about PANEXA. In fact, don't even think about it at all. Pretend you never heard of PANEXA, and never will. Drop this magazine immediately, and get the hell out of here as fast as you fucking can. Go on, get out of here. You'll thank me.

If you should become aware of a pregnant woman who has handled PANEXA, attempt to warn the peoples of earth of the mind-numbing horror that is about to unfold. Also, drink plenty of liquids.

IMPORTANT INFORMATION FOR SQUIRRELS

PANEXA has been known in a few cases (0.0087%) to cause Excessively Floppy Tail Syndrome (EFTS). If you are a squirrel, and suspect you may be suffering from EFTS, immediately call the EFTS Hotline at 1-800-867-5309. **Pediatric use:** Expired PANEXA may be disposed of by feeding to children in a bowl with milk.

SIDE EFFECTS

Most patients (2%) tolerate treatment with PANEXA well, especially when compared with prisoners of war of comparable size and weight. However, like all drugs, PANEXA can produce some notable side effects, all of which are probably really, really terrific and nothing that anyone should be concerned about, let alone notify any medical regulatory commission about. Most side effects of PANEXA, or their sufferers, are usually short-lived, and are rarely so fatal that the remains can no longer be identified, provided good dental records are available. Some known side effects are:
Respiratory system: Shortness of breath; longness of breath; kinetic balloon-like lung expansion; really geeky laughs.
Digestive system: Explosive diarrhea; upset stomach; bitter, withdrawn stomach; prehensile colon; achy butt; shiny, valuable feces composed of aluminum and studded with diamonds and sapphire.
Eyes/senses: Everything you think you see becomes a Tootsie Roll to you; night vision; taste hallucinations (where everything tastes 'gamey' or 'oakey'); inability to distinguish the colors 'taupe' and 'putty'; sudden enjoyment of really bad music, like Kenny G or some crap; thinking everything is so damn funny all the time.
Muscular/Skeletal: Real live skeleton walking around inside you; buttock muscles mirroring the actions of jaw muscles; magnetization of the rib cage; musical spine disorder (MSD); skin might turn blue, wither, and fall off—or just get really thick and spongy (muppet-like).
Other: Loss of sexual desire and/or desirability; rising of the lights, the vapors; the willies; susceptibility to wedgies; no rhythm; dresses for shit, and can't hold a job to save your life; blue sweats; symptoms that look like scurvy, but louder; and the compulsion to address everyone nearby as "Cap'n."

PANEXA is a registered trademark of MERD Pharmaceutical Group.

Why Pharma Commercials Are a Bad Idea: The Patient Is Often Wrong

Though we're now accustomed to drug ads on TV, it wasn't always that way: the FDA relaxed the rules governing drug ads in 1997, leading to a flood of pharma commercials. The reasoning, we were told, was to "empower" patients to learn more about medical options.

Never mind that drug ads are as uninformative and image-oriented as Calvin Klein ads (and much less sexy). The ultimate problem is that people—while ignorant of professional medical standards—routinely overestimate their ability to judge medical practice.

Take eye exams. After optometry was deregulated in the 1980s, large chain stores started offering eye tests in order to sell prescription eyeglasses. Such places usher patients into a room with high-tech-looking equipment, show them a series of eye charts, and write out a prescription in fifteen minutes. Patients, not knowing any better, believe they've had a medically thorough exam. But regardless of the technology used, minimum medical standards dictate that examinations can't last less than twenty minutes and be adequate. Brief exam-based prescriptions will often improve sight in the short term but decrease visual acuity in the long run. Yet, if the exam takes longer than a patient expects, he'll erroneously infer that the service provider is incompetent.

This fact—or "information asymmetry" in the parlance—is well known among companies selling eyeglasses. If they genuinely wanted to educate patients, they would tell them that exams need to take longer and show them why. But doing so would come at the expense of profits: longer exams means fewer of them, and less convenience (at least in the short term) for consumers. Since corporations are *by law* required to maximize profit for shareholders, the customers' long-term interests lose out.

What's true for marketing eyeglasses is likewise true for pharmaceutical advertising. The pretensions of "empowerment" thus assume a cruel irony, for drug ads only encourage the people most vulnerable to the lure of a quick fix—the sick and disabled—to rely all the more on faulty assumptions.

[*Stay Free!* #16, Summer 1999]

Corporate Mascots, Then and Now

ADVERTISING is like a hitman, and a hitman's job is to aim for the head or the heart. Either does the job pretty well. But in the advertisers' case, history shows us that hearts are better targets than brains. As we discussed in section 1, intellectual arguments don't work for advertisers because they invite reason and evaluation. The sweet, dumb heart, however, is more trusting, vulnerable, and willing to take candy and hop in a stranger's van.

We can see this process playing out in the evolution of a well-known mascot: the Michelin Man. Michelin is a tire brand, and while there are certainly many qualitative and technological differences between tires, these differences are too esoteric to be a truly effective selling point. Hence, a recognizable mascot helps consumers remember Michelin.

The Michelin Man most of us know is a friendly, happy-go-lucky lug who appears fun and pleasingly huggable. He looks bouncy and rubbery but otherwise barely suggests tires. He's white, for example, a color almost never associated with modern tires (early rubber tires were white). A black, burly tire man would likely intimidate white suburban tire purchasers, and he would have diffi-

culty driving in nice parts of town without getting pulled over. The modern Michelin Man has big, friendly eyes, chubby cheeks, and a happy, smiling mouth. His head looks like it could be from a cartoon baby turtle, or perhaps an earthworm pup. He's not someone you go to to get advice about radials— he's a jovial pal who's up for pushing you in a tire swing.

But he wasn't always like that. The Michelin Man came to life as Bibendum, from the latin verb *bibi*, meaning "to drink." Why? Because, Bibendum drank up road hazards: broken glass, nails, shards of bone, rocks, what have you. Bibendum was born in 1898, when roads were far worse and blowouts on those early tires were far more common. Michelin wanted to tout the toughness of their tires, and created a mascot to personify this selling point.

Early Bibendum looked quite differ- ent, partially because of the technology of the day. Many and more narrow tires make up his body: modern tires are much wider. But, more important, the way ad- vertisers target audiences have changed. The original Bibendum wore a pince-nez and had cuff links and a big cigar: he  looked basically like the mummy of Teddy Roosevelt or per- haps some Gilded Age plutocrat. If you saw him squeakily lum- bering down a hall toward you, you'd likely soil yourself and bolt for the nearest window.

In early ads, Bibendum is raising a glass of shards, shivs, and other sharp hazards, preparing to decant them in his mouth and choke them down with masochistic glee. Imagining this act is the sort of thing that might haunt your mind late at night, robbing you of precious sleep. Bibendum wasn't sup- posed to be cute. He was based on the template of rich, powerful men—men to be feared and respected, not cuddled. This Bibendum was aimed at the head: tough, like the tires, imposing, respectable, a worthy adversary or ally.

Yet, over the years, his image softened. Bibendum lost his robber-baron accessories and settled into an innocent nudity. He gained wide, childlike eyes, and the gaping, glass-guzzling maw grew into a blubbery, marshmallow belly. This evolution— or, perhaps more accurately, de-evolution—happened because advertisers realized it made no sense to have a mascot deliver a compelling argument; a character that people remembered fondly, that instilled warm fuzzy feelings, was more effective.

Bibendum is by no means the only corporate mascot to have undergone cutification; many other high-minded concepts have found themselves herded into the cute camp, all gaining similar traits and losing the traits that made them logical mascots for the given product.

Grimace, the large, purple being who has, until quite recently, been the evangelist for the sugary chemical slurries that McDonald's euphemistically calls "shakes," is a prime example. In the 1970s, Grimace was a hideous junkie hooked on McDonald's shakes, willing to commit almost any atrocity to get one more suck from that fat, striped straw. An extra pair of arms helped him steal shakes from others. He was a towering, shake-addled hexapod, purple in color but black in spirit.

This devious Grimace is now long gone. Grimace lost his extra arms, his face took on an angelic simper, and his relationship to McDonald's shakes became one of love, not need. In the wake of a national obesity epidemic, the change is sensible. But it demonstrates something deeper:

Don't challenge your customer. McDonaldland, once popu-lated with a variety of foils for the protagonist Ronald McDon-ald to face off against, soon became populated only with happy, bland friends of Ronald. Why provide any sort of conflict, plot, or moral decision, when you can simply have an unwavering, unified front?

This pattern occurs over and over, in a variety of ways. Sometimes the original mascot is supplemented with a cute side-kick, as in the case of the imposing, authoritative, yet still surprisingly jolly Green Giant, who was given Sprout, a lit-tle leafy green fellow who, unlike his big green progenitor, poses minimal risk to lives and property.

These cute mascots have absolutely nothing to do with the product or its intended audience. Take the Dow Scrubbing Bubbles bathroom cleaner product, and their scrubbing bub-bles. Those cute, fun bubbles speed all over that bathtub like a swarm of adorable, hygienic robots. (As a kid, I desperately wanted scrubbing bub-bles as pets.) And yet you'd think that a can of toxic chemicals would be precisely the kind of product you'd want to avoid marketing to children.

We'd like to think we're practical, rational people, a hope that becomes wishful thinking when we realize an infantilized, anthropomorphized creature is somehow able to make us melt.

Small wonder, then, that when it comes to selling stuff, cute and comforting beats odd and challenging. Feelings trump ar-guments, and wuv beats love, every time.

Key Questions

1. When banker J. P. Morgan Jr. was under investigation by the Senate in 1933, what did his handlers do to boost his public image?

   a. Arranged for media to photograph Morgan with a circus midget sitting on his knee.

   b. Circulated a colorful pamphlet about Morgan's misadventures with his adorable chimp, Kujo.

   c. Hired a group of wheelchair-bound orphans to appear in a newsreel about Morgan's charitable deeds.

   d. Scripted a radio drama in which Morgan portrays a lovable oaf named Benson who struggles against all odds to find work.

2. Which of the following statements about Milton Hershey, founder of Hershey Chocolate Co., is false?

   a. Hershey promoted chocolate as "more sustaining than meat."

   b. Hershey tried to convince the federal government that chocolate should be considered a food rather than candy for tax purposes.

   c. Hershey forbade employees from referring to chocolate as candy.

   d. Hershey held quarterly chocolate parties and encouraged his staff to lunch on milk chocolate.

3. Which of the following tactics did Coca-Cola strategists in Germany *not* employ to maintain the Nazi market for Coke during World War II?

a. Maneuvered to win appointments in the Nazi government, which allowed Coke officials to supervise all soft-drink plants in Germany and captured territories.

b. Invented a more German-sounding beverage, Fanta.

c. Placed a swastika on bottle caps sold in Germany.

d. Made Coca-Cola's business "essential" to the Nazi cause by distributing free bottles of carbonated water for emergency use.

4. Why did Procter & Gamble promote Darkie toothpaste in 1985?

a. To help a P&G subsidiary in South Africa broaden its market.

b. Darkie had been purchased by Colgate, and P&G hoped that by secretly publicizing the relationship, it could portray its leading competitor as racist.

c. Someone already owned the rights to Sambo.

d. To use it as a branding tool for its new line of tartar control products.

5. According to David Green, senior VP of marketing for McDonald's USA, why is Coca-Cola nutritious?

a. Because "it is providing water, and I think that is part of a balanced diet."

b. Because it contains citric acid, which kills bacteria in the stomach lining.

c. Because it is carbonated, and carbonation facilitates digestion.

d. Because "I feed my daughter nothing but Coke and she's in great shape!"

6. What did the duties of Ford Motor Company's Sociological Department include?

    a. Impromptu visits to workers' homes, where it investigated family drinking habits, sex lives, home cleanliness, and leisure time.

    b. Boosting the results of Ford's attitude survey, which showed employee morale to be low.

    c. Identifying union sympathizers and promptly firing them.

    d. Training Ford foremen in the fine arts of persuasion, or "human engineering."

7. In 1990, Operation PUSH launched a Nike boycott for the company's "zero policy": zero African-American executives, zero Nike advertisements in African-American-owned media outlets, and zero African-American professional-service providers. How did Nike respond?

    a. Suggested that the boycott had been instigated by its major competitor, Adidas.

    b. Argued that African-Americans constituted a mere 10 percent of their consumers.

    c. Ignored PUSH altogether.

    d. Hired Spike Lee to do another series of commercials.

Answers

1. A. John Faber, "J. P. Morgan and the Midget," *Great News Photos and the Stories Behind Them*, 2nd ed. (New York: Dover, 1978), p. 56.

2. D. Joel Glenn Brenner, *The Emperors of Chocolate* (New York: Random House, 1999).

3. C. Mark Pendergrast, *For God, Country, and Coca-Cola* (New York: Touchstone, 1993), pp. 226–28.

4. B. In 1989, Colgate changed the name to Darlie, with a new logo. Alecia Swasy, *Soap Opera: The Inside Story of Procter & Gamble* (New York: Times Books, 1993), pp. 162–63.

5. A. Daniel Zoll, "A British Libel Trial Puts McDonald's on the Grill," *San Francisco Bay Guardian*, January 29, 1997; reprinted at www.afn.org/~iguana/archives/1997_03/19970309.html.

6. A. The attitude survey—which was designed to show increased morale, and therefore boost morale—was conducted by Elmo Roper, not the Sociological Department. "Human engineering" was taught in a series of conferences held by Henry Ford II. Loren Baritz, *Servants of Power: A History of the Use of Social Science in Industry* (Middletown, CT: Wesleyan University Press, 1960), pp. 33–34, 153–54, 183; Carol Gelderman, *Henry Ford: The Wayward Capitalist* (New York: Dial Press, 1982), p. 240.

7. B. Nike suggested that Reebok, not Adidas, instigated the boycott. Spike Lee was hired as part of a "crisis management" response to the early 1990s "sneaker wars," in which inner-city kids robbed and killed for coveted Air Jordans.

Adventures in Medialand 6.

I WAS WALKING through the posh Brooklyn neighborhood of Park Slope for the millionth time when I noticed something: the cars lined up on this residential street were overwhelmingly SUVs. Park Slope is known as an enclave of affluent liberals, the kind who shop for green housewares and get their produce at the Food Coop. So it struck me as a beautiful example of consumers' skewed sense of values. The negative environmental impact of an SUV grossly outweighs any gain from purchasing, say, recycled paper products or non-toxic kitty litter. (Besides, the north end of Park Slope has excellent public transit; there is little reason to own a car there at all.)

This gave me an idea: make fake municipal NO SUV PARK-ING signs that look just like the real thing. We could use bolts to attach them to the regular parking signs, and SUV drivers circling for a coveted free parking spot might think twice about where they stopped.

My friends dug the idea, so I printed some NO SUV PARK-ING signs on plastic boards, and also created a parody ticket to place on SUVs in the targeted areas.

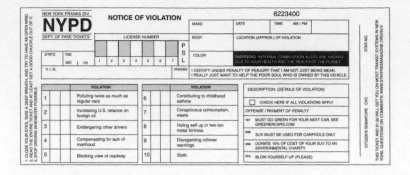

Then, on a designated evening, about twenty of us set out in pairs to hang the signs and ticket cars throughout the neighborhood. A couple of hours later, we reconvened at a nearby watering hole and gabbed about the experience. The next day I sent out a press release and the prank ended up reaping a ton of media coverage—attention that was ultimately much more important for spreading a message than the isolated interactions with neighborhood drivers. Journalists used the story as a "hook" for discussing the pitfalls of America's move toward larger and larger vehicles, for our increased reliance on foreign oil, and for associated threats to human health and the environment. Perhaps more important, media coverage also helped spread an image of SUVs as decadent, wasteful, and—horrors!—increasingly unfashionable.

Did this stunt change the world or prompt any of the targeted SUV owners to immediately stop driving their car? Probably not, but then there's no reason it should. Why would a public interest message accomplish more than the average advertisement? A typical national advertising campaign has millions of dollars and teams of educated professionals behind it. And yet the average ad not only fails to change the world, but fails to make any noticeable difference on any person's life. This doesn't make advertising a failure; ads work through "feather" effects: small, barely noticeable changes that over time and through repetition stand to add up to something more powerful.

The same can be said of efforts like our SUV stunt. They contribute to a climate of opposition, of critical public sentiment, that—combined with, say, newspaper exposés, crash studies stats, and global warming reports—can ultimately have a real impact. By "have a real impact," I mean provoke legislative change. Public outrage has a shelf life: people can protest an issue for only so long before surrendering and getting on with their lives. The only way to make something stick is to have the government put it in writing: to lower CAFE (corporate average fuel economy) standards, to restrict tobacco claims, to place real limits on advertising in schools, and the like.

Even if our SUV prank accomplished nothing—even if no media outlets reported it and few people noticed it at all—it was worth doing. I met some interesting people, had some good stories to tell, and even got quite a bit of exercise. Moreover, we found a way to socialize that doesn't center around consuming stuff—no small feat, in this day and age.

The minor acts of protest we highlight in this section tell a similar story: one of everyday people finding creative ways to subvert, exploit, or merely survive the machine. While none of them changed the world or even pointed to actual solutions, they made us laugh—and, at the very least, provide inspiration for the Davids fighting Goliaths out in the field.

Buyer Beware

HOW DO SUPERMARKET SHOPPERS REACT WHEN YOU PLACE FOREIGN OBJECTS IN THEIR BASKETS?

by Gaylord Fields

S EVERAL RECENTLY published studies con-
clude that supermarkets are geared to lull the
average shopper into a trancelike state and that this glassy-eyed
mesmerization makes the customer purchase more goods. This
comes as no surprise to this writer, as these results parallel my
findings of thirty years ago when I undertook several experiments in social psychology under the guise of adolescent
pranksterism.

The time: the early 1970s. The place: a typical Upper West
Side of Manhattan supermarket, which, for those unacquainted
with New York City commercial real estate, took up approximately the same square footage as the produce section of a
typical modern-day American megamarket. The researchers:
initially a trio of bored thirteen-year-olds, later pared to one
nascent social scientist and scores of anonymous shoppers and
checkout clerks, to whom I offer belated and collective thanks.

Phase One

During our initial forays into the local supermarkets of choice,
we gauged the level of cooperation of our host sites. In plainer

language, my cohorts and I were determining what we could get away with under the vigilant eye of the ubiquitous convex mirror (this is pre-surveillance-camera 1973). This mostly consisted of such activities as jamming our pockets full of a name-brand caramel candy and placing rolls of bathroom tissue in freezer cases. We attracted little attention from the busy shoppers or even (make that especially) from the store management and, in the process, developed the sangfroid, dexterity, and stealth needed for the successful completion of our operation.

Phase Two

For this part of the experiment, my colleagues' participation was no longer necessary, because if any member of our group were to be perceived as a member of a band of teenage males, we would attract unwanted attention. This science-minded young adult would have to go it alone. For it is here that the experiment commences in earnest, and I will link my findings

with the studies of those who followed me, as briefly cited in paragraph one.

The experiment was simply designed: It would involve the surreptitious placement of various individual supermarket goods in the handbasket or cart of a targeted shopper (the "subject") by the experimenter (namely, this writer). I would then follow the subject to a position directly behind him or her in the checkout line and observe whether he or she completed the shopping transaction by purchasing the introduced foreign product (the "item").

As we scientists are merely human, I can now admit to having breached protocol a bit to speculate as to what results I would find. I presumed that the fewer goods in the basket, the more likely the subject would be to reject the item. I also presumed a similar correlation between the unusualness of the item and its rejection. Thus, my initial thought was to play it close to the vest by introducing leading brands—a box of Tide brand detergent or Ritz brand snack crackers—into heavily laden carts. Expecting to be emboldened by some degree of success (the purchase of the item by the subject), I would then, over a period of time, increase the risk of discovery: more unusual items, such as a packet of Airwick brand room deodorizers and Knorr brand chicken bouillon cubes, would be introduced into a basket holding a scant four or five goods.

Conclusion

In approximately one year of trials, run on an average of twice a week, not one subject rejected the item or even regarded it strangely; all items were purchased without question. It mattered not one iota whether it was an incredibly commonplace and ubiquitous item, such as a roll of Scott brand bathroom tissue, or a more arcane item, such as a meat thermometer.

Forty items or four, the compliance rate was an astounding 100 percent! Everyone bought what was put in the basket without even a second's hesitation.

Unfortunately, my teen foray into the social sciences was curtailed by a variety of factors, namely the overwhelmingly one-sided data collected, the distractions of an increasingly challenging high school curriculum, and my awakening to the fact that I could have introduced a yelping schnauzer and her litter of suckling pups into a subject's cart without notice. But foremost was the knowledge that if my experiments were to be discovered by those who might refuse to understand the gravity of my mission, I would soon cease to have the protection of my juvenile status guaranteed by the laws of the state of New York once I reached the age of eighteen. I await phase three of my experiment, to commence sometime after the year 2030, when this writer's senescence will be the cloak under which to resume operation, and there will be an even wider palette of items to foist upon a new generation of shoppers.

[*Stay Free!* #21, Fall 2003]

True Gentleman Urinates on Dumpster

JASON TORCHINSKY TOURS THE PLAYBOY MANSION

LAST WEEK I received an invitation from Johnnie Walker to "The Journey of Taste." This Journey was to take place at none other than the Playboy Mansion. I was suitably impressed, not just with the details of the event but that the Johnnie Walker Company was insightful and sensitive enough to realize that I, Jason Torchinsky, was among the "true gentlemen" in Los Angeles. Their feat in deducing this was even more extraordinary when one considers the scene in which I received the invite: it is after 11:00 a.m., I'm barely awake, still unshowered, and standing in the living room with one hand firmly in my underpants. Yes, I thought to myself as I walked barefoot through the remains of a pizza that littered the floor, I'd be delighted to have "my share of the Scotch" with you, fellow gentlemen!

After my euphoria at being mistaken for a "true gentleman" had worn off, I began to think about this event. What was Johnnie Walker up to? Obviously, he felt that people of my age, sex, and income just weren't drinking as much Scotch as they could be. Well, they're right. I have no interest in Scotch, largely for the same reason that this invite seems so insipid: Scotch reeks of dorky white guys trying to seem like wealthier dorky white guys. The Johnnie Walker Company is playing on some sort of extinct idea of young manhood: the sort that wrote letters to *Playboy* inquiring about the best hi-fi to buy or what kind of gift one brings to a day of yachting—a type of man I haven't even heard of since I found my dad's book of *Playboy* party jokes.

Still, as posturing and dorky as the event promised to be, it was still the Playboy Mansion, which was probably worth seeing for the hell of it, and there was going to be free food and booze, so why not? I made reservations for three.

The day came, although my two friends chickened out at the last minute, so I put on my tie (they said I had to wear one) and headed out alone. When I got to the UCLA parking lot where we were to take the shuttle to the Playboy Mansion, I reaffirmed my status as a "true gentleman" by taking a leak behind a Dumpster. Then I scanned around the area, looking for where I was to find the bus; it wasn't hard, as I soon noticed a large group of be-sport-coated and necktied twenty-five- to thirty-five-year-old males, most of whom could charitably be called "dipshits."

I wandered into the group, where this very frat-type crowd was animatedly discussing the night ahead, speculating on the presence of Playmates and complaining about possibly fictitious girlfriends. I heard one group of dorks talking about how they used to hang out around the UCLA area where we were waiting, but that was "before all the gangs." Gangs? In Westwood? I'm no expert, but I think the only real danger from gangs anyone could face out there would be a long, tedious lecture on the benefits of vegetarianism. The scariest-looking place around was a B-rated falafel restaurant.

We boarded the bus, which had darkly tinted windows, perhaps to keep us from finding out the exact location of the Playboy Mansion. I asked around a bit to see how people had found out about this event. Lots of them called the number, which they were informed of by friends; a few others received invites like the one I got, making me very curious as to what sort of "impressionable, vain doofus" mailing list I'm on.

We pulled into the Playboy Mansion's parking lot, which displayed a novelty yellow-diamond traffic sign that read "Playmates at Play." Classy. We got off the bus and were led into a massive tent full of other "true gentlemen" (and a smattering of "true gentlewomen") as well as a bar and buffet table.

Before I even had a chance to start plotting where I was going to stash extra food and booze for the ride home, a genuine *Playboy* Playmate appeared and told us to follow her if we wanted a tour of the Playboy Mansion grounds.

The tour was actually quite compelling. Did you know there's a zoo at the Playboy Mansion? Mostly it seems to be peacocks, rabbits, and spider monkeys, but it's sure as hell a zoo. And the highest concentration of redwoods in Southern California is on Hef's 5.5 acres. It's all very lush, but we were told not to try and go hiding in the woody areas: the place is crawling with cameras and gigantic goons packed into expensive suits.

The most important fact I learned was this: Hugh Hefner's Donkey Kong high score is 1,689,000. I learned this at the last stop on our tour, the mansion's little Game Cottage. It was in this small building packed with pool tables, video games, and *Playboy*-themed pinball machines that I realized something about the Playboy mansion. It's a thirteen-year-old boy's dream come true: naked women, video games, and people to clean up after you. The game room was the ultimate basement rec room, complete with heavy brown furniture, a giant novelty $5 bill with Hef's picture in it, and those strange statues of Charlie

Chaplin and W. C. Fields with oversize heads that, up until this point, I had seen only as displays in luggage stores.

The tour was now over, and, on cue, two heavies appeared by the door to make sure none of us "true gentlemen" would try to swipe an ashtray or puke on the pool table. Our Playmate led us back to the "Journey of Taste" and we were shuffled into a gigantic tent, filled with rows of tables, known as the "tasting tent."

Each place setting at the table had six glasses of Scotch, a questionnaire, and a little "tasting notes" card. At the front of the room was a large video screen and a podium. A woman named Barbara got up and welcomed us, then forcefully reminded us to fill out the questionnaire.

The questionnaire wanted to know things like which booze brands "I would never willingly drink." (Why was that "willingly" in there? Was that a threat?) And "What was the main message you took away from tonight's presentation regarding Johnnie Walker?" (I answered: "Be true to yourself" and "Avoid contact with mucous membranes. For external use only.") A guy near me wondered aloud if this was all a "big marketing thing." Man, you just can't get anything past some people!

A kilted man named Ian Lowe took the podium. He was one of Johnnie Walker's brand ambassadors and had a "billion-liter" production record, which the crowd eagerly applauded. The crowd also sycophantically applauded the first mention of Johnnie Walker and the fact that Johnnie Walker made the world's bestselling whiskey. Ian then told us that "drinking was compulsory" and made some lame joke about being tipsy, which the crowd ate up, eager to prove to their surrounding people just how much they appreciated that dry Scottish wit.

He then started to play a video about the history of Scotch

and the Johnnie Walker Company. The video was fairly straight-foward, with lots of pretty scenery of Scotland, but the reverence with which the audience was viewing it all was a bit disturbing. If the same thing were on PBS or the Learning Channel one night, I'd find it difficult to believe anyone would have paused for more than the time it takes to fumble for the remote.

After the video, the guided tasting began in full force: he spoke about each of the whiskeys in front of us, showed how to "nose" it, how to check its "legs" (i.e., its viscosity: tilt it in the glass and see how long it takes to slide back). I saw scores of people doing this with fierce intensity, but I have no clue what was supposed to be seen. One man called me "tough guy" when he didn't think I was drinking my Scotch fast enough. I liked this guy because he put away all his whiskey before most of the crowd was even finished checking the rich amber color of the first Scotch.

"My fingers smell like a pencil," he told the bored-looking woman next to him. Later he announced that the whole room smelled "like a fish."

One somewhat ironic turn of the tasting came when our kilted leader warned the crowd to drink Scotch without snob-bery. It seems like snobbery is almost unavoidable whenever you describe any alcohol as "heather," but he backed up his wish by telling the crowd that any way to drink Scotch is right because "we want your money."

By now the crowd was getting rowdy. After several attempts to recapture their waning interest with a scintillating discus-sion of blended whiskeys, class was dismissed and everyone left for free food.

I went to the bathroom, which looked like it was hewn out of the living rock and, sure enough, had an entire closet full of fluffy bathrobes for the mansion's preferred guests. I was delighted to find a forgotten questionnaire, as mine had already been collected. The person had some good responses: the only thing he or she disliked about the event was "the musty smell in the tasting tent." And when asked to rate specific parts on a scale of 1 to 5, everything got a 5 except "the food" and "the people attending."

Finally the evening ended, and all us "true gentlemen" were herded back into vans with startling efficiency. The tents were dismantled with remarkable speed, too, leaving no trace that such an incredible "Journey of Taste" had occurred. But you could tell it had happened by looking at the gentlemen boarding the vans. They had a new gleam in their eyes. A new power. A new confidence. At least some of them. Most on my bus were just drunk, wondering where the mansion's "blowjob closets" were. Those were the harmless ones. As for the rest, well . . . women of Los Angeles, take cover. If anyone offers to buy you a Johnnie Walker Black Label Scotch served at room temperature in the proper kind of glass for nosing, Mace him and run away.   [*Stay Free!* #17, Summer 2000]

Letter to the Creative Pretzel Eater's Club

COMPANIES THAT TARGET kids love to hold contests in order to build up databases of customers. They use these databases not only to market their own goods but to sell the information to other businesses.

As long as businesses are collecting files on our future, we might as well make the best of it. Here's a letter by Damian Chadwick, one way to respond to a kiddie contest.

Creative Pretzel Eater's Club

Folks just love to enjoy Snyder's Old Fashioned Hard Pretzels in many taste-tempting ways. What is your favorite way of enjoying our pretzels? Write Snyder's Creative Pretzel Eater's Club, P.O. Box 917, Hanover, PA 17331, and tell us! We'll send you your official Membership Card.

Snyder's Creative Pretzel Eater's Club
P.O. Box 917
Hanover, PA 17331

To whom it may concern:

It gives me great pleasure to register my brother, Willie Molecule, with the Snyder's Pretzels Creative Pretzel Eater's

Club. He has dozens of bizarre and "creative" methods of eating Snyder's pretzels. The following is just a sample.

He reenacts the Last Supper with his family, using only Snyder's pretzels.

He builds a miniature Eiffel Tower out of pretzels, and then eats it without using his hands.

He soaks them in Pepsi and eats them with a spoon.

He breaks them apart into letter shapes and arranges them into a story on his carpet, then eats them.

He mixes them in a blender with applesauce and whiskey.

He has an overactive salivary gland, and soaks pretzels in his mouth until they are soft enough to swallow whole. This helps him to keep his drooling under control.

He feeds them to his dog, forces the dog to throw up, and then eats the pretzels half digested.

He packs them into his underwear and leaves them there for about a week and then eats them.

He licks off all the salt first, then bakes them into a pie, which he eats after sniffing glue for two hours.

He buries them in the backyard on the full moon, then forgets about them until the next full moon, when he digs them up, eats them, and buries another batch.

He doesn't eat them at all, but soaks them in kerosene and sets them on fire, inhaling the fumes until he loses consciousness.

Sometimes I worry about him, but I know it's all for the best. Snyder's pretzels are a wholesome, nutritious snack no matter how he eats 'em.

Sincerely,

Jack Molecule
Brooklyn, NY   **[Stay Free! #12, Fall 1996]**

Anal-yzing Car Consumption

by Kembrew McLeod

H ERE'S A ROAD TRIP GAME that won't exactly change the world, but at least you'll get to laugh at SUV drivers' expense. Take almost any SUV name (the Ford Explorer, for instance), add "Anal" to the title, and—presto!—you have the Anal Explorer, or the Anal Rodeo, or whatever. There's something about SUVs that make them more conducive to this semiotic game of revenge, far better than cars (the Anal Civic doesn't really work, nor does the Anal Camry). That's because most SUV names are all about dominance and penetration: of nature, puny cars, or pedestrians. If SUVs are the tops of the vehicular world, then I guess that makes the rest of us bottoms, and if you've ever had an Anal Blazer on your ass, you know what I'm talking about.

Top 10 SUVs

The Anal Navigator

The Anal Explorer

The Anal Excursion

The Anal Pathfinder

The Anal Blazer

The Anal Expedition

The Anal Trooper

The Anal Rodeo

The Anal Wrangler

The Anal Charger

Incidentally, the same dynamic also applies to RVs, which, between their gas guzzling, massive size, and dangerous road behaviors, are exponentially more obnoxious than SUVs. And eight times out of ten during the summer you'll find an RV hauling an SUV, which means you might see an Anal Wrangler mounted behind an Anal Prowler.

Top 5 RVs

The Anal Vacationer

The Anal Executive

The Anal Prowler

The Anal Jamboree

The Anal Revolution

[*Stay Free!* #21, Fall 2003]

Prankster
Sir Jon Hargrave
Speaks

SIR JOHN HARGRAVE is the founder of the humor website Zug.com and is about as close to being the Prime Minister of Pranks as anyone is likely to be. In fact, he legally changed his first name to the honorific "Sir." Congress, credit card companies, Wal-Mart, and the Super Bowl—he has pranked them all. The author of *Prank the Monkey: The ZUG Book of Pranks*, Hargrove has appeared on Comedy Central, *The Tonight Show with Jay Leno*, MSNBC, TechTV, and the BBC, so even grandparents and other Luddites may have heard of him and his pranking ways.

This is a really basic question, but what do you like about pranks?

JOHN: Pranks turn the power structure on its head. A prank allows the little guy to have a place. When a telemarketer calls your house, usually you're the victim. But when you can turn it into a prank, and tell the telemarketer that the person they're looking for is dead from a horrible accident and string the telemarketer along for ten or fifteen minutes, that's a way of kind of getting back at the system.

I'm a big fan of telling telemarketers I'm not allowed to have cell phones in the underwater prison. What do you think makes a good prank? Can you break it down into specific criteria?

I have a saying: "The bigger the butt cheek, the funnier the fall." In other words, the bigger and more powerful the target is, the funnier it is when that target is taken down. That's why Michael Moore's stuff is so satisfying.

But the funny thing about what I do is that I am the man. I'm a middle manager at an ad agency.

Using your rules regarding power differentials, what sorts of organizations and companies do you seek out for pranks?

I like to go after credit card companies because there's something inherently evil about them: they have essentially created a business on people's poor financial planning. What really gets me is that the security is so terrible. They don't really protect your data. One of my favorite things to do is to get credit cards in other people's names. It's very easy: all you need is a credit card in your name, then you request additional card numbers. They're supposed to check up on the names, but they never do. I have credit cards in Ashton Kutcher's name and Charles Manson's. Right now I'm carrying in my wallet a credit card in the name of Barack Obama.

Wow!

It's great: now I'm doing this series of pranks about Barack Obama. I just sent one of his campaign staffers a case of my book from Amazon, and I sent along a personal note: "Thanks for doing a great job, keep it up! —Barack." Somebody needs to thank these guys, they're slaving away, and it's hot. They'll check the Amazon sales receipt, and it's going to have Barack Obama's credit card.

I like to target large corporations, anybody that pisses us all off: the Wal-Marts, the Starbucks of the world. Any of those large organizations have a loophole, that chink in the armor where you can get in there and do something to them.

What's a prank you've done on one of these large companies that you're particularly fond of?

There was the Starbucks prank. You know the old line about how there are so many Starbucks, the only place you could open a new one would be inside a Starbucks? Well, I wanted to see what would happen if we opened a Starbucks inside an existing Starbucks. I got the Starbucks apron, I made a name tag, I had the whole Starbucks uniform. I brought in a coffeepot, an espresso maker, a cappuccino maker, my laptop, recording equipment, a camera, and all the accoutrements: milk, cream, and things like that. I went to the counter and asked for a pound of freshly ground coffee. Then I sat down in the large comfy chair, set up my stuff, and started brewing my Starbucks coffee.

You did buy the coffee.

Right, I bought the coffee, so I'm a paying customer: that's what I mean by finding the loophole. The employees couldn't see us well, so for ten minutes or so, I was able to brew a full pot of coffee. But then when the hot steam came out of the espresso maker—I was steaming the milk—the manager came over because it was kind of making a racket. He tells me I have to leave. We had an exchange and then he went away. I got up and walked around offering a free top-off to all the customers. That's another thing that bothers me. You go to a Waffle House, and they'll top your coffee off, but Starbucks can't afford to give you an extra half a cup? Come on.

So I was giving free top-offs to everybody, trying to give foamer top-offs. But the customers were afraid of me even though I was wearing all the Starbucks stuff, and no one was taking me up on my offer. Then the police showed up. My cappuccino maker's steam is spewing out, my shit's lying all over the Starbucks, the police are escorting me out, and then the carafe falls and shatters on the ground. It was a mess, it was terrible. The cops got us all outside, and we managed to talk them down from arresting us.

Arresting you for what?

Exactly. So I wrote a little note to Starbucks letting them know we opened up a Starbucks Express. I had a whole concept: Starbucks Express would be where you'd go to get a simple cup of coffee so you wouldn't have to wait in line behind a guy getting a triple-decaf soy latte. Starbucks sent a cease-and-desist letter telling me if I ever used their logo again or set foot in one of their stores, there'd be trouble. And I was just trying to be helpful!

What would you consider your favorite prank?

I really like the Michael Jackson one. We faked an appearance of Michael Jackson in Boston while he was living in Bahrain. So we hired an actor to play fake Michael, and we hired another actor to play his son, "Blanket." Remember how he kept his kid covered in that blanket? I tried to hire a midget, but it's really hard to find a midget on short notice. We ended up hiring a really small Hispanic man. So I've got a Hispanic man who spoke no English with a blanket over his head, a fake Michael, and a totally crazy entourage. I was his handler, a guy was playing his bodyguard, people were playing his friends, and I got a whole camera crew—the

Credit Card Security Prank

John Hargrave believes that "credit card security" is an oxymoron and, in two simple pranks, set out to prove it.

In his first experiment, he tested how carefully retail clerks checked his signature when processing a credit card purchase. Eschewing his own name—or even any name at all—Hargrave "signed" with a variety of gibberish. He filled the signature area with a crosshatch pattern; he inserted a doodle of a smiling whale; and he once simply wrote "Please check ID"—all of which were mindlessly approved. His reign of terror continued unabated until he tried to sign "NOT AUTHORIZED" for $15,000 in flat-screen TVs.

He then turned his attention to the security of account information. Do you really need to remember your mother's maiden name when you want information from a phone operator? No, it turns out you do not. Hargrave set out to access his account while demonstrating little or no knowledge of the account. On his first attempt he simply used a fake maiden name ("Swarthington"). The operator resisted, until he indicated that the name was simply part of a longer, faker name.

> **Hargrave:** That's my mother's maiden name, Swarthington-Stocktoston . . . Is that not what you have?

> **VISA:** I don't see that kind of information. Oh, okay . . . I got it. So you want to have a credit line increase?

Unfortunately, distracted by the ease of his progress, Hargrave started pestering the operator without obtaining any useful information. In fact, he became so infatuated with his own silliness that the call fell short of succeeding. The second time around he didn't make the same mistake:

Hargrave: I need to make an inquiry about my balance.

VISA: All right, sir. In order to maintain security, may I please have your mother's maiden name?

Hargrave: Yeah. That's [mumbles something unintelligible].

VISA: [Pause] Okay, and how can I help you, sir?

Hargrave: Um, can you tell me, uh, my current balance?

VISA: I show the current balance as . . . $7,618.62.

Despite hearing nothing resembling a name at all, the operator not only gave up Hargrave's balance, she then *told him his mother's maiden name*—certainly something to think about if you are estranged from Mom but need to transfer a balance on short notice.

—Charles Star

whole thing. The original plan was that he and his entourage were going to walk from his hotel and into this really fancy upscale mall. Then he was going to throw up in the mall. This was because there was this event out there in Bahrain where he had gone out and thrown up, and we were playing off that. We alerted the media that he was going to be there.

By coincidence that night there was this huge charity concert with Gladys Knight. We went over to the concert with Michael and the entourage in a limo (we had rented a limo). I found the concert organizers and said, "I'm Michael Jackson's handler, and he'd love to go to the concert tonight." They were looking at me skeptically, but I managed to convince them.

They ended up giving us a balcony with private seating— and this was a $10,000-a-plate charity dinner. The mayor of Boston was there, and all these high rollers were there. It was nuts: people were always coming up and trying to sneak a look at Michael with us keeping them out.

What are a couple of good, easy pranks that people reading this book could try without too much planning?

There's the old trick with direct mail: when you get return envelopes that you can really mail, stuff them full of whatever you want and send them back. It costs the company some nominal amount per envelope, but it just feels good.

Now you can't do the old tape-a-cinder-block-to-them anymore, right?

Yeah, that does not work: the post office will just throw it away if the envelope is affixed to something. But you can stuff it full, and I like to make it as heavy as I can. For my book, I tried this, and I used the heaviest metals I could get.

Several teaspoons of tuna are probably good too.

Sure, though I understand it's a federal offense to mail poo:
it's classified as biowaste, so it's illegal.

That's good to know.

Another good one is shop dropping. You bring things into a
store like Wal-Mart or any store you have a beef with. For example, I forced Wal-Mart to sell me pornography. I brought
some porno mags into the Wal-Mart, put them on the shelf,
went back through the checkout, and had them ring it all up
for me.

**What did they do when you came through the line with
pornography? Did they scan them?**

Well, of course the scanner didn't pick them up, but they
keyed them in and sold them to me.

If you don't like your public utility, another good prank is
to pay bills in pennies. With Quicken or other software, it's
very easy to print out huge stacks of checks with small random amounts on them. I did that: I used hundreds of small
checks to pay my electric bill.

Did they complain? Did you hear back from them about that?

Uh, yeah. I started out like that, and I got more and more aggressive: I have sort of a beef with my electric company. My
electric company is named "nStar" so I got a credit card with
the name FUK U NSTAR. I started paying my nStar bill with
my FUK U NSTAR credit card. It ended with me blowing up
a giant photo of my FUK U NSTAR credit card, taking this
five-by-eight-foot card to the company headquarters, and
trying to pay my bill with it. I took it to an extreme I guess
most people wouldn't have.

MeBay!

eBAY FOR FUN AND PROFIT

by Joe Garden

WHEN I STARTED eBaying, it was just a way to make a few bucks and get rid of some of the detritus that consumes my life. With neither a digital camera or scanner, I tried to hold customers' interest by peppering product descriptions with humor and non sequiturs. From this point, it seemed like a natural extension to take every half-formed idea and vague concept and turn it into a finished work that would be published instantly.

"Creative" auctions are in fact not allowed on eBay. However, in my experience, auctions that didn't attract bids were the only ones that got shut down. "DNA" (final price: $31), "Peanut Butter Sandwich" (final price: $4.50), and "New Swear Word" (final price: $21) failed to raise an eyebrow. But "Bells, Whistles" was shut down with two days left and no bids.

I strongly recommend eBay as a valuable outlet for impulse writing and exorcising creative frustrations.

Befriend the Legendary Joe Garden

Starting bid: $4.99
Final price: $17.50

Hello. My name is Joe Garden. I am a writer. A secretary. A lover of fineries. But more than anything, I am a nice guy. The kind of person you can walk through the zoo with and talk about nothing for hours. The kind of person that will watch movies with you but will only offer commentary at the most appropriate moments. The kind of person who will help you move if there's nothing too heavy and he isn't too busy. You know. The good sort.

And, besides all this, I am legendary. The item I am offering is unique indeed. I am offering the chance to purchase my friendship.

Why do you need to purchase? you might ask. Perhaps you find yourself with a great deal of time on your hands with no one to spend it with. Or maybe you want my friendship for bragging rights to lord over your existing friends. Maybe you're just unlovable. Whatever the reason, I am the man for the job. Assuming, of course, you meet the reserve price.

I don't know much about you. I really don't have to. So far as I'm concerned, we may never come into physical contact, but you can count on me for a phone call and a Christmas card. If you need a friend, or at least a friend of a more legendary status, this is the auction for you. I'm not here to judge you. I will not question your motives. As soon as the check clears, I will be there for you, friend. Should the bid top $150, I will throw in a photo opportunity with me so you can show other people a picture of you with your friend, the legendary Joe Garden. Shipping is, of course, free, as friendship is a metaphysical quality which flows freely between borders. Thank you for your bid.

DNA from a Writer from *The Onion*!

Starting bid: $9.99
Final price: $31.00

As an amateur scientist in the cloning field, you may be looking for just the right person to replicate. Well, look no further! I am Joe Garden, relatively healthy male, 30, and I am a writer for *The Onion*. As such, I am creative, intelligent, and as erudite—or coarse—as the occasion demands.

While I am happy to propagate in nonconventional ways, I do not want to feel cheated. For all I know, you could start a Joe Garden farm and sell the babies. Well, that's fine, but I want my cut.

I will send you whatever you deem necessary to unbind the modern Prometheus: cheek scrapings, blood sample, hair, skin flakes, etc. Please note: Any DNA transmitted in this transaction is done so with the understanding that Joe Garden does not agree to undertake any financial responsibility for the resultant offspring. Shipping charge is dependent on the sample required.

Bid now and bid high. This is a limited offer. Should the high bid top $150, I'll throw in an 8" x 10" photograph to show the little Joe what he's made of. Thank you.

Are You Running for Public Office?

Starting bid: $0.99
No bids

That's great. Public service is the most noble calling one can pursue, right next to buying records at a rummage sale and selling them at a record fair for 200x what you paid for it.

But how can you get your message across? Good question.

My name is Joe Garden. I am an editor for a popular newspaper and website. In the course of a given week, I reach up to 3 million people. And statistically speaking, most of those people can vote. What website and newspaper? If you have to ask, you are obviously incapable of using Google, and do not deserve my attention.

I'm not promising I will be sympathetic to you or your cause. I am not promising to present your cause in a sympathetic manner. However, you will have my ear for the entire meal. Make the most of it.

Stipulations:

1. The meal MUST be in New York City metropolitan area.

2. I must agree to the restaurant.

3. The restaurant will be Peter Luger Steak House in Brooklyn.

4. It must be after normal business hours.

5. Winning bidder must make the reservation.

6. Winning bidder picks up the check.

7. Winning bidder will not make any noises of objection when I order drinks, dessert, or take the leftovers home with me.

8. This offer is not good to publicists trying to work a play, film, or band, unless they are large enough that someone outside of New York will have heard of it.

There is no reserve on this auction. Remember, you have the potential to reach up to 3 million people, so bid accordingly. My interest will be reflected in your bid.

A Unique Haiku That Will Be Yours Alone

Starting bid: $1.00
Final price: $14.50

Hello. My name is Joe Garden. I am, by trade, a writer. I have not won any awards, but that is because I have chosen not to do so. Awards are like a subsistence diet of cotton candy. The initial giddy high is amazing, but the sickness which follows leaves you hollow. Words are my paints; the keyboard, my brush; the screen, and, invariably, the paper it is printed on, is my canvas.

I love . . . to create.

One form—genre, if you will—I am particularly adept at is the haiku. Originating from the mysterious Orient, this highly structured poem is like a flashcube in the darkness, illuminating a scene or an item briefly, but leaving an indelible mark on your eyes, which are, of course, the windows to the soul.

I love to touch the soul. Please, allow me to touch yours. For a low starting price (with no reserve) I will sculpt, as it were, a haiku that is entirely unique and will be yours to cherish.

Please note that the haiku will be on a subject of my own choosing, for I am not a trained monkey that flings verse onto paper and calls it genius. I will write on what inspires me. Non-unique samples are available on request.

For yourself. For a gift. For posterity. Consider this to be your contribution to the arts, and to your soul. Thank you for your attention. **[*Stay Free!* #18, Spring 2001]**

Advertise on My Colon!!!!

Perhaps you've seen news stories about budding entrepreneurs who use eBay to sell ad space on their foreheads—or on their faces, bald heads, or pregnant bellies. Alhough some of the early adopters earned thousands of dollars in addition to headlines, latecomers found the auctions not nearly so lucrative, with bidding hovering around a dollar or two, at most.

In 2005, at the height of the fad, and at the risk of my dignity, I decided to step into the fray and auction off ad space on my colon—an opportunity, I pitched, to see advertising in a space where it truly belongs.

Administrators at eBay, however, didn't appreciate the joke, and canceled the auction within days.
[blog.stayfreemagazine.org, February 3, 2005]

Planning your next ad campaign? You've seen ads on foreheads, arms, bikini bottoms, and pregnant bell here's a chance to put advertising where it truly belongs. At 36 years old, my colon is healthy, robust, and bear your message! Through a unique process of laser imaging, I will imprint your company logo on my b where it shall remain for a minimum of 14 days.

Though invisible to the average eye, my colon will be viewed by an affluent audience of medical professiona. Overpriced pharmaceuticals, diuretics, and Frito-Lay products are a natural fit, but keep in mind that docto enjoy a wide array of luxury products, too.

THIS IS LIKE THE STORY YOU HAVE HEARD ABOUT: Seen on MSNBC, WBTW TV 13 Myrtle Beach, WFXB Fox 43 Myrtle Beach, WPDE TV 15 Myrtle Beach, WIS T 10 Columbia, South Carolina.

NO RESERVE! SERIOUS BIDS ONLY. The price of this auction includes GUARANTEED MEDIA COVERAGE from a wide array of newspapers and television news programs offering upbeat, superficial coverage of advertising's latest assaults on the public psyche.

Disclaimer: As the owner of my colon, I reserve the right to reject advertising for anything inappropriate or offensive. This includes but is not limited to cigarette companies, bigbox retailers, and dildos. A portion of the proceeds go to the American Cancer Society. Thanks for all your support!

Drive-thru Entertainment

HERE'S A PRANK for everyone to try in their hometown: it's simple, relatively easy, and fairly low-risk.

You know the big, illuminated menus virtually all fast-food drive-thrus have, usually a good distance from the grab-your-food window? Our prank simply involves adding appropriate-looking but hopefully trouble-inducing signage to those menus. We have several samples here, designed to fit in with the graphical styles of most fast-food chains, or at least look like governmental, mandated signage.

So, here's the process:

1. Download one or more of our signs from our website, www.adnauseam.info (or make your own!).

2. Print it out in color.

3. Spray-mount it to card stock or foam core.

4. Sneak over to a drive-thru menu late at night. Find a nice flat area for your sign. Using more spray mount, get the back of the sign nice and sticky. Place it on the menu, making sure it holds.

5. Leave. Or hide and listen to see what happens.

Depending on the sign, it may be ignored; it may repulse or inconvenience the staff. Who knows? Most likely, the inherent apathy of the staff should ensure the sign will remain in place at least an hour or so.

ATTENTION CONSUMERS:

STATE LAW REQUIRES THIS ESTABLISHMENT TO INFORM YOU OF THE PERCENTAGE OF HORSEMEAT USED IN ITEMS SOLD FOR HUMAN CONSUMPTION.

THIS ESTABLISHMENT'S AVERAGE PERCENTAGE OF HORSEMEAT IS: 24% /LB.

SIGN COMPLIES WITH SR REG #445, 441, AND SH REG #53.
Inquiries may be addressed to Board of Health and Sanitation.

Key Questions

1. Match the following with the correct euphemisms:

   i. Starbucks employees   a. team members

   ii. Disney employees   b. cast members

   iii. Wal-Mart employees   c. associates

   iv. Saturn employees   d. partners

2. How did the producers of *Super Jockey*, a late-1990s Japanese game show, determine the duration of a given sponsor's commercial?

   a. Dogs chased a child around a track and the sponsor got as much time as it took the dogs to catch the child.

   b. By dunking a bikini-clad woman in scalding hot water and seeing how long she could stay submerged; the sponsor was allowed the same length of time.

   c. Amateur marksmen shot at live bunnies; for each wounded, the sponsor received ten seconds.

   d. The sponsor's hired rep was forced to wrestle one of several wild boars; the advertisement remained until the rep screamed, "Mercy!"

3. The man in the Toyota T-shirt in this Internet screen shot appears on the page:

   a. To taunt friends and family members of the victim.

b. To distract readers' attention away from the web article and toward the Toyota brand.

c. Coincidentally: the placement of the ad to this particular article was unintentional.

d. B and C.

4. It is against Home Depot store policy for:

a. Employees to call the police on any customer caught shoplifting.

b. Subcontractors to install hot water heaters or hardwood or tile floors, or perform other home services without botching the job.

c. Department managers to answer the phone.

d. Employees to correctly answer customer questions in the hardware, electrical, or painting aisles.

5. Which of the following is NOT a commercially available board game?

a. *Public Assistance: Why Bother Working for a Living?*—Players try to collect as much money as possible without getting a job.

b. *Serial Killer*—Kill as many babies as possible and avoid getting captured in a death-penalty state.

c. *Battle to Baghdad*—"Conquer Baghdad and take out Saddam Hussein."

d. *War on Terror*—"Liberate the world" by destroying opponents before they destroy you.

6. A prank billboard in Orange County, Florida, proclaiming "All religions are fairy tales" led to what results?

a. The local restaurant that usually advertised in the spot faced drastic sales declines on Easter Sunday.

b. The local restaurant that usually advertised in the spot posted its own sign, which read, "Celebrate Jesus' rebirth with our $4.99 omelette!"

c. The billboard company removed the offending ad, upon receiving complaints.

d. A and C.

7. In 1976, Joey Skaggs pulled a controversial prank by advertising what sort of business in *The Village Voice*?

a. A detective agency only for Jews.

b. A horse accountant.

c. A taxi service of the mind.

d. A "cathouse for dogs."

8. During the 1972 election campaign, how was a Nixon ad, run in *The Wall Street Journal*, the focus of a prank?

a. The name "Nixon" on the ad was changed to "Numbnuts."

b. A border of American flags and swastikas was included on the ad.

c. Nixon was shown with a pair of devil horns.

d. The copy included a vehement anti-Vietnam diatribe.

9. Where do birds that nest in supermarkets go to the bathroom?

a. It depends on what sex they are.

b. In their little bird pants.

c. All over the produce.

d. On the frozen poultry, with contempt.

e. There is no one correct answer.

Answers

1. Starbucks, D; Disney, B; Wal-Mart, C; Saturn, A.

2. B. Neil Strauss, "Critic's Notebook: A Japanese TV Show That Pairs Beauty and Pain," *The New York Times*, July 14, 1998. query.nytimes.com/gst/fullpage.html?res=9401E2 D81331F937A25754C0A96E958260&sec=&spon=&page wanted=all.

3. D.

4. A. "Man Says Home Depot Fired Workers for Catching Thieves," *Koco 5*, June 4, 2007. www.koco.com/news/ 13441545/detail.html.

5. B. Serial Killer, designed in the early 1990s, is now out of print. "The World's Most Controversial Boardgames," *Deputydog*, January 1, 2008. deputy-dog.com/2008/01/17/ the-worlds-most-controversial-boardgames.

6. D. "Business Owners, Customers Upset Over Controversial Billboard," WFTV.com, March 28, 2008. www.wftv.com/ news/15735444/detail.html.

7. D. This stunt earned Skaggs the wrath of the ASPCA, the Bureau of Animal Affairs, the NYPD vice squad, and the creepy interest of far more people than you'd think.

8. B. The ad had been altered and the change wasn't noticed until after the paper had been distributed. *The Wall Street Journal* attributed the alteration to someone in the layout department, issued an apology, and fired the accused. V. Vale and Andrea Juno, eds., *ReSearch #11: Pranks* (San Francisco: V/Search Publications, 1987), p. 135.

9. E. www.flickr.com/photos/23687760@N07/2259307910/in/set-72157603894276653/.

Bird spotted at a
Safeway in Fairfax,
Virginia

Postscript

S O T H I S I S W H E R E we were planning on tidy-
ing everything up with a grand solution that will
solve all the ills of consumer culture without hampering anyone's freedom to shop. But then our cat started a fire in the office, burning those pages before we could get them off to the
publisher.

Which is to say that solving the problem of consumer culture would be like solving the problem of society. The sources
of many of the problems discussed in this book are so complex
and so embedded in the American psyche that there is no unified solution.

We can do more than sit on our duffs and pray, however. As
mentioned in the previous section, we're big fans of the calculated prank. But pranks, at their best, are tools for influencing
public opinion and culture; protest, controversy, and satire can
take one only so far. At the end of the day, someone needs to
step up to the plate and get something in writing—to change
corporate bylaws, to pass legislation, to set new boundaries and
rules. This kind of work is a lot less sexy, but it's crucial in
countering the excesses of commercialization.

Frankly, we've never been particularly good at this ourselves.
Fortunately, there are other people in the universe, people who
have formed groups and organizations that systematically work

to reform the powers that be. We've listed a few of them below. Anyone interested in getting involved in battling media giants is encouraged to contact them. Our side can certainly use all the help we can get.

CCFC: Campaign for a Commercial-Free Childhood

53 Parker Hill Ave.
Boston, MA 02120
www.commercialexploitation.org

The go-to group for anything related to kids. Since its founding in 2000, the CCFC has evolved into a substantial opponent of marketing to kids, sparking popular protests against junk-food advertising, school commercialization, and media sexualization of children. The group's website lists a number of campaigns currently in progress as well as handy tips like the *CCFC's Guide to Commercial-Free School Book Fairs*.

The Center for a New American Dream

6930 Carroll Ave.
Suite 900
Takoma Park, MD 20912
(301) 891-3683
newdream@newdream.org
www.newdream.org

This liberal organization aims to help Americans "consume responsibly to protect the environment, enhance quality of life, and promote social justice." This group tends to focus more on changing individual buying habits and behavior than some of the other groups (kinda like a health-food store that sells more than just food).

Center for Screen-Time Awareness

1200 29th Street
N.W. Lower Level #1
Washington, DC 20007
www.tvturnoff.org

The name of this organization—which sponsors the annual TV Turnoff Week—is almost a parody of political correctness. But the group does some important work in helping children find ways to play and socialize in the real world. The group's latest project: fighting the saturation coverage of televisions in airports.

Commercial Alert

P.O. Box 19002
Washington, DC 20036
www.commercialalert.org

Commercial Alert reaches across the political spectrum to parties on the left and right who share a concern for rampant commercialism. The group's modus operandi is the carefully coordinated press release, often signed by a slew of dignitaries, opposing the latest corporate assaults on humanity: US Airways ads targeting "captive" passengers; undisclosed television product placements; a plan by the school board of Seminole County, Florida, to pipe in radio commercials on school buses. Although the group is much less active than it was under founder Gary Ruskin, it remains an important national organization fighting many of these efforts.

Corporations and Health Watch

response@corporationsandhealth.org

www.corporationsandhealth.org

A collaboration between researchers at the City College of New York and the University of Michigan, Corporations and Health Watch studies the impact of corporate practices on public health and helps develop policies to mitigate harm stemming from those practices. It also assesses public service efforts. For example, the project has studied campaigns to improve SUV fuel efficiency, stop the Patient Channel from advertising drugs to hospitalized patients, and remove Coca-Cola from Seattle schools.

Free Press

40 Main Street, Suite 301

Florence, MA 01062

www.freepress.net

Free Press is "a national, nonpartisan organization working to reform the media." Internet neutrality, independent ownership, and public media are their bread and butter. Free Press is large and better organized than your average lefty umbrella group. Plus they have fun conferences!

No Free Lunch

P.O. Box 26605

Brooklyn, NY 11202

www.nofreelunch.org

A not-for-profit organization founded on a novel premise: that medical practice should be based on science rather than commercial promotion. The group's mission is largely educational, informing health-care providers and the general public about the various ways that drug company money perverts medicine. One project is a "pen amnesty" program. The group offers "No Free Lunch" pens in exchange for pharmaceutical-sponsored pens and paraphernalia.

Notes

1: How Advertising Works

The Psychology of Advertising

1. Robert B. Cialdini, *Influence: The Psychology of Persuasion* (New York: Quill/ William Morrow, rev. ed., 1993), p. 191.

2. "Just (get paid to) do it: Fake fans swooshing with pride, keeping Nike happy," Reuters, January 25, 1999. sportsillustrated.cnn.com/tennis/1999/australian_open/news/ 1999/01/25/nike_fans.

3. Rob Walker, "The Hidden (in Plain Sight) Persuaders," *The New York Times Magazine*, December 5, 2004. www.nytimes.com/2004/12/05/magazine/05BUZZ.html.

4. Cialdini, pp. 171–72; Nicholas Bakalar, "Ugly Children May Get Parental Short Shrift," *The New York Times*, May 3, 2005. www.nytimes.com/2005/05/03/health/ 03ugly.html.

5. Thomas Hine, *The Total Package: The Evolution and Secret Meanings of Boxes, Bottles, Cans and Tubes* (New York: Little, Brown, 1995), p. 212.

Image Is Everything: Why the Adman Prefers Images

1. Anirban Nayak, "Leslie Stahl: From Behind the Podium," *The Tech* 27, June 2, 2000. tech.mit.edu/V120/N27/Leslie_Stahl.27f.html.

Truth in Advertising Case Study

1. Melvin S. Hattiwick, *How to Use Psychology for Better Advertising* (Englewood Cliffs, NJ: Prentice Hall, 1950), pp. 338–39.

2. Ibid.

Brand Magic

1. S. Hwang, "Sugar Fix: Nutrament, Debunked as a 'Fitness' Drink, Is Reborn in the Slums," *The Wall Street Journal*, November 22, 1994.

2. Ellen Bryon and Stephen Miller, "Richard Q. Kress (1927–2006): 'Norelco Man' Boldly Marketed Electric Shavers. A 'Gotcha!' Television Ad Nicked Blade Competitors . . ." (obituary), *The Wall Street Journal*, November 25, 2006, p. A6.

3. Hwang, "Sugar Fix."

2: How Consumer Culture Shapes People

A Slow-Creeping Brain Death

1. "Turning into digital goldfish," *BBC News*, February 22, 2002. news.bbc.co.uk/1/hi/sci/tech/1834682.stm.

2. Jane Healy, *Endangered Minds: Why Children Don't Think and What We Can Do about It* (New York: Touchstone, 1999). Morley Safer, "The Millennials Are Coming!" *60 Minutes*, www.cbsnews.com/sections/i_video/main500251.shtml?id=3486473n. Scott Shuster, "Wake Up! The Speech Is Over!: TV Has Conquered Short Attention Span . . ." www.businessconferences.com/Resources/WakeUpTheSpeechIsOver.doc. Jeff Davidson, *The Complete Guide to Public Speaking* (New York: John Wiley, 2003), pp. 50, 275. George C. Dehne, "The New Student Generation: Are We Ready? Do We Care?" www.dehne.com/news_research/research_new_student.html. "Welcoming the New Millennials: MBA Programs Adjust to the Next Generation, and Their Parents," *The Wall Street Journal*, December 4, 2007, Career Journal, p. B9.

3. "End-User Study on Email Hygiene," co-sponsored by The Radicati Group, Inc. & Mirapoint, Inc., April 2005. www.issa-sac.org/info_resources/ISSA_20051020_Mirapoint _Email_Hygiene_User_Study.pdf.

4. www.businessconferences.com/attention-span.htm.

5. This statistic is bunk. See www.straightdope.com/columns/070907.html (accessed September 7, 2007).

Regarding Media Violence

1. The tendency of media reports of suicide to inspire copycat suicides is also known as the Werther effect. For example, see Cialdini, pp. 144–147; "Preventing Suicide: A Resource for Media Health Professionals," World Health Organization (2000), www.who .int/entity/mental_health/media/en/426.pdf; Jeannette De Wyze, "Why Do They Die?" *San Diego Weekly Reader*, March 31, 2005, www.sandiegoreader.com/news/2005/mar/31/why-do-they-die.

The Media Made Them Do It

1. "Learning to Live with TV," *Time*, May 28, 1979. www.time.com/time/magazine/article/0,9171,947316,00.html.

2. Lee Margulies, "Child's Death Prompts MTV to Retool 'Beavis,'" *Los Angeles Times*, October 14, 1993.

3. "Cartoon on MTV Blamed for Fire," Associated Press, *The New York Times*, October 10, 1993, Section 1, p. 30.

4. "Ban on TV Advert After Children Hurt in 'Copycat' Slapping Craze," *The Guardian*, March 12, 1992, p. 6.

5. Ben Macintyre, "Copycat killer held in Nebraska," *The Times* (London), November 5, 1994.

6. Rhonda Cook, "Woman on trial for murder said to be fan of violent film . . ." *Atlanta Journal and Constitution*, February 10, 1997, p. 4B.

7. "Deaths prompt Fresh-Up to pull ad," *The Dominion* (Wellington, New Zealand), December 30, 1997, p. 3.

8. "'Wrestling' Case Draws Life Sentence," CBSNews.com, March 9, 2001. www .cbsnews.com/stories/2001/03/09/national/main277536.shtml.

9. David Sapsted, "Ships Warned over 'Titanic' Stunt Mimics," *The Daily Telegraph*, June 25, 1998, International, p. 20; Edwin McDowell, "Allure of 'Titanic,' Minus Ice, Is Packing Cruise Ship Cabins," *The New York Times*, March 29, 1998. query.nytimes.com/ gst/Fullpage.html?res=9C04E6DD123BF93AA15750COA96E958260, accessed on September 24, 2008.

10. Michael deCourcy Hinds, "Not Like the Movie: A Dare Leads to Death," *The New York Times*, October 19, 1993, A:1.

11. Vincent LoBrutto, *Stanley Kubrick: A Biography* (Cambridge, MA: Da Capo Press, 1999), p. 368.

12. "Man Sets Wife Afire, Milwaukee Police Say," UPI, *The New York Times*, October 10, 1984, Section A, p. 12; Neal Karlen with Michael Reese, "A Copycat Assault?" *Newsweek*, October 22, 1984, p. 38.

13. Renee Graham, "Beavis: A Bow, Not a Surrender," *The Boston Globe*, October 20, 1993, National/Foreign, p. 6.

14. Frank Mankiewicz and Joel Swerdlow, *Remote Control: Television and the Manipulation of American Life* (New York: Times Books, 1978), p. 53.

15. Ibid, pp. 240–41.

16. The safe-driving PSA starring James Dean can be found on YouTube as of April 18, 2008, at www.youtube.com/watch?v=DZXhaDXvFfc.

3: Consumer Culture and Society

1. Jack Neff, "P&G Pulls Children's Body Spray Advertising: Product Carries 'Keep Out of Reach of Children' Warning," *Advertising Age*, June 10, 2005. adage.com/abstract .php?article_id=46011.

2. Ezra Caraeff, "I Hate You Princess Cruise Lines," *The Portland Mercury*, October 16, 2007. blogtown.portlandmercury.com/2007/10/i_hate_you_princess_cruise _lin.php.

3. "Study of Americans' Media Use Finds Web Finally Passing Newspapers," Associated Press, *Editor & Publisher*, December 15, 2006. www.editorandpublisher.com/eandp/ news/article_display.jsp?vnu_content_id=1003522187.

4. Patrick di Justo, "Infoporn: Despite the Web, Americans Remain Woefully Ill-Informed," *Wired*, June 27, 2007. www.wired.com/culture/culturereviews/magazine/15-07/ st_infoporn.

5. In 2003 and 2004, Wal-Mart was listed as #1 on *Fortune* magazine's "Most Admired Company in America" listing: www.walmartfacts.com/content/default .aspx?id=4; and the store is ranked #11 at "2007 [the World's Fifty] Most Innovative Companies," *BusinessWeek*. bwnt.businessweek.com/interactive_reports/most_ innovative/index.asp.

Shopping for Cancer

1. Theo Francis and Ellen Byron, "Flu Economy Takes Unexpected Turn," *The Wall Street Journal*, April 3, 2008, B1.

4: Behind the Scenes

Coca-Cola and the Case of the Disappearing Water Glass

1. Daniel Eisenberg, "A New-Age Drink War Starts as Soda Flops," *Time*, December 2000. www.time.com/time/magazine/article/0,9171,998783,00.html.

2. Ed Sealover, "Mandatory water cuts likely; City prepared to move to phase two," *Colorado Springs Gazette*, June 8, 2002. findarticles.com/p/articles/mi_qn4191/is_20020608/ai_n10005875; also, City of Durham, North Carolina, "Water Management—Water Conservation Information." www.ci.durham.nc.us/departments/wm/water_update.cfm (accessed May 13, 2008).

3. *Arena*, June 1, 2001. www.accessmylibrary.com/coms2/summary_0286-10659675_ITM.

4. David F. Gallagher, "Word for Word/Deep Water: 'Just Say No to H$_2$0' (Unless It's Coke's Own Brew)," *The New York Times*, September 2, 2001. query.nytimes.com/gst/fullpage.html?res=9D04E1D81E30F931A3575AC0A9679C8B63.

5: Down the Memory Hole

Subliminal Seduction

1. Wilson Bryan Key, *The Clam-Plate Orgy and Other Subliminal Techniques for Manipulating Your Behavior* (New York: Signet, 1981), pp. 2–3.

2. Ibid., p. 7.

3. Daniel Horowitz, *Vance Packard and American Social Criticism* (Chapel Hill, NC: University of North Carolina Press, 1994), p. 165.

4. Jack Haberstroh, *Ice Cube Sex: The Truth About Subliminal Advertising* (Notre Dame, IN: Cross Cultural Publications, 1994), p. 90.

5. Ibid., p. 84.

The Idiot Consumer

1. Age 14? ad is from *Advertising and Selling*, September 13, 1934, p. 20.

2. Kenneth M. Goode and Harford Powel Jr., *What About Advertising?* (New York: Harper, 1927), p. 117.

3. Roland Marchand, *Advertising the American Dream: Making Way for Modernity, 1920–1940* (Berkeley: University of California Press, 1985), p. 69.

4. *Printers' Ink Monthly*, February 1933, p. 71. Quoted in Marchand, p. 86.

5. Quoted in Otis Pease, *Responsibilities of American Advertising: Private Control and Public Influence, 1920–1940* (New Haven: Yale University Press, 1958), p. 179.

6. *Printers' Ink*, December 14, 1933, p. 9.

7. *Printers' Ink*, July 20, 1933, pp. 8–9.

8. *Printers' Ink*, December 14, 1933, p. 9.

9. Pease, p. 177.

10. *New Yorker*, March 11, 1933, p. 45. library.duke.edu/digitalcollections/adaccess .BH1683/pg.1/.

11. John Caples, "Why It Is Not Clever to Write Clever Ads," *Advertising & Selling*, May 13, 1931, p. 24.

12. *Printers' Ink*, January 30, 1936, p. 50.

13. *Printers' Ink*, December 23, 1926, pp. 82–83.

14. *Printers' Ink*, September 14, 1933, pp. 30–31.

15. *Printers' Ink*, October 19, 1933, p. 111.

16. *Printers' Ink*, January 30, 1936, pp. 82–83.

17. *Printers' Ink*, February 13, 1936, p. 100.

18. Albert T. Poffenberger, *Psychology in Advertising* (Chicago: A. W. Shaw, 1925), p. 330.

19. Stuart Chase in *Forum*, January 1928, p. 29.

20. Frank Crowninshield, May 31, 1934, starts p. 7; quote on p. 8.

Acknowledgments

Carrie McLaren

I did the good bulk of work on this book while pregnant and feeling something akin to brain damaged. So I'm not sure I could have written anything coherent for the new material without the help of my assistant, Sara Vogel. Sara read and edited everything Jason and I wrote for the book, and her insights and suggestions were instrumental in shaping what could have been a hodgepodge of articles into a cohesive piece.

It is a grave injustice that Alexandra Ringe has nothing in this book. (Long story.) Alexandra worked on *Stay Free!* for many years and helped transform the zine into a quality magazine. *Stay Free!* wouldn't have been what it was without her. She's a brilliant editor, a gifted writer, and a dear friend.

I also owe a great deal to Jim Hanas, who took over Adult Education—*Stay Free!*'s Brooklyn-based lecture series—while I was on leave this year.

There have been so many excellent contributors to *Stay Free!* over the years that I dare not even try to thank them, for fear that I'll leave someone out. I want to thank David Cross and William Moree, though, for arranging a photo shoot for this book.

Shout-outs are also due to Katie Gately; Brewster Kahle; my

agent, Daniel Greenberg; my editor at FSG, Denise Oswald, and her assistant, Jessica Ferri. Thanks, guys.

Last but never least, my beloved, Charles Star. Charles not only performed his marital duty of reading and commenting on the book but has supported me thoughout our years together in one harebrained scheme after another (including the rearing of our son, Sidney). Charles knows how I feel about public displays of affection, so suffice it to say: you are my Pushkin.

Jason Torchinsky

I'm always secretly amazed when any large project manages to get completed. In this case, I really should swap amazement for gratitude, as Carrie and I certainly could not have done this without lots of help from lots of people.

Of course, I'll echo Carrie's essentials: our agent, Daniel Greenberg; Denise Oswald and Jessica Ferri at FSG. And I'd like to add Charlotte Strick in FSG's art department for taking a risk and letting me design the cover, and Jenny Carrow for her help with that as well. And the woman at that airline counter who mailed me a barf bag.

I especially want to thank contributors Chris Boznos (for indulging my automotive obsessions) and Alan Benson (just because I've known him so long). My comedy collective, the Van Gogh-Goghs (Alan again, Galen Black, T. Mike Childs, Charles Rempel, and Rob Terrell) I should thank since I'm pretty sure I learned something from all of them. And I'd like to thank the Onion News Network writing staff, who have been good about keeping me disciplined, whether they realize it or even care. I'm going to thank Mark Allen, Mark Frauenfelder, and Tom Jennings here as well, not because they did anything to help me with the book, but because they all provided some important extra-book experiences and opportunities that must have helped me do this in some way.

Most important is, of course, my partner, Sally. She not only endured many nights of my cognitive absence as I worked on the book, but also was always available for giving me insight, suggestions, and eye rolls as the subject demanded. Plus, she helped this project even more directly by taking many of the photos you see in the book, as well as the photo used for the cover. She already knows I love her dearly, but it's always nice to see that in print.

And though Carrie and I agreed we'd not thank each other, for fear it would sound weird, I'm going to thank Carrie anyway. I'm delighted our creative partnership has endured for so long, and I'm excited to see what we do next. She makes me proud.

Carrie McLaren

Carrie would like to add that, while she still doesn't think she and Mr. Torchinsky should thank each other in the acknowledgments, she has always envied Jason's genius and couldn't have asked for a better partner or friend.